MW01247446

IF FOUND, PLEASE CONTACT THE OWNER
OF THIS BOOK.

....
NAME

....
ADDRESS

....
PHONE NUMBER

....
EMAIL

Journaling

With Sunday Scripture

A Book for All Seasons
2024 Liturgical Year

Linda Kracht

Fortifying Families of Faith

Cover, photography, illustrations, design and layout by Kelly Anne Bauer

ISBN: 978-0-9827080-6-4

Contact Information:
Fortifying Families of Faith, LLC
St. Paul, MN 55116-6354
www.fortifyingfamiliesoffaith.com
info@fortifyingfamiliesoffaith.com

DEDICATION

To my husband, Dave, for requesting this journal.
To you for journaling with scripture.

PRAYER FOR FAMILIES

Lord God, from you every family in heaven and on earth takes its name. Father, you are Love and Life. Through your Son Jesus Christ - born of woman and through the Holy Spirit — fountain of divine charity; grant that every family on earth may become for each successive generation a true shrine of life and love.

Grant that your grace may guide the thoughts and actions of husbands and wives for the good of their families and of all the families in the world. Grant that the young may find in the family solid support for their human dignity and for their growth in truth and love. Grant that love, strengthened by the grace of the sacrament of marriage, may prove mightier than all the weakness and trials through which our families sometimes pass.

Through the intercession of the Holy Family of Nazareth, grant that the Church may fruitfully carry out Her worldwide mission in the family and through the family. Through Christ our Lord, who is the Way, the Truth and the Life forever and ever. Amen. + Saint John Paul II

Table of Contents

St. Paul the Apostle

"Let us not become weary in doing good, for at the proper time we will reap a harvest if we do not give up. Finally, be strong in the Lord and in his mighty power. Put on the full armor of God so that you can take your stand against the devil's schemes."

Galations: 6:9

Introduction

Whether you purchased this journal or received it as a gift, your personal commitment to understanding Holy Scriptures and its application to everyday life will be rewarded. Personal growth occurs slowly and consistently when we rely on effective tools and methods. Take time to reflect on each Sunday's Scripture readings; consider how it speaks to you personally; and then answer the reflection questions to the best of your ability.

The Sunday Readings are used with permission from the **USCCB Lectionary for the Mass.** The Mass readings are often announced prior to the start of each Mass and this will be helpful when alternate Sunday readings are used. *Alternate Readings* are designated in **bold or *italic bold* fonts.** "The Lectionary for the Mass Readings is arranged in two cycles, one for Sundays and one for weekdays. The Sunday cycle is divided into three years: **A, B, and C.** Year A relies heavily on the Gospel of Matthew; Year B uses the Gospel of Mark [and chapter 6 of the Gospel of John] and Year C uses the Gospel of Luke. The Gospel of John is read during the Easter season in all three years. **The 2024 Sundays employ Cycle B.** The weekday cycle is divided into two years: Year I and Year II. Year I is read in odd-numbered years and Year II in even-numbered years ." [USCCB] **Cycle II is used for the 2024** Weekday Masses.

Did you know that the **Liturgical Year** has seven Seasons: **Advent; Christmas and Epiphany; Lent; Easter; Pentecost; Ordinary Time 1; and Ordinary Time 11**. The Liturgical Year begins with the First Sunday of Advent and concludes on the 34th Sunday of Ordinary Time [or the 33rd Sunday when the calendar year is a leap year] The *colors* of the seasons are on full display - we see them on the celebrant's vestments; church banners and streamers and various altar cloths. This **Journal** uses proprietary Stained Glass Photos framed with the identifying colors of each Liturgical Season to divide the seasons visually. **Purple** is used during the seasons of Advent and Lent. This color represents waiting; hopeful expectation; and our need for purification and penance. The color **Rose** is used only for the Third Sunday of Advent [Gaudete Sunday] and the Fourth Sunday of Lent [Laetare Sunday]. Rose results from mixing purple with white; therefore it's meaning is twofold. It represents our need for penitence [purple] and the forthcoming joyfulness and gratitude we will experience because of the gloriousness and triumph of the specific feast days [represented by the color white] of Jesus' birth; His Resurrection from the dead; and other special feast days. **Red** represents royalty, fire, death and martyrdom and is used for Pentecost Sunday; Palm Sunday; Good Friday; and select Holy Days of Obligation or other special feast days. **Green** symbolizes new life and growth [in the Church] and is used during Ordinary Times [I & II]. **Gold** and **Silver** represent God's glory and are only used for select feast days. As already stated, the Stained Glass Photos showcase the start of each new Liturgical Season.

Please set aside time to answer the questions about the seasonal Images.

Answers regarding the Liturgical Images can be found on my website: fortify ingfamiliesoffaith.com. [Click on Blog]. The photos were taken at the Church of the Nativity of Our Lord, St. Paul, MN [built in 1928] by Joan Welter Czaia, Daystar Design. Father Patrick Hipwell, pastor, gave permission for the taking of and use of these images for this journal.

The Mass has two *main parts* and two *framing parts*: the *Liturgy of the Word* and the *Liturgy of the Eucharist*. The *Introductory Rite* and the *Concluding Rite* comprise the two framing rites. The *Liturgy of the Word* includes bible readings, the Homily, the Creed, and Intercessory Prayers. The *Liturgy of the Eucharist* includes the Eucharistic Prayer and the Communion Rite. The complete order of the Mass includes: **The Introductory Rites** [the Entrance; the Greeting; the Sign of the Cross; the Penitential Act; the Gloria; and the Collect]. **The Liturgy of the Word** follows next and consists **of** the First Reading; the Responsorial Psalm; the Second Reading (on Sundays and solemnities); the Gospel Acclamation; the Gospel; the Homily; the Profession of Faith (spoken on Sundays, Solemnities, & special occasions) or the Creed and the Universal Prayer. **The Liturgy of the Eucharist** is the *source and summit* of our Christian life. [CCC #324] It includes the Presentation of the Gifts; the Preparation of the Altar; the Prayer over the Offerings; the Eucharistic Prayer; the Preface, the Holy, Holy, Holy; the *first half* of the Eucharistic Prayers including the Consecration; and the Mystery of Faith. The Final Rites include the Second Half of the Eucharistic Prayers: including the Doxology; The Lord's Prayer, the Sign of Peace; the Lamb of God; followed by the distribution of Holy Communion and the Prayer After Communion. The Mass ends with a **Concluding Rite** which include optional announcements; the Final Blessing and the Dismissal. See page X for the outline.

This journal encourages you to take homily notes. These notes will help you retain the homilist's theological lessons. If you need additional space, use the extra pages starting on page 270. Most homilies are fairly short and to the point while others are lengthy and richly detailed. These longer homilies may require more writing space. Date your *extra* notes on the back pages in order to connect them to the right Sunday.

Answer the *Reflection Questions* before or after Mass. Many homilies will help you answer the reflection questions but when they don't, please still try to answer the questions to the best of your ability. There are generally no right or wrong answers.

Dave and I learned to pray with scripture - commonly referred to as *Lectio Divina* - while attending the Catechetical Institute of the Archdiocese of St. Paul/Mpls [Class of John Paul ll]. "It is especially necessary that listening to God should become a life-giving encounter. The ancient and ever valid tradition of Lectio Divina draws from the biblical text the living Word which questions, directs and shapes our lives." [JP ll] You can learn to *pray with scriptures* with this book's Sunday and Weekly scriptures references. The steps for Lectio Divina include: read the scripture passage at a normal rate. Read it again; but more slowly. Mull over the words. Focus on a phrase or word *that jumps out* for you. Reflect on that phrase or word; ask God to explain its importance or depth. Give thanks to God for the new insight you may have. Finish up with a final reading of the verses or passage. Conclude with prayers of praise, petition, thanksgiving, and gratitude to God. The process is fairly simple, so give it a try. *"Do not be afraid; I go before you."* You will be grateful for the time you spent reflecting on God's word.

Virtue Section. Near the end of each Sunday Section, the author challenges you to *arm yourself* with a specific virtue for the new Week based on one of the Sunday readings. If you prefer to choose your own virtue of the week, please do so. You are not bound to my virtue selection. The goal of the virtuous life is to *become like God* [CCC 1803]. All of us are called; may we listen and obey joyfully and virtuously. In order to continue striving for the virtuous life we will have to give up certain things - either temporarily or permanently; we will have to choose goodness; we will have to pray for God's help; and we will have to do penance whenever we fail to act rightly; and we will be called to help others. In other words, we will have to fast, to pray, to give alms, and do penance in order to become more virtuous. It is a choice. We will either choose to live for God or live for self.

The Book of Sirach [15: 14-17] teaches "God in the beginning created human beings / and made them subject to their own free choice./ If you choose, you can keep the commandments;/ loyalty is doing the will of God./ Set before you are fire and water;/ to whatever you choose, stretch out your hand. / Before everyone are life and death,/ whichever they choose will be given them." [New American Bible, revised edition] The fire represents vice; worldliness; and unhappiness whereas the water represents grace; virtue; happiness; and godliness. Lists of the Theological & Cardinal Virtues; more common human virtues; and the Corporal & Spiritual Works of Mercy] can be found on pages 266 .

The **Prayer Section** incorporates prayers for home or Church use. The **Penance Section** allows you to record when you receive the Sacrament of Reconciliation. This will help you track this Sacrament.

Fortifying Families of Faith has been in the business of providing helpful resources for parents and adolescents since 2008. Our feature works [in English and Spanish] include: *A Book for All Seasons*; *Daughters and Sons Forever* [book and workbook]; *Black and White* [a First Communion & Confirmation resource[; *Surviving College*; and *Mothers Forever, Fathers Forever*. We hope that works express the words from Joshua 24:15: "As for me and my household, we will praise and serve the Lord."

May the 2024 Liturgical Seasons be a year of grace and spiritual growth for you and your family.

Linda Kracht, Founder, Fortifying Families of Faith

Phone: 651-470-3699
www. fortifyingfamiliesoffaith.com
info@fortifyingfamiliesoffaith.com

The Order of the Mass

The Introductory Rites
Entrance
Greeting & the Sign of the Cross
Penitential Act
Glory to God
Collect

The Liturgy of the Word
First Reading
Responsorial Psalm
Second Reading (on Sundays and solemnities)
Gospel Acclamation
Gospel
Homily
Profession of Faith (Sundays, solemnities, & special occasions) or Creed Universal
Prayer

The Liturgy of the Eucharist
Presentation of the Gifts and Preparation of the Altar
Prayer over the Offerings
Eucharistic Prayer
Preface
Holy, Holy, Holy
First half of prayer, including Consecration
Mystery of Faith
Second half of prayer, ending with Doxology
The Lord's Prayer
Sign of Peace
Lamb of God
Communion
Prayer after Communion

Concluding Rites
Optional announcements
Greeting and Blessing
Dismissal

ADVENT

The SEASON of ADVENT

Advent is a reminder that Jesus will come again to *judge* the living and the dead. It is a season of *repentance, prayer,* and of *faithful, patient waiting* on our Lord. Consider how you will *watch and wait* for the arrival of the Son of God this Season. "Advent is also a time to consider how we *think with* God. Christ is born to us; we are born from the Church to God's presence. Be not afraid to look up and to allow the Holy Spirit to overshadow you. Christ wants to be conceived in our hearts for the glory of God and the wellbeing of our neighbors. May we stand faithfully united as we watch and wait in hopeful expectation of Christ's second coming." [St. Pope JP ll]

Each week of Advent offers us the opportunity to develop/renew our Weekly Spiritual Plan with regard to almsgiving, fasting, prayer and penance, and virtue development.

"God in the beginning created human beings / and made them subject to their own free choice./ If you choose, you can keep the commandments;/ loyalty is doing the will of God./ Set before you are fire and water;/ to whatever you choose, stretch out your hand. / Before everyone are life and death,/ whichever they choose will be given them."

Sirach 15:14-17 [New American Bible, revised edition]

What do *fire* and *water* represent?

. . . .
. . . .
. . . .
. . . .
. . . .
. . . .
.

Study the Stained Glass Window for Advent [see previous page]. List the different *signs* of Advent that you found; explain how they represent Advent.

. . . .
. . . .
. . . .
. . . .
. . . .

First Sunday of Advent

First Reading: *Isaiah* 63:16B-17, 19B; 64:2-7

You, LORD, are our father,/ our redeemer you are named forever./ Why do you let us wander, O LORD, from your ways,/ and harden our hearts so that we fear you not?/ Return for the sake of your servants,/ the tribes of your heritage./ Oh, that you would rend the heavens and come down/ with the mountains quaking before you,/ while you wrought awesome deeds we could not hope for,/ such as they had not heard of from of old./ No ear has ever heard, no eye ever seen, any God but you/ doing such deeds for those who wait for him./ Would that you might meet us doing right,/ that we were mindful of you in our ways!/ Behold, you are angry,/ and we are sinful;/ all of us have become like unclean people,/ all our good deeds are like polluted rags;/ we have all withered like leaves,/ and our guilt carries us away like the wind./ There is none who calls upon your name,/ who rouses himself to cling to you;/ for you have hidden your face from us/ and have delivered us up to our guilt./ Yet, O LORD, you are our father;/ we are the clay and you the potter:/ we are all the work of your hands.

Second Reading: *1 Corinthians 1:3-9*

Brothers and sisters: Grace to you and peace from God our Father and the Lord Jesus Christ. I give thanks to my God always on your account for the grace of God bestowed on you in Christ Jesus, that in him you were enriched in every way, with all discourse and all knowledge, as the testimony to Christ was confirmed among you, so that you are not lacking in any spiritual gift as you wait for the revelation of our Lord Jesus Christ. He will keep you firm to the end, irreproachable on the day of our Lord Jesus Christ. God is faithful, and by him you were called to fellowship with his Son, Jesus Christ our Lord.

Gospel Reading: *Mark 13:33-37*

Jesus said to his disciples: "Be watchful! Be alert! You do not know when the time will come. It is like a man traveling abroad. He leaves home and places his servants in charge, each with his own work, and orders the gatekeeper to be on the watch. Watch, therefore; you do not know when the Lord of the house is coming, whether in the evening, or at midnight, or at cockcrow, or in the morning. May he not come suddenly and find you sleeping. What I say to you, I say to all: 'Watch!'"

First Sunday of Advent

Homily Notes:

....
....
....
....
....
....
....
....
....
....
....
....
....
....
....
....
....
....
....
....
....
....
....
....
....
....
....
....

First Sunday of Advent

December 3, 2023

Reflection Questions for Each of the Readings:

1. *Based on the First Reading:* What is Isaiah appealing for [from God]? Explain in your own words what Isaiah means when stating: *God is the potter and we are the clay.*

2. *Based on the Second Reading:* What does it mean to be in fellowship with God? What gifts has God has bestowed on you?

3. *Based on the Gospel Reading:* This reading URGES us to be alert. Other translations tell us to be vigilant and pray. How is being alert and being vigilant similar yet different? How does prayer make you alert & vigilant?

3

Your Virtue Challenge:

The goal of the virtuous person is to become like God. [CCC 1803] This will require identifying ways to increase this virtue and reduce opposing vice; *fasting [avoiding]* from habits or practices that oppose it; *praying* for God's help; *helping* others; and *doing penance. Based on the Second Reading,* your Virtue Challenge for the week is to increase in the virtue of:

FAITH.

My Virtue Goals and Working Plan for the Week:

....

....

....

....

....

....

....

Daily Mass Readings for the Week:
Monday, December 4: St. John Damascene Isaiah 2:1-5; Matthew 8:5-11.
Tuesday, December 5: Isaiah 11:1-10/Luke 10:21-24.
Wednesday, December 6: Saint Nicholas Isaiah 25:6-10a; Matthew 15:29-37.
Thursday, December 7: Saint Ambrose Isaiah 26:1-6; Matthew 7:21, 24-27.
Friday, December 8: **Solemnity of the Immaculate Conception of the Blessed Virgin Mary Holy Day of Obligation See pages: 5-7.**
Saturday, December 9: Saint Juan Diego Cuauhtlatoatzin Isaiah 30:19-21, 23-26; Matthew 9:35- 10:1, 5a, 6-8.

4

Solemnity of the Immaculate Conception of the Blessed Virgin Mary, Patroness of the USA   December 8, 2023

First Reading: *Genesis 3:9-15, 20*

After the man, Adam, had eaten of the tree, the LORD God called to the man and asked him, "Where are you?" He answered, "I heard you in the garden; but I was afraid, because I was naked, so I hid myself." Then he asked, "Who told you that you were naked? You have eaten, then, from the tree of which I had forbidden you to eat!" The man replied, "The woman whom you put here with me-- she gave me fruit from the tree, and so I ate it." The LORD God then asked the woman, "Why did you do such a thing?" The woman answered, "The serpent tricked me into it, so I ate it."

Then the LORD God said to the serpent:/ "Because you have done this,/   you shall be banned from all the animals and from all the wild creatures; / on your belly shall you crawl,/   and dirt shall you eat all the days of your life./   I will put enmity between you and the woman,/   and between your offspring and hers;/   he will strike at your head,/   while you strike at his heel."/

The man called his wife Eve, because she became the mother of all the living.

Second Reading: *Ephesians 1:3-6, 11-12*

Brothers and sisters: Blessed be the God and Father of our Lord Jesus Christ, who has blessed us in Christ with every spiritual blessing in the heavens, as he chose us in him, before the foundation of the world, to be holy and without blemish before him. In love he destined us for adoption to himself through Jesus Christ, in accord with the favor of his will, for the praise of the glory of his grace that he granted us in the beloved.

In him we were also chosen, destined in accord with the purpose of the One who accomplishes all things according to the intention of his will, so that we might exist for the praise of his glory, we who first hoped in Christ.

Gospel Reading: *Luke 1:26-38*

The angel Gabriel was sent from God to a town of Galilee called Nazareth, to a virgin betrothed to a man named Joseph, of the house of David, and the virgin's name was Mary. And coming to her, he said, "Hail, full of grace! The Lord is with you." But she was greatly troubled at what was said and pondered what sort of greeting this might be. Then the angel said to her, "Do not be afraid, Mary, for you have found favor with God. Behold, you will conceive in your womb and bear a son, and you shall name him Jesus. He will be great and will be called Son of the Most High, and the Lord God will give him the throne of David his father, and he will rule over the house of Jacob forever, and of his Kingdom there will be no end." But Mary said to the angel, How can this be, since I have no relations with a man?" And the angel said to her in reply, "The Holy Spirit will come upon you, and the power of the Most High will overshadow you. Therefore the child to be born will be called holy, the Son of God. And behold, Elizabeth, your relative, has also conceived a son in her old age, and this is the sixth month for her who was called barren; for nothing will be impossible for God." Mary said, "Behold, I am the handmaid of the Lord. May it be done to me according to your word." Then the angel departed from her.

Homily Notes:

....
....
....
....
....
....
....
....
....
....
....
....
....
....
....
....
....
....
....

Reflection Questions for Each of the Readings:

1. *Based on the First Reading:* Shame makes us feel smaller and smaller; it also causes us to *hide* from God and others. Why are Adam and Eve hiding from God? Who did they *implicitly* blame for this shame? Who did they *explicitly* blame for their sin?

2. *Based on the Second Reading:* The reading teaches us that God wants us to experience a myriad of spiritual blessings and to achieve great things. What spiritual blessings have you already received? What spiritual blessings do you hope to receive in the future? What is your intended eternal destiny?

3. *Based on the Gospel Reading:* What does it mean to *feel troubled*? Why was Mary *troubled* by the angel's greeting? Contrast Mary's response to Eve's. Explain the I*mmaculate Conception in your own words.*

Second Sunday of Advent

First Reading: *Isaiah 40:1-5, 9-11*

Comfort, give comfort to my people,/ says your God./ Speak tenderly to Jerusalem, and proclaim to her/ that her service is at an end,/ her guilt is expiated;/ indeed, she has received from the hand of the LORD/ double for all her sins./

A voice cries out:/ In the desert prepare the way of the LORD!/ Make straight in the wasteland a highway for our God!/ Every valley shall be filled in,/ every mountain and hill shall be made low;/ the rugged land shall be made a plain,/ the rough country, a broad valley./ Then the glory of the LORD shall be revealed,/ and all people shall see it together;/ for the mouth of the LORD has spoken./

Go up on to a high mountain,/ Zion, herald of glad tidings;/ cry out at the top of your voice,/ Jerusalem, herald of good news!/ Fear not to cry out/ and say to the cities of Judah:/ Here is your God!/ Here comes with power/ the Lord GOD,/ who rules by his strong arm;/ here is his reward with him,/ his recompense before him./ Like a shepherd he feeds his flock;/ in his arms he gathers the lambs,/ carrying them in his bosom,/ and leading the ewes with care.

Second Reading: *2 Peter 3:8-14*

Do not ignore this one fact, beloved, that with the Lord one day is like a thousand years and a thousand years like one day. The Lord does not delay his promise, as some regard "delay," but he is patient with you, not wishing that any should perish but that all should come to repentance. But the day of the Lord will come like a thief, and then the heavens will pass away with a mighty roar and the elements will be dissolved by fire, and the earth and everything done on it will be found out.

Since everything is to be dissolved in this way, what sort of persons ought you to be, conducting yourselves in holiness and devotion, waiting for and hastening the coming of the day of God, because of which the heavens will be dissolved in flames and the elements melted by fire. But according to his promise we await new heavens and a new earth in which righteousness dwells. Therefore, beloved, since you await these things, be eager to be found without spot or blemish before him, at peace.

Gospel Reading: *Mark 1:1-8*

The beginning of the gospel of Jesus Christ the Son of God.
As it is written in Isaiah the prophet:/ *Behold, I am sending my messenger ahead of you; / he will prepare your way./ A voice of one crying out in the*

8

Second Sunday of Advent

December 10, 2023

desert:/   "Prepare the way of the Lord, make straight his paths."

John the Baptist appeared in the desert proclaiming a baptism of repentance for the forgiveness of sins. People of the whole Judean countryside and all the inhabitants of Jerusalem were going out to him and were being baptized by him in the Jordan River as they acknowledged their sins. John was clothed in camel's hair, with a leather belt around his waist. He fed on locusts and wild honey. And this is what he proclaimed: "One mightier than I is coming after me. I am not worthy to stoop and loosen the thongs of his sandals. I have baptized you with water; he will baptize you with the Holy Spirit."

Homily Notes:

....
....
....
....
....
....
....
....
....
....
....
....
....
....
....
....
....
....
....
....

Second Sunday of Advent

Reflection Questions for Each of the Readings:

1. *Based on the First Reading*: Empathy allows us *enter into* someone else's pain and share their suffering. What is Jerusalem suffering from? Who will comfort her? How will she be comforted?

2. *Based on the Second Reading*: What does this reading urge us to do? Why is it urging us to do this?

3. *Based on the Gospel Reading*: Explain who John the Baptist is? Why is he significant? Look up some facts about John the Baptist online and make note of them here.

Your Virtue Challenge:

The goal of the virtuous person is to become like God. [CCC 1803] This will require identifying ways to increase this virtue and reduce opposing vice; *fasting [avoiding]* from habits or practices that oppose it; *praying* for God's help; *helping* others; and *doing penance. Based on the Second Reading,* your Virtue Challenge for the week is to increase in the virtue of:

COMPASSION

My Virtue Goals and Working Plan for the Week:

....

....

....

....

....

....

....

Daily Mass Readings for the Week:

Monday, December 11: **Saint Damasus I** Isaiah 35:1-10; Luke 5:17-26.

Tuesday, December 12: **Our Lady of Guadalupe** Zechariah 2:14-17 or Revelation 11:19a; 12:1-6a, 10ab; Luke 1:26-38 or 1:39-47.

Wednesday, December 13: **Saint Lucy** Isaiah 40:25-31; Matthew 11:28-30.

Thursday, December 14: **Saint John of the Cross** Isaiah 41:13-20; Matthew 11:11-15.

Friday, December 15: Isaiah 48:17-19; Matthew 11:16-19.

Saturday, December 16: Sirach 48:1-4, 9-11; Matthew 17:9a, 10-13.

First Reading: *Isaiah 61:1-2a,10-11*

The spirit of the Lord GOD is upon me/   because the LORD has anointed me;/   he has sent me to bring glad tidings to the poor,/   to heal the broken hearted,/   to proclaim liberty to the captives/   and release to the prisoners,/   to announce a year of favor from the LORD/   and a day of vindication by our /God

I rejoice heartily in the LORD,/   in my God is the joy of my soul;/ for he has clothed me with a robe of salvation/   and wrapped me in a mantle of justice,/   like a bridegroom adorned with a diadem,/   like a bride bedecked with her jewels./   As the earth brings forth its plants,/   and a garden makes its growth spring up,/   so will the Lord GOD make justice and praise/   spring up before all the nations.

Second Reading: *1 Thessalonians 5:16-24*

Brothers and sister: Rejoice always. Pray without ceasing. In all circumstances give thanks, for this is the will of God for you in Christ Jesus. Do not quench the Spirit. Do not despise prophetic utterances. Test everything; retain what is good. Refrain from every kind of evil.

May the God of peace make you perfectly holy and may you entirely, spirit, soul, and body, be preserved blameless for the coming of our Lord Jesus Christ. The one who calls you is faithful, and he will also accomplish it.

Gospel Reading: *John 1:6-8; 19-28*

A man named John was sent from God. He came for testimony, to testify to the light, so that all might believe through him. He was not the light, but came to testify to the light.

And this is the testimony of John. When the Jews from Jerusalem sent priests and Levites to him to ask him, "Who are you?" he admitted and did not deny it, but admitted, "I am not the Christ." So they asked him, "What are you then? Are you Elijah?" And he said, "I am not." "Are you the Prophet?" He answered, "No." So they said to him, "Who are you, so we can give an answer to those who sent us? What do you have to say for yourself?" He said:/   "I am *the voice of one crying out in the desert,/   'make straight the way of the Lord',* as Isaiah the prophet said." Some Pharisees were also sent. They asked him, "Why then do you baptize if you are not the Christ or Elijah or the Prophet?" John answered them, "I baptize with water; but there is one among you whom you do not recognize, the one who is coming after me, whose sandal strap I am not worthy to untie." This happened in Bethany across the Jordan, where John was baptizing.

Homily Notes:

....
....
....
....
....
....
....
....
....
....
....
....
....
....
....
....
....
....
....
....
....
....

Reflection Questions for Each of the Readings:

1. *Based on the First Reading*: Bishop Barron teaches that God created us to give praise and worship to Him alone; if/when we stop praising/worshipping God we will end up giving false praise and worship to self or someone or something else. What things do many people praise and worship today? What are the consequences of this false worship?

2. *Based on the Second Reading*: What does this reading urge us to do? How do we quench the Spirit?

3. *Based on the Gospel Reading:* How did John pave the way for the Messiah? Why did he baptize with water?

Your Virtue Challenge:

       The goal of the virtuous person is to become like God. [CCC 1803] This will require identifying ways to increase this virtue and reduce opposing vice; *fasting [avoiding]* from habits or practices that oppose it; *praying* for God's help; *helping* others; and *doing penance. Based on the Second Reading,* your Virtue Challenge for the week is to increase in the virtue of:

BLAMELESSNESS

My Virtue Goals and Working Plan for the Week:

....

....

....

....

....

....

....

Daily Mass Readings for the Week:
Monday, December 18: Jeremiah 23:5-8; Matthew 1:18-25.
Tuesday, December 19: Judges 13:2-7, 24-25a; Luke 1:5-25
Wednesday, December 20: Isaiah 7:10-14; Luke 1:26-38.
Thursday, December 21: **Saint Peter Canisius** Song of Songs 2:8-14 or Zephaniah 3:14-18a; Luke 1:39-45.
Friday, December 22: 1 Samuel 1:24-28; Luke 1:46-56.
Saturday, December 23: **Saint John of Kanty** Malachi 3:1-4, 23-24; Luke 1:57-66.

14

First Reading: *2 Samuel 7:1-5, 8b-12, 14a, 16*

When King David was settled in his palace, and the LORD had given him rest from his enemies on every side, he said to Nathan the prophet, "Here I am living in a house of cedar, while the ark of God dwells in a tent!" Nathan answered the king, "Go, do whatever you have in mind, for the LORD is with you." But that night the LORD spoke to Nathan and said: "Go, tell my servant David, 'Thus says the LORD: Should you build me a house to dwell in?'

"'It was I who took you from the pasture and from the care of the flock to be commander of my people Israel. I have been with you wherever you went, and I have destroyed all your enemies before you. And I will make you famous like the great ones of the earth. I will fix a place for my people Israel; I will plant them so that they may dwell in their place without further disturbance. Neither shall the wicked continue to afflict them as they did of old, since the time I first appointed judges over my people Israel. I will give you rest from all your enemies. The LORD also reveals to you that he will establish a house for you. And when your time comes and you rest with your ancestors, I will raise up your heir after you, sprung from your loins, and I will make his kingdom firm. I will be a father to him, and he shall be a son to me. Your house and your kingdom shall endure forever before me; your throne shall stand firm forever.'"

Second Reading: *Romans 16:25-27*

Brothers and sisters: To him who can strengthen you, according to my gospel and the proclamation of Jesus Christ, according to the revelation of the mystery kept secret for long ages but now manifested through the prophetic writings and, according to the command of the eternal God, made known to all nations to bring about the obedience of faith, to the only wise God, through Jesus Christ be glory forever and ever. Amen.

Gospel Reading: *Luke 1:26-38*

The angel Gabriel was sent from God to a town of Galilee called Nazareth, to a virgin betrothed to a man named Joseph, of the house of David, and the virgin's name was Mary. And coming to her, he said, "Hail, full of grace! The Lord is with you." But she was greatly troubled at what was said and pondered what sort of greeting this might be. Then the angel said to her, "Do not be afraid, Mary, for you have found favor with God.

"Behold, you will conceive in your womb and bear a son, and you shall name him Jesus. He will be great and will be called Son of the Most High, and the Lord God will give him the throne of David his father, and he will rule over the house of Jacob forever, and of his kingdom there will be no end." But Mary said to the angel, "How can this be, since I have no relations with a man?" And the angel said to her in reply, "The Holy Spirit will come upon you, and the power of the Most High will over- shadow you. Therefore the child to be born will be called holy, the Son of God.  And behold, Elizabeth, your rela- tive, has also conceived a son in her old age, and this is the sixth month for her who was called barren; for nothing will be impossible for God." Mary said, "Behold, I am the handmaid of the Lord. May it be done to me according to your word." Then the angel departed from her.

Homily Notes:

....
....
....
....
....
....
....
....
....
....
....
....
....
....
....
....
....
....
....
....

Fourth Sunday of Advent

Reflection Questions for Each of the Readings:

1. *Based on the First Reading*: What promises did God make with David? Why was David prohibited from building the temple? Who eventually ordered the construction of the Great Temple in Jerusalem and when was it built?

2. *Based on the Second Reading*: "Paul's gospel reveals the mystery kept secret for long ages: justification and salvation through faith." [USCCB] Explain what that means to you in your own words.

3. *Based on the Gospel Reading*: Why was Mary startled and troubled? What was her response despite the *unknowns*?

Your Virtue Challenge:

The goal of the virtuous person is to become like God. [CCC 1803] This will require identifying ways to increase this virtue and reduce opposing vice; *fasting [avoiding]* from habits or practices that oppose it; *praying* for God's help; *helping* others; and *doing penance*. *Based on the Second Reading*, your Virtue Challenge for the week is to increase in the virtue of:

THOUGHTFULNESS

My Virtue Goals and Working Plan for the Week:

....

....

....

....

....

Daily Mass Readings for the Week:

Monday, December 25: **Solemnity of the Nativity of the Lord - Holy Day of Obligation** See pages 19 - 27.

Tuesday, December 26: **Feast of Saint Stephen** Acts 6:8-10; 7:54-59; Matthew 10:17-22.

Wednesday, December 27: **Feast of Saint John** 1 John 1:1-4; John 20:1a, 2-8.

Thursday, December 28: **Feast of The Holy Innocents** 1 John 1:5-2:2; Matthew 2:13-18.

Friday, December 29: **Saint Thomas Becket** 1 John 2:3-11; Luke 2:22-35

Saturday, December 30: 1 John 2:12-17; Luke 2:36-40.

MERRY CHRISTMAS!

Angels & Shepherds by Rembrandt

"On this night, the Ancient yet ever new proclamation of the Lord's birth rings out. It rings out for those keeping watch, like the shepherds in Bethlehem two thousand years ago; it rings out for those who have responded to Advent's call and who, waiting watchfully, are ready to welcome the joyful tidings which in the liturgy become our song. Today is born our Savior." Pope John Paul II: Excerpt from the Christmas Midnight Mass - 2000 AD

"At long last, Christ is born. At long last, Advent is over. We have the Christ. He, the Son of God, became man so that we might become like God." St. Irenaeus

18

CHRISTMAS AND EPIPHANY

CHRISTMAS AND EPIPHANY

The Nativity of the Lord

"O Child, who willed to have for your crib a manger; O Creator of the universe, who stripped yourself of divine glory; O Redeemer, who offered your vulnerable body in sacrifice for the salvation of humanity! May the radiance of your birth light up the night of the world. May the power of your message of love thwart the proud snares of the evil one. May the gift of your life make us understand ever more clearly the worth of the life of each human being. Too much blood is still being shed on the earth! Too much violence and too many conflicts trouble the peaceful coexistence of nations! You come to bring us peace. You are our peace! You alone can make of us "a people purified" and belonging to you for ever, a people "zealous for good deeds" (Titus 2:14). For to us a Child is born, to us a son is given! What an unfathomable mystery is hidden in the humility of this Child! We would like to touch him; we would like to embrace him. You, Mary, who keep watch over your all-powerful Son, grant us your eyes to contemplate him with faith; grant us your heart to worship him with love. In his simplicity, the Child of Bethlehem teaches us to rediscover the real meaning of our existence; he teaches us "to live sober, upright and godly lives in this world" (Titus 2:12). O Holy Night, so long awaited, which has united God and man for ever! You rekindle our hope. You fill us with ecstatic wonder. You assure us of the triumph of love over hatred, of life over death. For this reason we remain absorbed in prayer. In the luminous silence of your Nativity, you, Emmanuel, continue to speak to us. And we are ready to listen to you." *Excerpt from the Christmas Homily of Pope John Paul ll: Midnight Mass, 2003*

Our response to the Advent call prepares us to receive the joyful tidings that today the Savior of the world is born in Bethlehem. Who is Jesus? How do we prove we are His disciples?

....

....

....

....

....

Study the Stained Glass Window for *Christmas* [previous page]. List the different *signs* of Christmas that you find. Explain how they represent Christmas.

....

....

....

....

Solemnity of the Nativity of the Lord
The Vigil Mass   December 24, 2023

The **Bold Headings** [see above] [pages 21-27] indicate whether the readings on the pages below are for the Vigil, Night, Dawn or Day Mass for Christmas.

First Reading: *Isaiah 62:1-5*

For Zion's sake I will not be silent,/ for Jerusalem's sake I will not be quiet,/ until her vindication shines forth like the dawn/ and her victory like a burning torch./

Nations shall behold your vindication,/ and all the kings your glory;/ you shall be called by a new name/ pronounced by the mouth of the LORD./ You shall be a glorious crown in the hand of the LORD,/ a royal diadem held by your God./ No more shall people call you "Forsaken,"/ or your land "Desolate,"/ but you shall be called "My Delight,"/ and your land "Espoused."/ For the LORD delights in you/ and makes your land his spouse./ As a young man marries a virgin,/ your Builder shall marry you;/ and as a bridegroom rejoices in his bride/ so shall your God rejoice in you.

Second Reading: *Acts of the Apostles 13:16-17, 22-25*

When Paul reached Antioch in Pisidia and entered the synagogue, he stood up, motioned with his hand, and said, "Fellow Israelites and you others who are God-fearing, listen. The God of this people Israel chose our ancestors and exalted the people during their sojourn in the land of Egypt. With uplifted arm he led them out of it. Then he removed Saul and raised up David as king; of him he testified, I have found David, son of Jesse, a man after my own heart; he will carry out my every wish.' From this man's descendants God, according to his promise, has brought to Israel a savior, Jesus. John heralded his coming by proclaiming a baptism of repentance to all the people of Israel; and as John was completing his course, he would say, 'What do you suppose that I am? I am not he. Behold, one is coming after me;

Gospel Reading: *Matthew 1:1-25 or 1:18-25*

The book of the genealogy of Jesus Christ, the son of David, the son of Abraham.

Abraham became the father of Isaac, Isaac the father of Jacob, Jacob the father of Judah and his brothers. Judah became the father of Perez and Zerah, whose mother was Tamar. Perez became the father of Hezron, Hezron the father of Ram, Ram the father of Amminadab. Amminadab became the father of Nahshon, Nahshon the father of Salmon, Salmon the father of Boaz, whose mother was Rahab. Boaz became the father of Obed, whose mother was Ruth. Obed became the father of Jesse, Jesse the father of David the king.

David became the father of Solomon, whose mother had been the wife of Uriah. Solomon became the father of Rehoboam, Rehoboam the father of Abijah, Abijah the father of Asaph. Asaph became the father of Jehoshaphat, Jehoshaphat the father of Joram, Joram the father of Uzziah. Uzziah became the father of Jotham, Jotham the father of Ahaz, Ahaz the father of Hezekiah. Hezekiah became the father of Manasseh, Manasseh the father of Amos, Amos the father of Josiah. Josiah became the father of Jechoniah and his brothers at the time of the Babylonian exile.

After the Babylonian exile, Jechoniah became the father of Shealtiel, Shealtiel the father of Zerubbabel, Zerubbabel the father of Abiud. Abiud became the father of Eliakim, Eliakim the father of Azor, Azor the father of Zadok. Zadok became the father of Achim, Achim the father of Eliud, Eliud the father of Eleazar. Eleazar became the father of Matthan, Matthan the father of  Jacob, Jacob the father of Joseph, the husband of Mary. Of her was born Jesus who is called the Christ.

Thus the total number of generations from Abraham to David is fourteen generations; from David to the Babylonian exile, fourteen generations; from the Babylonian exile to the Christ, fourteen generations.

Now **this is how the birth of Jesus Christ came about. When his mother Mary was betrothed to Joseph, but before they lived together, she was found with child through the Holy Spirit. Joseph her husband, since he was a righteous man, yet unwilling to expose her to shame, decided to divorce her quietly. Such was his intention when, behold, the angel of the Lord appeared to him in a dream and said, "Joseph, son of David, do not be afraid to take Mary your wife into your home. For it is through the Holy Spirit that this child has been conceived in her. She will bear a son and you are to name him Jesus, because he will save his people from their sins." All this took place to fulfill what the Lord had said through the prophet:/ *Behold, the virgin shall conceive and bear a son, / and they shall name him Emmanuel,* which means "God is with us." When Joseph awoke, he did as the angel of the Lord had commanded him and took his wife into his home. He had no relations with her until she bore a son, and he named him Jesus.**

Solemnity of the Nativity of the Lord
The Night Mass
December 25, 2023

First Reading: *Isaiah 9:1-6*

The people who walked in darkness/ have seen a great light;/ upon those who dwelt in the land of gloom/ a light has shone./ You have brought them abundant joy/ and great rejoicing,/ as they rejoice before you as at the harvest,/ as people make merry when dividing spoils./ For the yoke that burdened them,/ the pole on their shoulder,/ and the rod of their taskmaster/ you have smashed, as on the day of Midian./ For every boot that tramped in battle,/ every cloak rolled in blood,/ will be burned as fuel for flames./ For a child is born to us, a son is given us;/ upon his/ shoulder dominion rests./ They name him Wonder-Counselor, God-Hero,/ Father-Forever, Prince of Peace./ His dominion is vast/. and forever peaceful,/ from David's throne, and over his kingdom,/ which he confirms and sustains/ by judgment and justice,/ both now and forever./ The zeal of the LORD of hosts will do this!

Second Reading: *Titus 2:11-14*

Beloved: The grace of God has appeared, saving all and training us to reject godless ways and worldly desires and to live temperately, justly, and devoutly in this age, as we await the blessed hope, the appearance of the glory of our great God and savior Jesus Christ, who gave himself for us to deliver us from all lawlessness and to cleanse for himself a people as his own, eager to do what is good.

Gospel Reading: *Luke 2:1-14*

In those days a decree went out from Caesar Augustus that the whole world should be enrolled. This was the first enrollment, when Quirinius was governor of Syria. So all went to be enrolled, each to his own town. And Joseph too went up from Galilee from the town of Nazareth to Judea, to the city of David that is called Bethlehem, because he was of the house and family of David, to be enrolled with Mary, his betrothed, who was with child. While they were there, the time came for her to have her child, and she gave birth to her firstborn son. She wrapped him in swaddling clothes and laid him in a manger, because there was no room for them in the inn.

Now there were shepherds in that region living in the fields and keeping the night watch over their flock. The angel of the Lord appeared to them and the glory of the Lord shone around them, and they were struck with great fear. The angel said to them, "Do not be afraid; for behold, I proclaim to you good news of great joy that will be for all the people. For today in the city of David a savior has been born for you who is Christ and Lord. And this will be a sign for you: you will find an infant wrapped in swaddling clothes and lying in a manger." And suddenly there was a multitude of the heavenly host with the angel, praising God and saying:

"Glory to God in the highest/ and on earth peace to those on whom his favor rests./"

First Reading: *Isaiah 62:11 - 12*

See, the LORD proclaims/ to the ends of the earth:/ say to daughter Zion,/ your savior comes!/ Here is his reward with him,/ his recompense before him./ They shall be called the holy people,/ the redeemed of the LORD,/ and you shall be called "Frequented,"/ a city that is not forsaken.

Second Reading: *Titus 3:4-7*

Beloved: When the kindness and generous love/ of God our savior appeared,/ not because of any righteous deeds we had done/ but because of his mercy,/ He saved us through the bath of rebirth/ and renewal by the Holy Spirit,/ whom he richly poured out on us/ through Jesus Christ our savior,/ so that we might be justified by his grace/ and become heirs of eternal life.

Gospel Reading: *Luke 2:15-20*

When the angels went away from them to heaven, the shepherds said to one another, "Let us go, then, to Bethlehem to see this thing that has taken place, which the Lord has made known to us." So they went in haste and found Mary and Joseph, and the infant lying in the manger. When they saw this, they made known the message that had been told them about this child. All who heard it were amazed by what had been told them by the shepherds. And Mary kept all these things, reflecting on them in her heart. Then the shepherds returned, glorifying and praising God for all they had heard and seen, just as it had been told to them.

Solemnity of the Nativity of the Lord
Mass during the Day   December 25, 2023

First Reading: *Isaiah 52:7-10*

How beautiful upon the mountains/ are the feet of him who brings glad tidings,/ announcing peace, bearing good news,/ announcing salvation, and saying to Zion,/ "Your God is King!"/

Hark! Your sentinels raise a cry,/ together they shout for joy,/ for they see directly, before their eyes,/ the LORD restoring Zion./ Break out together in song,/ O ruins of Jerusalem!/ For the LORD comforts his people,/ he redeems Jerusalem./ The LORD has bared his holy arm/ in the sight of all the nations;/ all the ends of the earth will behold/ the salvation of our God.

Second Reading: *Hebrews 1:1-6*

Brothers and sisters: In times past, God spoke in partial and various ways to our ancestors through the prophets; in these last days, he has spoken to us through the Son, whom he made heir of all things and through whom he created the universe,/ who is the refulgence of his glory,/ the very imprint of his being,/ and who sustains all things by his mighty word./ When he had accomplished purification from sins,/ he took his seat at the right hand of the Majesty on high,/ as far superior to the angels as the name he has inherited is more excellent than theirs./

For to which of the angels did God ever say: / *You are my son; this day I have begotten you?* / Or again: / *I will be a father to him,/ and he shall be a son to me?* And again, when he leads the firstborn into the world, / he says:/ *Let all the angels of God worship him.*

Gospel Reading: *John 1:1-18 or **1:1-5, 9-14***

In the beginning was the Word,/ and the Word was with God,/ and the Word was God./ He was in the beginning with God./ All things came to be through him,/ and without him nothing came to be./ What came to be through him was life,/ and this life was the light of the human race;/ the light shines in the darkness,/ and the darkness has not overcome it./ A man named John was sent from God. He came for testimony, to testify to the light, so that all might believe through him. He was not the light, but came to testify to the light. **The true light,/ which enlightens everyone, / was coming into the world./ He was in the world,/ and the world came to be through him,/ but the world did not know him./ He came to what was his own,/ but his own people did not accept him./ But to those who did accept him he gave power to become children of God, to those who believe in his name, who were born not by natural generation nor by hu-**

man choice nor by a man's decision but of God./   And the Word became flesh/   and made his dwelling among us,/   and we saw his glory,/   the glory as of the Father's only Son,/   full of grace and truth. John testified to him and cried out, saying, "This was he of whom I said, 'The one who is coming after me ranks ahead of me because he existed before me.'" From his fullness we have all received, grace in place of grace, because while the law was given through Moses, grace and truth came through Jesus Christ. No one has ever seen God. The only Son, God, who is at the Father's side, has revealed him.

Homily Notes:

....
....
....
....
....
....
....
....
....
....
....
....
....
....
....
....
....
....
....
....

Solemnity of the Nativity of the Lord
Mass at Day   December 25, 2023

Reflection Questions for Each of the Readings:

1. *Based on the First Reading*: "The vision of God's majesty was so overwhelming to Isaiah that military and political power faded into insignificance. He constantly called his people back to a reliance on God's promises and away from vain attempts to find security in human plans and intrigues. This vision also led him to insist on the ethical behavior that was required of human beings who wished to live in the presence of such a holy God." [USCCB] Does this apply today to believers? Explain your answer.

2. *Based on the Second Reading*: "Titus teaches the community of believers to serve as *a leaven for Christianizing the social world*. Good works are the evidence of believers' faith in God; those who engage in religious controversy are, after suitable warning, to be ignored." Titus 3:8 & 3:9-11. [USCCB] How does this apply to us today?

3. *Based on the Gospel Reading*: How do you explain [or describe] Jesus to other people? Why is he called *the Word*? What does the *Word* accomplish?

Feast of the Holy Family of Jesus, Mary, Joseph
December 31, 2023

First Reading: *Sirach 3:2-6, 12-14* **or** *Genesis 15:1-6; 21:1-3*

Sirach 3:2-6, 12-14

God sets a father in honor over his children;/ a mother's authority he confirms over her sons./ Whoever honors his father atones for sins,/ and preserves himself from them./ When he prays,/ he is heard;/ he stores up riches who reveres his mother./ Whoever honors his father is gladdened by children,/ and,/ when he prays,/ is heard./ Whoever reveres his father will live a long life;/ he who obeys his father brings comfort to his mother.

My son,/ take care of your father when he is old;/ grieve him not as long as he lives./ Even if his mind fail,/ be considerate of him; / revile him not all the days of his life; / kindness to a father will not be forgotten,/ firmly planted against the debt of your sins.

Genesis 15:1-6; 21:1-3

The word of the LORD came to Abram in a vision, saying: "Fear not, Abram! I am your shield; I will make your reward very great." But Abram said, "O Lord GOD, what good will your gifts be, if I keep on being childless and have as my heir the steward of my house, Eliezer?" Abram continued, "See, you have given me no offspring, and so one of my servants will be my heir." Then the word of the LORD came to him: "No, that one shall not be your heir; your own issue shall be your heir." The Lord took Abram outside and said, "Look up at the sky and count the stars, if you can. Just so," he added, "shall your descendants be." Abram put his faith in the LORD, who credited it to him as an act of righteousness.

The LORD took note of Sarah as he had said he would; he did for her as he had promised. Sarah became pregnant and bore Abraham a son in his old age, at the set time that God had stated. Abraham gave the name Isaac to this son of his whom Sarah bore him.

Second Reading: *Colossians* **3:12-17 or** *3:12-21* **or** *Hebrews 11:8; 11-12; 17-19*

Colossians **3:12-17 or** *3:12-21*

Brothers and sisters: Put on, as God's chosen ones, holy and beloved, heartfelt compassion, kindness, humility, gentleness, and patience, bearing with one another and forgiving one another, if one has a grievance against another; as the Lord has forgiven you, so must you also do. And over all these put on love, that is, the bond of perfection. And let the peace of Christ control your hearts, the peace into which you were also called in one body. And be thankful. Let the word of Christ dwell in you

richly, as in all wisdom you teach and admonish one another, singing psalms, hymns, and spiritual songs with gratitude in your hearts to God. And whatever you do, in word or in deed, do everything in the name of the Lord Jesus, giving thanks to God the Father through him.

Wives, be subordinate to your husbands, as is proper in the Lord. Husbands, love your wives, and avoid any bitterness toward them. Children, obey your parents in everything, for this is pleasing to the Lord. Fathers, do not provoke your children, so they may not become discouraged.

Hebrews: 11: 8, 11-12, 17-19

Brothers and sisters: By faith Abraham obeyed when he was called to go out to a place that he was to receive as an inheritance; he went out, not knowing where he was to go. By faith he received power to generate, even though he was past the normal age --and Sarah herself was sterile-- for he thought that the one who had made the promise was trustworthy. So it was that there came forth from one man, himself as good as dead, descendants as numerous as the stars in the sky and as countless as the sands on the seashore.

By faith Abraham, when put to the test, offered up Isaac, and he who had received the promises was ready to offer his only son, of whom it was said, "Through Isaac descendants shall bear your name." He reasoned that God was able to raise even from the dead, and he received Isaac back as a symbol.

Gospel Reading: *Luke 2:22-40 or **2:22, 39-40***

When the days were completed for their purification according to the law of Moses, They took him up to Jerusalem to present him to the Lord, just as it is written in the law of the Lord, *Every male that opens the womb shall be consecrated to the Lord,* and to offer the sacrifice of a *pair of turtledoves or two young pigeons,* in accordance with the dictate in the law of the Lord.

Now there was a man in Jerusalem whose name was Simeon. This man was righteous and devout, awaiting the consolation of Israel, and the Holy Spirit was upon him. It had been revealed to him by the Holy Spirit that he should not see death before he had seen the Christ of the Lord. He came in the Spirit into the temple; and when the parents brought in the child Jesus to perform the custom of the law in regard to him, He took him into his arms and blessed God, saying: "Now, Master, you may let your servant go/ in peace, according to your word,/ for my eyes have seen your salvation,/ which you prepared in sight of all the peoples,/ a light for revelation to the Gentiles,/ and glory for your people Israel." The child's father-and mother were amazed at what was said about him; and Simeon blessed them and said to Mary his mother, "Behold, this child is destined for the fall and rise of many in Israel, and to be a sign that will be contradicted — and you yourself a sword will pierce — so that the thoughts of many hearts may be revealed." There was also a prophetess, Anna, the daughter of Phanuel, of the tribe of Asher. She was advanced in years, having lived seven years with her husband after her marriage, and then as a widow until she was eighty-four. She never left the temple, but worshiped night and day with fasting and prayer. And coming forward at that very

time, she gave thanks to God and spoke about the child to all who were awaiting the redemption of Jerusalem.

When they had fulfilled all the prescriptions of the law of the Lord, they returned to Galilee, to their own town of Nazareth. The child grew and became strong, filled with wisdom; and the favor of God was upon him.

Homily Notes:

....
....
....
....
....
....
....
....
....
....
....
....
....
....

Feast of the Holy Family of Jesus, Mary, Joseph
December 31, 2023

Reflection Questions for Each of the Readings:

1. *Based on the First Reading:* Which reading was proclaimed during Mass? What did you learn from this reading?

2. *Based on the Second Reading:* Which reading was proclaimed during Mass? What did you learn from this reading?

3. *Based on the Gospel Reading:* Why did Mary and Joseph take Jesus to Jerusalem? Explain what happened in your own words.

Feast of the Holy Family of Jesus, Mary, Joseph
December 31, 2023

Your Virtue Challenge:

The goal of the virtuous person is to become like God. [CCC 1803] This will require identifying ways to increase this virtue and reduce opposing vice; *fasting [avoiding]* from habits or practices that oppose it; *praying* for God's help; *helping* others; and *doing penance. Based on the Second Reading,* your Virtue Challenge for the week is to increase in the virtue of:

OBEDIENCE
[to parents, or other rightful authority]

My Virtue Goals and Working Plan for the Week:

....

....

....

....

....

Daily Mass Readings for the Week:

Monday, January 1: **Solemnity of Mary, the Holy Mother of God** Numbers 6:22-27; Galatians 4:4-7; Luke 2:16-21 See next page.

Tuesday, January 2: **Saints Basil the Great and Gregory Nazianzen** 1 John 2:22-28; John 1:19-28.

Wednesday, January 3: The **Most Holy Name of Jesus** 1 John 2:29-3:6; John 1:29-34.

Thursday, January 4: **Saint Elizabeth Ann Seton** 1 John 3:7-10; John 1:35-42.

Friday, January 5: **Saint John Neumann** 1 John 3:11-21; John 1:43-51.

Saturday, January 6: **Saint André Bessette** 1 John 5:5-13; Mark 1:7-11 or Luke 3:23-38 or 3:23, 31-34, 36, 38.

Solemnity of Mary, the Holy Mother of God

January 1, 2024

Note: This year, *The Solemnity of Mary* is not a declared Holy Day of Obligation; however, many Catholics will attend the Solemnity Mass.

First Reading: *Numbers 6:22-27*

The LORD said to Moses: "Speak to Aaron and his sons and tell them: This is how you shall bless the Israelites. Say to them:/   The LORD bless you and keep you!/   The LORD let his face shine upon you, /   and be gracious to you!/   The LORD look upon you kindly and give you peace!/   So shall they invoke my name upon the Israelites, and I will bless them."

Second Reading: *Galatians 4:4-7*

Brothers and sisters: When the fullness of time had come, God sent his Son,   born of a woman, born under the law,   to ransom those under the law,   so that we might receive adoption as sons. As proof that you are sons,   God sent the Spirit of his Son into our hearts,   crying out, "Abba, Father!" So you are no longer a slave but a son,   and if a son then also an heir, through God.

Gospel Reading: *Luke 2:16-21*

The shepherds went in haste to Bethlehem and found Mary and Joseph, and the infant lying in the manger. When they saw this,   they made known the message   that had been told them about this child. All who heard it were amazed   by what had been told them by the shepherds. And Mary kept all these things, reflecting on them in her heart. Then the shepherds returned,   glorifying and praising God   for all they had heard and seen,   just as it had been told to them.

When eight days were completed for his circumcision,   he was named Jesus, the name given him by the angel   before he was conceived in the womb.

Solemnity of Mary, the Holy Mother of God

Homily Notes:

....
....
....
....
....
....
....
....
....
....
....
....
....
....
....
....
....
....
....
....
....
....
....
....
....
....
....
....
....
....

Reflection Questions for Each of the Readings:

1. *Based on the First Reading*: The Book of Numbers provides a very beautiful blessing that we can pray with our loved ones as they leave home for work, school, or other activities. Use it this week.

2. *Based on the Second Reading*: Explain who is an heir. According to this reading, who do we share this *honorable right* with?

3. *Based on the Gospel*: "Mary kept all these things, reflecting on them in her heart." Some Bibles use the word *ponder* rather than *reflect*. Is there a difference between the two words? When and how do you reflect on God's word? What do you think the shepherds relayed to Mary and Joseph that moved them to reflecting on Jesus' birth?

Solemnity of The Epiphany of the Lord

First Reading: *Isaiah 60:1-6*

Rise up in splendor, Jerusalem!/ Your light has come,/ the glory of the Lord shines upon you./ See, darkness covers the earth,/ and thick clouds cover the peoples;/ but upon you the LORD shines,/ and over you appears his glory./ Nations shall walk by your light,/ and kings by your shining radiance./ Raise your eyes and look about;/ they all gather and come to you:/ your sons come from afar,/ and your daughters in the arms of their nurses. /

Then you shall be radiant at what you see,/ your heart shall throb and overflow,/ for the riches of the sea shall be emptied out before you,/ the wealth of nations shall be brought to you./ Caravans of camels shall fill you,/ dromedaries from Midian and Ephah;/ all from Sheba shall come/ bearing gold and frankincense,/ and proclaiming the praises of the LORD.

Second Reading: *Ephesians 3:2-3a, 5-6*

Brothers and sisters: You have heard of the stewardship of God's grace that was given to me for your benefit, namely, that the mystery was made known to me by revelation. It was not made known to people in other generations as it has now been revealed to his holy apostles and prophets by the Spirit: that the Gentiles are coheirs, members of the same body, and copartners in the promise in Christ Jesus through the gospel.

Gospel Reading: *Matthew 2:1-12*

When Jesus was born in Bethlehem of Judea, in the days of King Herod, behold, magi from the east arrived in Jerusalem, saying, "Where is the newborn king of the Jews? We saw his star at its rising and have come to do him homage." When King Herod heard this, he was greatly troubled, and all Jerusalem with him. Assembling all the chief priests and the scribes of the people, He inquired of them where the Christ was to be born. They said to him, "In Bethlehem of Judea, for thus it has been written through the prophet:
And you, Bethlehem, land of Judah,/ are by no means least among the rulers of Judah;/ since from you shall come a ruler,/ who is to shepherd my people Israel."/ Then Herod called the magi secretly and ascertained from them the time of the star's appearance. He sent them to Bethlehem and said, "Go and search diligently for the child. When you have found him, bring me word, that I too may go and do him homage." After their audience with the king they set out. And behold, the star that they had seen at its rising preceded them, until it came and stopped over the place where the child was. They were overjoyed at seeing the star, and on entering the house they saw the child with Mary his mother. They prostrated themselves and did him homage. Then they opened

their treasures and offered him gifts of gold, frankincense, and myrrh. And having been warned in a dream not to return to Herod, they departed for their country by another way.

Homily Notes:

....

....

....

....

....

....

....

....

....

....

....

....

....

....

....

....

....

....

....

....

....

....

....

....

....

....

....

....

Reflection Questions for Each of the Readings:

1. *Based on the First Reading*: Isaiah was a great prophet of the Old Testament. Who is Isaiah talking about? What is the role of a prophet?

2. *Based on the Second Reading*: Who are the Gentiles coheirs with? Define coheir.

3. *Based on the Gospel Reading*: What do each of the Magi's gifts [Gold, Frankincense, & Myrrh] represent? Why did the Magi have to return home another way? Where did the Magi come from?

Your Virtue Challenge:

The goal of the virtuous person is to become like God. [CCC 1803] This will require identifying ways to increase this virtue and reduce opposing vice; *fasting [avoiding]* from habits or practices that oppose it; *praying* for God's help; *helping* others; and *doing penance. Based on the Second Reading,* your Virtue Challenge for the week is to increase in the virtue of:

STEWARDSHIP
[of God's Gifts]

My Virtue Goals and Working Plan for the Week:

....
....
....
....
....
....

Daily Mass Readings for the Week:

Monday, January 8: **Feast of The Baptism of the Lord** Pages 41 - 43.

Tuesday, January 9:1 Samuel 1:9-20; Mark 1:21-28 or 1 Samuel 1:1-8; 9-20; Mark 1:14-20; 21-28.

Wednesday, January 10: 1 Samuel 3:1-10, 19-20; Mark 1:29-39.

Thursday, January 11: 1 Samuel 4:1-11; Mark 1:40-45.

Friday, January 12: 1 Samuel 8:4-7, 10-22a; Mark 2:1-12.

Saturday, January 13: **Saint Hilary** 1 Samuel 9:1- 4, 17-19; 10:1a; Mark 2:13-

17.

On the Feast of the Epiphany

Homily of Pope Benedict XVI; Vatican Basilica; Sunday, 6 January 2013

Dear Brothers and Sisters,

The Wise Men from the East who, guided by the star, made their way to the manger of Bethlehem, are only the beginning of a great procession which winds throughout history. Thus the liturgy reads the Gospel which relates the journey of the Wise Men, together with the magnificent prophetic visions of the sixtieth chapter of the Book of Isaiah and Psalm 71, which depict in bold imagery the pilgrimage of the peoples to Jerusalem. Like the shepherds, who as the first visitors to the newborn Child in the manger, embodied the poor of Israel and more generally those humble souls who live in deep interior closeness to Jesus, so the men from the East embody the world of the peoples, the Church of the Gentiles – the men and women who in every age set out on the way which leads to the Child of Bethlehem, to offer him homage as the Son of God and to bow down before him.

The Church calls this feast "Epiphany" – the appearance of the Godhead. If we consider the fact that from the very beginning men and women of every place, of every continent, of all the different cultures, mentalities and lifestyles, have been on the way to Christ, then we can truly say that this pilgrimage and this encounter with God in the form of a Child is an epiphany of God's goodness and loving kindness for humanity (cf. Tit 3:4).

Based on the account of Matthew, we can gain a certain idea of what sort of men these were, who followed the sign of the star and set off to find that King who would establish not only for Israel but for all mankind a new kind of kingship. What kind of men were they? These men who set out towards the unknown were, in any event, men with a restless heart. Men driven by a restless quest for God and the salvation of the world. They were filled with expectation, not satisfied with their secure income and their respectable place in society. They were looking for something greater. They were no doubt learned men, quite knowledgeable about the heavens and probably possessed of a fine philosophical formation. But they desired more than simply knowledge about things. They wanted above all else to know what is essential. They wanted to know how we succeed in being human. And therefore they wanted to know if God exists, and where and how he exists. Whether he is concerned about us and how we can encounter him. Nor did they want just to wanted above all else to know what is essential. They wanted to know how we succeed in being human. And therefore they wanted to know if God exists, and where and how he exists. Whether he is concerned about us and how we can encounter him. Nor did they want just to know. They wanted to understand the truth about selves and about God and the world. Their outward pilgrimage was an expression of their inward journey, the inner pilgrimage of their hearts. They were men who sought God and were ultimately on the way towards him. They were seekers after God. Faith's inner pilgrimage towards God occurs above all in prayer. Saint Augustine once said that prayer is ultimately nothing more than the realization and radicalization of our yearning for God. Instead of "yearning", we could also translate the word as "restlessness" and say that prayer would detach us from our false security, from our being enclosed within material and visible realities, and would give us a restlessness for God and thus an openness to and concern for one another. Let us return to the Wise Men from the East. These were also, and above all, men of courage, the courage and humility born of faith. Courage was needed to grasp the meaning of the star as a sign to set out, to go forth

– towards the unknown, the uncertain, on paths filled with hidden dangers. We can imagine that their decision was met with derision: the scorn of those realists who could only mock the reveries of such men. The Wise Men followed the star, and thus came to Jesus, to the great Light which enlightens everyone coming into this world (cf. John 1:9). As pilgrims of faith, the Wise Men themselves became stars shining in the firmament of history and they show us the way. The saints are God's true constellations, which light up the nights of this world, serving as our guides. Saint Paul, in his Letter to the Philippians, told his faithful that they must shine like stars in the world (cf. 2:15).

Feast of the Baptism of the Lord

January 8, 2024

First Reading: *Isaiah 42:1-4, 6-7* or *Isaiah 55:1-11*

Thus says the LORD:/ Here is my servant whom I uphold,/ my chosen one with whom I am pleased,/ upon whom I have put my spirit;/ he shall bring forth justice to the nations,/ not crying out, not shouting,/ not making his voice heard in the street./ a bruised reed he shall not break,/ and a smoldering wick he shall not quench,/ until he establishes justice on the earth;/ the coastlands will wait for his teaching./

I, the LORD, have called you for the victory of justice,/ I have grasped you by the hand;/ I formed you, and set you/ as a covenant of the people,/ a light for the nations,/ to open the eyes of the blind,/ to bring out prisoners from confinement,/ and from the dungeon, those who live in darkness.

Isaiah 55:1-11

Thus says the LORD:/ All you who are thirsty,/ come to the water!/ You who have no money,/ come, receive grain and eat;/ come, without paying and without cost,/ drink wine and milk!/ Why spend your money for what is not bread,/ your wages for what fails to satisfy?/ Heed me, and you shall eat well,/ you shall delight in rich fare./ Come to me heedfully,/ listen, that you may have life./ I will renew with you the everlasting covenant,/ the benefits assured to David./ As I made him a witness to the peoples,/ a leader and commander of nations,/ so shall you summon a nation you knew not,/ and nations that knew you not shall run to you,/ because of the LORD, your God,/ the Holy One of Israel, who has glorified you.

Seek the LORD while he may be found,/ call him while he is near./ Let the scoundrel forsake his way,/ and the wicked man his thoughts;/ let him turn to the LORD for mercy;/ to our God, who is generous in forgiving./ For my thoughts are not your thoughts,/ nor are your ways my ways, says the LORD./ As high as the heavens are above the earth / so high are my ways above your ways/ and my thoughts above your thoughts./

For just as from the heavens/ the rain and snow come down/ and do not return there/ till they have watered the earth,/ making it fertile and fruitful,/ giving seed to the one who sows/ and bread to the one who eats,/ so shall my word be/ that goes forth from my mouth;/ my word shall not return to me void,/ but shall do my will,/ achieving the end for which I sent it.

Second Reading: *Acts of the Apostles 10:34-38* **or** *1 John 5:1-9*

Peter proceeded to speak to those gathered in the house of Cornelius, saying: "In truth, I see that God shows no partiality. Rather, in every nation whoever fears him and acts uprightly is acceptable to him. You know the word that he sent to the Israelites as he proclaimed peace through Jesus Christ, who is Lord of all, what has happened all over Judea, beginning in Galilee after the baptism that John preached, how God anointed Jesus of Nazareth with the Holy Spirit and power. He went about doing good and healing all those oppressed by the devil, for God was with him."

1 John 5:1-9

Beloved: Everyone who believes that Jesus is the Christ is begotten by God, and everyone who loves the Father loves also the one begotten by him. In this way we know that we love the children of God when we love God and obey his commandments. For the love of God is this, that we keep his commandments. And his commandments are not burdensome, for whoever is begotten by God conquers the world. And the victory that conquers the world is our faith. Who indeed is the victor over the world but the one who believes that Jesus is the Son of God? This is the one who came through water and blood, Jesus Christ, not by water alone, but by water and blood. The Spirit is the one who testifies, and the Spirit is truth. So there are three that testify, the Spirit, the water, and the blood, and the three are of one accord. If we accept human testimony, the testimony of God is surely greater. Now the testimony of God is this, that he has testified on behalf of his Son.

Gospel Reading: *Mark 1:7-11*

This is what John the Baptist proclaimed: "One mightier than I is coming after me. I am not worthy to stoop and loosen the thongs of his sandals. I have baptized you with water; he will baptize you with the Holy Spirit."

It happened in those days that Jesus came from Nazareth of Galilee and was baptized in the Jordan by John. On coming up out of the water he saw the heavens being torn open and the Spirit, like a dove, descending upon him. And a voice came from the heavens, "You are my beloved Son; with you I am well pleased."

Feast of the Baptism of the Lord

January 8, 2024

Homily Notes:

Reflection Questions for Each of the Readings:
1. *Based on the First Reading*: What is Isaiah foretelling?

2. *Based on the Second Reading*: Explain partiality. How does God prove his impartiality? How does partiality attack our human dignity?

3. *Based on the Gospel Reading*: Why did John baptize with water? Explain what the baptism by the Holy Spirit means?

Ordinary Time

The Church will enter **Ordinary Time** after Epiphany next Sunday even though next Sunday is already considered to be the Second Sunday of Ordinary Time! An explanation of Ordinary Time can be found on page 46.

TIME AFTER EPIPHANY

Explanation of Ordinary Time

The weeks of Ordinary Time [of the Liturgical Calendar] take us through the life of Christ. This becomes another opportunity for our personal conversion and growth in Christ; and living in the life of Christ. Ordinary Time is a period in which the *mysteries of Christ* are called to penetrate ever more deeply into history until all things are finally *caught up in Christ*. The goal, toward which all of history is directed, is represented by the final Sunday in Ordinary Time: the Solemnity of Our Lord Jesus Christ, King of the Universe.[1]

In 1955, Pope Pius XI declared that the Baptism of the Lord was to be celebrated on the last day of the Season of Christmas; therefore, the following Monday would normally mark the first day of Ordinary Time [OT]. However, this year, the Church celebrates Jesus' Baptism on Monday with the previous Sunday being the Feast of the Epiphany [still within the Season of Christmas/Epiphany]. Therefore, the Second Sunday of Ordinary Time is actually this year's first Sunday within Ordinary Time despite being referred to as the Second Sunday. Yes, the Liturgical Calendar gets confusing sometimes.

Most of our life [living] actually happens during the ordinary time of every year - Liturgical or Calendar. It's important to know that Ordinary Time [the name] is not meant to connote *insignificance*. It's important to reflect on how and why every day matters. Note that there is no First Sunday of Ordinary Time this Liturgical Year; rather it starts with the Second Sunday due to the layout of the 2024 Calendar Year.

We can all grow in our faith and personal life everyday - even during ordinary times. Collect your thoughts on how you can do this and write them down below.

....
....
....
....

The Stained Glass image depicts Ordinary Time. What symbols, images, and colors depict Ordinary Time? List them below.

....
....
....
....
....
.

References:

[1] USCCB https://www.usccb.org/prayer-worship/liturgical-year/ordinary-time

Second Sunday of Ordinary Time

First Reading: *1 Samuel 3:3b-10, 19*

Samuel was sleeping in the temple of the LORD where the ark of God was. The LORD called to Samuel, who answered, "Here I am." Samuel ran to Eli and said, "Here I am. You called me." "I did not call you, " Eli said. "Go back to sleep." So he went back to sleep. Again the LORD called Samuel, who rose and went to Eli. "Here I am, " he said. "You called me." But Eli answered, "I did not call you, my son. Go back to sleep."

At that time Samuel was not familiar with the LORD, because the LORD had not revealed anything to him as yet. The LORD called Samuel again, for the third time. Getting up and going to Eli, he said, "Here I am. You called me." Then Eli understood that the LORD was calling the youth. So he said to Samuel, "Go to sleep, and if you are called, reply, Speak, LORD, for your servant is listening." When Samuel went to sleep in his place, the LORD came and revealed his presence, calling out as before, "Samuel, Samuel!" Samuel answered, "Speak, for your servant is listening."

Samuel grew up, and the LORD was with him, not permitting any word of his to be without effect.

Second Reading: *1 Corinthians 6:13c-15a, 17-20*

Brothers and sisters: The body is not for immorality, but for the Lord, and the Lord is for the body; God raised the Lord and will also raise us by his power.

Do you not know that your bodies are members of Christ? But whoever is joined to the Lord becomes one Spirit with him. Avoid immorality. Every other sin a person commits is outside the body, but the immoral person sins against his own body. Do you not know that your body is a temple of the Holy Spirit within you, whom you have from God, and that you are not your own? For you have been purchased at a price. Therefore glorify God in your body.

Gospel Reading: *John 1:35-42*

John was standing with two of his disciples, and as he watched Jesus walk by, he said, "Behold, the Lamb of God." The two disciples heard what he said and followed Jesus. Jesus turned and saw them following him and said to them, "What are you looking for?" They said to him, "Rabbi" - which translated means Teacher -; "where are you staying?" He said to them, "Come, and you will see." So they went and saw where Jesus was staying, and they stayed with him that day. It was about four in the afternoon. Andrew, the brother of Simon Peter, was one of the two who heard John and followed Jesus. He first found his own brother Simon and told him, "We have found the Messiah"-

which is translated Christ. Then he brought him to Jesus. Jesus looked at him and said, "You are Simon the son of John; you will be called Cephas" — which is translated Peter.

Homily Notes:

....
....
....
....
....
....
....
....
....
....
....
....
....
....
....
....
....
....
....
....
....

Reflection Questions for Each of the Readings:

1. *Based on the First Reading*: Samuel is a pivotal figure in the Old Testament. "He bridges the gap between the period of the Judges and the monarchy, and guides Israel's transition to kingship." USCCB} How old was Samuel when God called him? How did Samuel's answer God's call?

2. *Based on the Second Reading:* Saint Pope JP ll wrote extensively about authentic love [God's Love] which is always free, full, faithful, fruitful and forever. Define immorality & explain how it opposes authentic love.

3. *Based on the Gospel Reading:* John called Jesus the *Lamb of God.* Explain the meaning of this title.

Your Virtue Challenge:

The goal of the virtuous person is to become like God. [CCC 1803] This will require identifying ways to increase this virtue and reduce opposing vice; *fasting [avoiding]* from habits or practices that oppose it; *praying* for God's help; *helping* others; and *doing penance. Based on the Second Reading,* your Virtue Challenge for the week is to increase in the virtue of:

CHASTITY & MODESTY

My Virtue Goals and Working Plan for the Week:

....

....

....

....

....

....

Daily Mass Readings for the Week:

Monday, January 15: 1 Samuel 15:16-23; Mark 2:18-22.

Tuesday, January 16: 1 Samuel 16:1-13; Mark 2:23-28.

Wednesday, January 17: **St. Anthony** 1 Samuel 17:32-33, 37, 40-51; Mark 3:1-6.

Thursday, January 18: 1 Samuel 18:6-9; 19:1-7; Mark 3:7-12.

Friday, January 19: 1 Samuel 24:3-21; Mark 3:13-19.

Saturday, January 20: **Sts. Fabian & Sebastian** 2 Samuel 1:1-4, 11-12, 19, 23-27; Mark 3:20-21.

First Reading: *Jonah 3:1-5, 10*

The word of the LORD came to Jonah, saying: "Set out for the great city of Nineveh, and announce to it the message that I will tell you." So Jonah made ready and went to Nineveh, according to the LORD'S bidding. Now Nineveh was an enormously large city; it took three days to go through it. Jonah began his journey through the city, and had gone but a single day's walk announcing, "Forty days more and Nineveh shall be destroyed," when the people of Nineveh believed God; they proclaimed a fast and all of them, great and small, put on sackcloth.

When God saw by their actions how they turned from their evil way, he repented of the evil that he had threatened to do to them; he did not carry it out.

Second Reading: *1 Corinthians 7:29-31*

I tell you, brothers and sisters, the time is running out. From now on, let those having wives act as not having them, those weeping as not weeping, those rejoicing as not rejoicing, those buying as not owning, those using the world as not using it fully. For the world in its present form is passing away.

Gospel Reading: *Mark 1:14-20*

After John had been arrested, Jesus came to Galilee proclaiming the gospel of God: "This is the time of fulfillment. The kingdom of God is at hand. Repent, and believe in the gospel."

As he passed by the Sea of Galilee, he saw Simon and his brother Andrew casting their nets into the sea; they were fishermen. Jesus said to them, "Come after me, and I will make you fishers of men." Then they abandoned their nets and followed him. He walked along a little farther and saw James, the son of Zebedee, and his brother John. They too were in a boat mending their nets. Then he called them. So they left their father Zebedee in the boat along with the hired men and followed him.

Third Sunday of Ordinary Time

Homily Notes:

....
....
....
....
....
....
....
....
....
....
....
....
....
....
....
....
....
....
....
....
....
....

Reflection Questions for Each of the Readings:

1. *Based on the First Reading*: Nineveh is the capital city of Israel's ancient enemy - which one? Jonah presumes God's love & mercy only extends to Israel. Was he right or wrong? Describe God's love & mercy.

2. Based on the Second Reading: Paul answered many spiritual/ theological questions for the Corinthians regarding marriage, life, faith, etc. Explain how these teachings still apply today.

3. Based on the Gospel Reading: This reading describes how Jesus *called* his apostles. Why did Jesus select these men? How does Jesus call his disciples today?

Your Virtue Challenge:

The goal of the virtuous person is to become like God. [CCC 1803] This will require identifying ways to increase this virtue and reduce opposing vice; *fasting [avoiding]* from habits or practices that oppose it; *praying* for God's help; *helping* others; and *doing penance. Based on the Second Reading,* your Virtue Challenge for the week is to increase in the virtue of:

COURAGE

My Virtue Goals and Working Plan for the Week:

....
....
....
....
....

Daily Mass Readings for the Week:
Monday, January 22: **Day of Prayer for the Legal Protection of Unborn Children** 2 Samuel 5:1-7, 10; Mark 3:22-30.
Tuesday, January 23: **Sts. Vincent & Marianne Cope.** 2 Samuel 6:12b-15, 17-19; Mark 3:31-35.
Wednesday, January 24: **Saint Francis de Sales** 2 Samuel 7:4-17; Mark 4:1-20.
Thursday, January 25: **The Conversion of Saint Paul the Apostle** Acts 22:3-16 or Acts 9:1-22; Mark 16:15-18.
Friday, January 26: **Sts. Timothy & Titus** 2 Timothy 1:1-8 or Titus 1:1-5; Mark 4:26-34.
Saturday, January 27: **Saint Angela Merici** 2 Samuel 12:1-7a, 10-17; Mark 4:35-41.

52

Fourth Sunday of Ordinary Time

First Reading: *Deuteronomy 18:15-20*

Moses spoke to all the people, saying: "A prophet like me will the LORD, your God, raise up for you from among your own kin; to him you shall listen. This is exactly what you requested of the LORD, your God, at Horeb on the day of the assembly, when you said, 'Let us not again hear the voice of the LORD, our God, nor see this great fire any more, lest we die.' And the LORD said to me, 'This was well said. I will raise up for them a prophet like you from among their kin, and will put my words into his mouth; he shall tell them all that I command him. Whoever will not listen to my words which he speaks in my name, I myself will make him answer for it. But if a prophet presumes to speak in my name an oracle that I have not commanded him to speak or speaks in the name of other gods, he shall die.'"

Second Reading: *1 Corinthians 7:32-35*

Brothers and sisters: I should like you to be free of anxieties. An unmarried man is anxious about the things of the Lord, how he may please the Lord. But a married man is anxious about the things of the world, how he may please his wife, and he is divided. An unmarried woman or a virgin is anxious about the things of the Lord, so that she may be holy in both body and spirit. A married woman, on the other hand, is anxious about the things of the world, how she may please her husband. I am telling you this for your own benefit, not to impose a restraint upon you, but for the sake of propriety and adherence to the Lord without distraction.

Gospel Reading: *Mark 1:21-28*

Then they came to Capernaum, and on the sabbath Jesus entered the synagogue and taught. The people were astonished at his teaching, for he taught them as one having authority and not as the scribes. In their synagogue was a man with an unclean spirit; he cried out, "What have you to do with us, Jesus of Nazareth? Have you come to destroy us? I know who you are—the Holy One of God!" Jesus rebuked him and said, "Quiet! Come out of him!" The unclean  spirit convulsed him and with a loud cry came out of him. All were amazed and asked one another, "What is this? A new teaching with authority.He commands even the unclean spirits and they obey him." His fame spread everywhere -

throughout the whole region of Galilee.

Homily Notes:

....
....
....
....
....
....
....
....
....
....
....
....
....
....
....
....
....
....
....
....
....
....

Reflection Questions for Each of the Readings:

1. *Based on the First Reading*: Moses is speaking to the Israelites about the need for faithful prophets. Did you know: The Sacraments of Baptism and Confirmation call us to be lay priests; prophets; and kings for others? Explain each of these roles below.

Fourth Sunday of Ordinary Time
January 28, 2024

2. Based on the Second Reading: St. Paul reminds us to try and reduce the many *distractions* we face everyday. Why are distractions a problem? How do they interfere with our lives?

3. Based on the Gospel Reading: The people were astonished at Jesus' teachings. Where does His authority come from? Imagine you are present in this scene. What are your thoughts or reactions?

Your Virtue Challenge:

The goal of the virtuous person is to become like God. [CCC 1803] This will require identifying ways to increase this virtue and reduce opposing vice; *fasting [avoiding]* from habits or practices that oppose it; *praying* for God's help; *helping* others; and *doing penance. Based on the Second Reading,* your Virtue Challenge for the week is to increase in the virtue of:

PEACEFULNESS

My Virtue Goals and Working Plan for the Week:

....
....
....
....
....

Daily Mass Readings for the Week:

Monday, January 29: 2 Samuel 15:13-14, 30; 16:5-13; Mark 5:1-20.
Tuesday, January 30: 2 Samuel 18:9-10, 14b, 24-25a, 30—19:3; Mark 5:21-43.
Wednesday, January 31: **Saint John Bosco** 2 Samuel 24:2, 9-17; Mark 6:1-6.
Thursday, February 1:1 Kings 2:1-4, 10-12; Mark 6:7-13.
Friday, February 2: **The Presentation of the Lord** Malachi 3:1-4; Hebrews 2:14-18; Luke 2:22-40 or 2:22-32.
Saturday, February 3: **Sts. Blaise & Ansgar** 1 Kings 3:4-13; Mark 6:30-34.

Fifth Sunday of Ordinary Time

February 4, 2024

First Reading: *Job 7:1-4, 6-7*

Job spoke, saying:/ Is not man's life on earth a drudgery?/ Are not his days those of hirelings?/ He is a slave who longs for the shade,/ a hireling who waits for his wages./ So I have been assigned months of misery,/ and troubled nights have been allotted to me./ If in bed I say,/ "When shall I arise?"/ then the night drags on;/ I am filled with restlessness until the dawn./ My days are swifter than a weaver's shuttle;/ they come to an end without hope./ Remember that my life is like the wind;/ I shall not see happiness again.

Second Reading: *1 Corinthians 9:16-19, 22-23*

Brothers and sisters: If I preach the gospel, this is no reason for me to boast, for an obligation has been imposed on me, and woe to me if I do not preach it! If I do so willingly, I have a recompense, but if unwillingly, then I have been entrusted with a stewardship. What then is my recompense? That, when I preach, I offer the gospel free of charge so as not to make full use of my right in the gospel. Although I am free in regard to all, I have made myself a slave to all so as to win over as many as possible. To the weak I became weak, to win over the weak. I have become all things to all, to save at least some. All this I do for the sake of the gospel, so that I too may have a share in it.

Gospel Reading: *Mark 1:29-39*

On leaving the synagogue Jesus entered the house of Simon and Andrew with James and John. Simon's mother-in-law lay sick with a fever. They immediately told him about her. He approached, grasped her hand, and helped her up. Then the fever left her and she waited on them.

When it was evening, after sunset, they brought to him all who were ill or possessed by demons. The whole town was gathered at the door. He cured many who were sick with various diseases, and he drove out many demons, not permitting them to speak because they knew him.

Rising very early before dawn, he left and went off to a deserted place, where he prayed. Simon and those who were with him pursued him and on finding him said, "Everyone is looking for you." He told them, "Let us go on to the nearby villages that I may preach there also. For this purpose have I come." So he went into their synagogues, preaching and driving out demons through-

Fifth Sunday of Ordinary Time

February 4, 2024

out the whole of Galilee.

Homily Notes:

....

....

....

....

....

....

....

....

....

....

....

....

....

....

....

....

....

....

....

....

....

Reflection Questions for Each of the Readings:

1. *Based on the First Reading*: Have you ever been innocent - like Job - yet were blamed for defeat; losses, or personal problems? What does Job teach us to do about false blame?

Fifth Sunday of Ordinary Time
February 4, 2024

2. *Based on the Second Reading*: Explain St. Paul's doxology: "To all, I became all, so that I might save all. I do everything for the sake of the Gospel, so that I may become its partner."

3. *Based on the Gospel Reading*: Jesus releases the sick from their physical and mental and spiritual bondage. Let's ask Jesus to heal us from our bondage to sin by going to regular Confession.

Your Virtue Challenge:
The goal of the virtuous person is to become like God. [CCC 1803] This will require identifying ways to increase this virtue and reduce opposing vice; *fasting [avoiding]* from habits or practices that oppose it; *praying* for God's help; *helping* others; and *doing penance. Based on the Second Reading,* your Virtue Challenge for the week is to increase in the virtue of:

HELPFULNESS

My Virtue Goals and Working Plan for the Week:

....
....
....
....
....

Daily Mass Readings for the Week:
Monday, February 5: **Saint Agatha** 1 Kings 8:1-7, 9-13; Mark 6:53-56.
Tuesday, February 6: **St. Paul Miki and Companions** 1 Kings 8:22-23, 27-30; Mark 7:1-13.
Wednesday, February 7: 1 Kings 10:1-10; Mark 7:14-23.
Thursday, February 8: **Sts. Jerome Emiliani & Josephine Bakhita** 1 Kings 11:4-13; Mark 7:24-30.
Friday, February 9: 1 Kings 11:29-32; 12:19; Mark 7:31-37.
Saturday, February 10: **Saint Scholastica** 1 Kings 12:26-32; 13:33-34; Mark 8:1-10.
58

Sixth Sunday of Ordinary Time

February 11, 2024

First Reading: *Leviticus 13:1-2, 44-46*

The LORD said to Moses and Aaron, "If someone has on his skin a scab or pustule or blotch which appears to be the sore of leprosy, he shall be brought to Aaron, the priest, or to one of the priests among his descendants. If the man is leprous and unclean, the priest shall declare him unclean by reason of the sore on his head.

"The one who bears the sore of leprosy shall keep his garments rent and his head bare, and shall muffle his beard; he shall cry out, 'Unclean, unclean!' As long as the sore is on him he shall declare himself unclean, since he is in fact unclean. He shall dwell apart, making his abode outside the camp."

Second Reading: *1 Corinthians 10:31-11:1*

Brothers and sisters, Whether you eat or drink, or whatever you do, do everything for the glory of God. Avoid giving offense, whether to the Jews or Greeks or the church of God, just as I try to please everyone in every way, not seeking my own benefit but that of the many, that they may be saved. Be imitators of me, as I am of Christ.

Gospel Reading: *Mark 1:40-45*

A leper came to Jesus and kneeling down begged him and said, "If you wish, you can make me clean." Moved with pity, he stretched out his hand, touched him, and said to him, "I do will it. Be made clean." The leprosy left him immediately, and he was made clean. Then, warning him sternly, he dismissed him at once.

He said to him, "See that you tell no one anything, but go, show yourself to the priest and offer for your cleansing what Moses prescribed; that will be proof for them."

The man went away and began to publicize the whole matter. He spread the report abroad so that it was impossible for Jesus to enter a town openly. He remained outside in deserted places, and people kept coming to him from everywhere.

Homily Notes:

....

....

....

....

59

....
....
....
....
....
....
....
....
....
....
....
....
....
....
....
....
....
....
....
....
....
....
....

Reflection Questions for Each of the Readings:

1. *Based on the First Reading*: Why were lepers isolated from their communities after contracting leprosy? Fear still isolates people from one another today. Name several instances of when this happened to you. What/ how can the faithful help relieve other people's suffering when it is caused by isolation?

2. *Based on the Second Reading*: Why are we often reluctant to *be imitators of Christ*?

3. *Based on the Gospel Reading:* Why did it become impossible for Jesus to walk openly around many towns? Why do the Gospel writers make note of the fact that Jesus *touches* everyone he heals? What should his example teach us?

Your Virtue Challenge:

The goal of the virtuous person is to become like God. [CCC 1803] This will require identifying ways to increase this virtue and reduce opposing vice; *fasting [avoiding]* from habits or practices that oppose it; *praying* for God's help; *helping* others; and *doing penance. Based on the Second Reading,* your Virtue Challenge for the week is to increase in the virtue of:

JUSTICE

My Virtue Goals and Working Plan for the Week:

....

....

....

....

....

Daily Mass Readings for the Week:
Monday, February 12: James 1:1-11; Mark 8:11-13.
Tuesday, February 13: James 1:12-18; Mark 8:14-21.
Wednesday, February 14: **Ash Wednesday:** see pages 60 - 63.
Thursday, February 15: Deuteronomy 30:15-20; Luke 9:22-25.
Friday, February 16: Isaiah 58:1-9a; Matthew 9:14-15.
Saturday, February 17: Isaiah 58:9b-14; Luke 5:27-32.

On Mercy   Lenten Reflection #1
Pope Francis; Wednesday General Audience, 12 October 2016

How can we be **witnesses of mercy**? We do not think that it is done with great efforts or superhuman actions. No, it is not so. The Lord shows us a very simple path, made by small actions which, nonetheless, have great value in his eyes, to the extent to which he has told us that it is by these actions we will be judged. In fact, one of the most beautiful pages from Matthew's Gospel brings us the lesson which we can, in every way, hold to be true as the "testament of Jesus" by the Evangelist, who had experienced the action of Mercy directly on himself.

Jesus says that every time we give food to the hungry and drink to the thirsty, cloth the naked and welcome the foreigner, visit the sick or imprisoned, we do the same to him (MT 25:31-46). The Church calls these actions "corporal works of mercy", because they assist people with their material necessities. There are seven other works of mercy called "spiritual", which pertain to other equally important needs, especially today, because they touch the person's soul, and often create the greatest suffering. We certainly remember a phrase which has entered into the common language: "Bear wrongs patiently". And there are troublesome people! It might seem like a minor thing which makes us smile, but instead contains a feeling of profound charity; it is the same for the other six [spiritual works of mercy], which are good to remember: counsel the doubtful, instruct the ignorant, admonish sinners, console the afflicted, pardon offences, pray to God for the living and the dead. These are daily things! "But I am afflicted..." "But God will help you, I don't have time...". No! I stop myself, I listen, I give my time and console him; that is an act of mercy, and it is done not only to him, it is done to Jesus!

In the following Catechesis, we will reflect on these works which the Church presents to us as the concrete way of living out mercy. Over the course of centuries, many simple people have put this into practice, giving their sincere witness of faith. The Church, after all, faithful to her Lord, nourishes a preferential love for the weakest. Often it is the people closest to us who need our help. We should not go out in search of some unknown business to accomplish. It is better to begin with the simplest, which the Lord tells us is the most urgent. In a world which, unfortunately, has been damaged by the virus of indifference, the works of mercy are the best antidote. In fact, they educate us to be attentive to the most basic needs of "the least of these my brethren" (MT 25:40), in whom Jesus is present. Jesus is always present there.

Where there is need, there is someone who has need, be it material or spiritual. Jesus is there. Recognizing his face in those who are in need is one way to really confront indifference. He allows us to be always vigilant, and avoid having Christ pass by without us recognizing him. It recalls to mind the words of St. Augustine: "Timeo Iesum ranseuntem" (Serm., 88, 14, 13): "I fear the Lord passing by", and I do not notice him; I fear that the Lord may pass before me in one of these little people in need, and I do not realize that it is Jesus. I fear that the Lord may pass by without my recognizing him! I wondered why St. Augustine said he feared the passing by of Jesus. The answer, unfortunately, is in our behavior: because we are often distracted, indifferent, and when the Lord closely passes us by, we lose the opportunity to encounter him. The works of mercy reawaken in us the need, and the ability, to make the faith alive and active with charity. I am convinced that, through these simple, daily actions, we can achieve a true cultural revolution, like there was in the past. If every one of us, every day, does one of these, this will be a revolution in the world! Everyone, each and every one of us...

Commentary:

Pope Francis' reflection [on Mercy] should prompt us to stop and consider how *you* and *I* are obligated to show mercy just as Christ is merciful to us. Consider who needs your mercy today, this week, this year. How will you show them your mercy? Describe how God has shown you His mercy.

....

....

....

....

....

....

....

....

Create in Me a Clean Heart, O God   Lenten Reflection #2

Excerpts from the Ash Wednesday Homily of St. Pope John Paul ll; 8 March 2000

"Create in me a clean heart, O God, and put a new and right spirit within me. Cast me not away from your presence, and take not your holy Spirit from me" (Psalm 51: 10-11).Today, Ash Wednesday, this is how the Psalmist, King David, prays: a great and powerful king in Israel, but at the same time frail and sinful. At the beginning of these 40 days of preparation for Easter, the Church puts his words on the lips of all who take part in the austere liturgy of Ash Wednesday. Create in me a clean heart, O God, ... take not your holy Spirit from me. We hear this plea echoing in our hearts, while in a few moments we will approach the Lord's altar to receive ashes on our forehead in accordance with a very ancient tradition."

"Earthly life is marked from its beginning by the prospect of death. Our bodies are mortal, that is, subject to the inevitable prospect of death. We live with this end before us: every passing day brings us inexorably closer to it. And death has something destructive about it. With death it seems that everything will end for us. And here, precisely in the face of this disheartening prospect, man, who is aware of his sin, raises a cry of hope to heaven: O God, "create in me a clean heart and put a new and right spirit within me. Cast me not away from your presence, and take not your holy Spirit from me".

"Today too, the believer who feels threatened by evil and death calls on God in this way, knowing that he has reserved for him a destiny of eternal life. He knows that he is not only a body condemned to death because of sin, but that he also has an immortal soul. Therefore he turns to God the Father, who has the power to create out of nothing; to God the Only-begotten Son, who became man for our salvation, died for us and now, risen, lives in glory; to God the immortal Spirit, who calls us to life and restores life. "Create in me a clean heart and put a new and right spirit within me".

"The whole Church makes the Psalmist's prayer her own. "Repent and believe in the Gospel". This invitation, which we find at the beginning of Jesus' preaching, introduces us into the Lenten season, a time to be dedicated in a special way to conversion and renewal, to prayer, to fasting and to works of charity. In recalling the experience of the chosen people, we too set out as it were to retrace the journey that Israel made across the desert to the Promised Land."

LENT

LENT

My Lenten Resolutions

1. Study the Stained Glass Window for *Lent* on the previous page. List the *signs* of Lent and explain why they represent Lent.

....

....

....

2. Our Lent practices should prepare us to receive Christ's rich spiritual blessings that come from His sacrifice on the Cross and Resurrection from the dead. Explain why Jesus willingly died for us on the Cross.

....

....

....

3. My Spiritual Resolutions For Lent:
[See *corporal & spiritual works of mercy* - page 266.] I will intentionally suffer with Christ and His Church this Lent by: *fasting; praying; giving alms, and doing penance.*

     Fasting teaches me to *detach* from the things that I cling to. My Lenten goal regarding fasting is:

....

....

     Prayer draws me closer to God. My Lenten goal regarding prayer is:

....

....

     Almsgiving helps the poor and needy and it also helps me grow in generosity and other virtues. My Lenten goal regarding almsgiving is:

....

....

     Penance heals me spiritually and mentally. My Lenten goal regarding Penance is:

....

....

Ash Wednesday

First Reading: *Joel 2:12-18*

Even now, says the LORD,/ return to me with your whole heart,/ with fasting, and weeping, and mourning;/ Rend your hearts, not your garments,/ and return to the LORD, your God./ For gracious and merciful is he,/ slow to anger, rich in kindness,/ and relenting in punishment./ Perhaps he will again relent/ and leave behind him a blessing,/ Offerings and libations/ for the LORD, your God.

Blow the trumpet in Zion!/ proclaim a fast,/ call an assembly;/ Gather the people,/ notify the congregation;/ Assemble the elders,/ gather the children/ and the infants at the breast;/ Let the bridegroom quit his room/ and the bride her chamber./ Between the porch and the altar/ let the priests, the ministers of the LORD, weep,/ And say, "Spare, O LORD, your people,/ and make not your heritage a reproach,/ with the nations ruling over them!/ Why should they say among the peoples,/ Where is their God?'"

Then the LORD was stirred to concern for his land and took pity on his people.

Second Reading: *2 Corinthians 5:20-6:2*

Brothers and sisters: We are ambassadors for Christ, as if God were appealing through us. We implore you on behalf of Christ, be reconciled to God. For our sake he made him to be sin who did not know sin, so that we might become the righteousness of God in him. Working together, then, we appeal to you not to receive the grace of God in vain. For he says:/ In an acceptable time I heard you,/ and on the day of salvation I helped you. Behold, now is a very acceptable time; behold, now is the day of salvation.

Gospel Reading: *Matthew 6:1-6, 16-18*

Jesus said to his disciples: "Take care not to perform righteous deeds in order that people may see them; otherwise, you will have no recompense from your heavenly Father. When you give alms, do not blow a trumpet before you, as the hypocrites do in the synagogues and in the streets to win the praise of others. Amen, I say to you, they have received their reward. But when you give alms, do not let your left hand know what your right is doing, so that your almsgiving may be secret. And your Father who sees in secret will repay you.

"When you pray, do not be like the hypocrites, who love to stand and pray in the synagogues and on street corners so that others may see them. Amen, I say to you, they have received their reward. But when you pray, go to your inner room, close the door, and pray to your Father in secret. And your Father who sees in secret will repay you."

"When you fast, do not look gloomy like the hypocrites. They neglect

Ash Wednesday

their appearance, so that they may appear to others to be fasting. Amen, I say to you, they have received their reward. But when you fast, anoint your head and wash your face, so that you may not appear to be fasting, except to your Father who is hidden. And your Father who sees what is hidden will repay you."

Homily Notes:

....
....
....
....
....
....
....
....
....
....
....
....
....
....
....
....
....
....
....
....
....
....
....
....

Ash Wednesday

Reflection Questions for Each of the Readings:

1. *Based on the First Reading:*: How does this reading apply to you?

2. *Based on the Second Reading:* How do we become effective ambassadors for Christ?

3. *Based on the Gospel Reading:* We are asked to unite ourselves to Jesus' fasting, suffering, passion and death for the next 40 days. Complete your Lenten resolutions [if you haven't done so] on page 66.

First Sunday of Lent

February 18, 2024

First Reading: *Genesis 9:8-15*

God said to Noah and to his sons with him: "See, I am now establishing my covenant with you and your descendants after you and with every living creature that was with you: all the birds, and the various tame and wild animals that were with you and came out of the ark. I will establish my covenant with you, that never again shall all bodily creatures be destroyed by the waters of a flood; there shall not be another flood to devastate the earth." God added: "This is the sign that I am giving for all ages to come, of the covenant between me and you and every living creature with you: I set my bow in the clouds to serve as a sign of the covenant between me and the earth. When I bring clouds over the earth, and the bow appears in the clouds, I will recall the covenant I have made between me and you and all living beings, so that the waters shall never again become a flood to destroy all mortal beings."

Second Reading: *1 Peter 3:18-22*

Beloved: Christ suffered for sins once, the righteous for the sake of the unrighteous, that he might lead you to God. Put to death in the flesh, he was brought to life in the Spirit. In it he also went to preach to the spirits in prison, who had once been disobedient while God patiently waited in the days of Noah during the building of the ark, in which a few persons, eight in all, were saved through water. This prefigured baptism, which saves you now. It is not a removal of dirt from the body but an appeal to God for a clear conscience, through the resurrection of Jesus Christ, who has gone into heaven and is at the right hand of God, with angels, authorities, and powers subject to him.

Gospel Reading: *Mark 1:12-15*

The Spirit drove Jesus out into the desert, and he remained in the desert for forty days, tempted by Satan. He was among wild beasts, and the angels ministered to him.

After John had been arrested, Jesus came to Galilee proclaiming the gospel of God: "This is the time of fulfillment. The kingdom of God is at hand. Repent, and believe in the gospel."

First Sunday of Lent

Homily Notes:

....
....
....
....
....
....
....
....
....
....
....
....
....
....
....
....
....
....
....
....
....
....
....
....
....
....

Reflection Questions for Each of the Readings:

1. *Based on the First Reading*: What is the significance of a covenant? Why did God create a covenant with Noah and Abraham?

2. *Based on the Second Reading*: Why did Jesus accept his suffering and death on the cross? Explain what it means to unite our suffering to Jesus.

3. *Based on the Gospel Reading*: Why did Jesus fast for forty days and nights? What is the significance of the number forty? Why does the Church ask us to fast at various times during Lent?

Your Virtue Challenge:

The goal of the virtuous person is to become like God. [CCC 1803] This will require identifying ways to increase this virtue and reduce opposing vice; *fasting [avoiding]* from habits or practices that oppose it; *praying* for God's help; *helping* others; and *doing penance. Based on the Gospel Reading,* your Virtue Challenge for the week is to increase in the virtue of:

TRUTHFULNESS

My Virtue Goals and Working Plan for the Week:

....

....

....

....

....

Daily Mass Readings for the Week:
Monday, February 19: Leviticus 19:1-2, 11-18; Matthew 25:31-46.
Tuesday, February 20: Isaiah 55:10-11; Matthew 6:7-15.
Wednesday, February 21: **Saint Peter Damian** Jonah 3:1-10; Luke 11:29-32.
Thursday, February 22: 1 Peter 5:1-4; Matthew 16:13-19.
Friday,February 23: **Saint Polycarp** Ezekiel 18:21-28; Matthew 5:20-2.6
Saturday, February 24: Deuteronomy 26:16-19; Matthew 5:43-48.

Second Sunday of Lent

First Reading: *Genesis 22:1-2, 9a, 10-13, 15-18*

God put Abraham to the test. He called to him, "Abraham!" "Here I am!" he replied. Then God said: "Take your son Isaac, your only one, whom you love, and go to the land of Moriah. There you shall offer him up as a holocaust on a height that I will point out to you."

When they came to the place of which God had told him, Abraham built an altar there and arranged the wood on it. Then he reached out and took the knife to slaughter his son. But the LORD's messenger called to him from heaven, "Abraham, Abraham!" "Here I am!" he answered. "Do not lay your hand on the boy," said the messenger. "Do not do the least thing to him.
I know now how devoted you are to God, since you did not withhold from me your own beloved son." As Abraham looked about, he spied a ram caught by its horns in the thicket. So he went and took the ram and offered it up as a holocaust in place of his son.

Again the LORD's messenger called to Abraham from heaven and said: "I swear by myself, declares the LORD, that because you acted as you did in not withholding from me your beloved son, I will bless you abundantly and make your descendants as countless as the stars of the sky and the sands of the seashore; your descendants shall take possession of the gates of their enemies, and in your descendants all the nations of the earth shall find blessing—all this because you obeyed my command."

Second Reading: *Romans 8:31b-34*

Brothers and sisters: If God is for us, who can be against us? He who did not spare his own Son but handed him over for us all, how will he not also give us everything else along with him?

Who will bring a charge against God's chosen ones? It is God who acquits us, who will condemn? Christ Jesus it is who died — or, rather, was raised — who also is at the right hand of God, who indeed intercedes for us.

Gospel Reading: *Mark 9:2-10*

Jesus took Peter, James, and John and led them up a high mountain apart by themselves. And he was transfigured before them, and his clothes became dazzling white, such as no fuller on earth could bleach them. Then Elijah appeared to them along with Moses, and they were conversing with Jesus. Then Peter said to Jesus in reply, "Rabbi, it is good that we are here! Let us make three

tents: one for you, one for Moses, and one for Elijah." He hardly knew what to say, they were so terrified. Then a cloud came, casting a shadow over them; from the cloud came a voice, "This is my beloved Son. Listen to him." Suddenly, looking around, they no longer saw anyone but Jesus alone with them.

As they were coming down from the mountain, he charged them not to relate what they had seen to anyone, except when the Son of Man had risen from the dead. So they kept the matter to themselves, questioning what rising from the dead meant.

Homily Notes:

....
....
....
....
....
....
....
....
....
....
....
....
....
....
....
....
....
....
....
....
....
....
....

Second Sunday of Lent

February 25, 2024

Reflection Questions for Each of the Readings:

1. *Based on the First Reading*: God blessed Abraham's *Fear of the Lord*. Explain the difference between *Fear of the Lord* [the virtue] and *being afraid of God* [as Adam and Eve in the Garden].

2. *Based on the Second Reading*: Explain Verse 31 in your own words.

3. *Based on the Gospel Reading*: Why did the apostles cower in fear at the Transfiguration? Were they exhibiting Fear of the Lord [virtue] or were they afraid?

Your Virtue Challenge:

The goal of the virtuous person is to become like God. [CCC 1803] This will require identifying ways to increase this virtue and reduce opposing vice; *fasting [avoiding]* from habits or practices that oppose it; *praying* for God's help; *helping* others; and *doing penance*. Based on the Gospel Reading, your Virtue Challenge for the week is to increase in the virtue of:

FEAR of The LORD

My Virtue Goals and Working Plan for the Week:

....

....

....

....

Daily Mass Readings for the Week:

Monday, February 26: Daniel 9:4b-10; Luke 6:36-38.
Tuesday, February 27: **Saint Gregory of Narek** Isaiah 1:10, 16-20; Matthew 23:1-12.
Wednesday, February 28: Jeremiah 18:18-20; Matthew 20:17-28.
Thursday, February 29: Jeremiah 17:5-10; Luke 16:19-31.
Friday, March 1: Genesis 37:3-4, 12-13a, 17b-28a; Matthew 21:33-43, 45-46.
Saturday, March 2: Micah 7:14-15, 18-20; Luke 15:1-3, 11-32.

First Reading: *Exodus 20:1-17* or **20:1-3, 7-8, 12-17**

In those days, God delivered all these commandments: "I, the LORD, am your God, who brought you out of the land of Egypt, that place of slavery. You shall not have other gods besides me. You shall not carve idols for yourselves in the shape of anything in the sky above or on the earth below or in the waters beneath the earth; you shall not bow down before them or worship them. For I, the LORD, your God, am a jealous God, inflicting punishment for their fathers' wickedness on the children of those who hate me, down to the third and fourth generation; but bestowing mercy down to the thousandth generation on the children of those who love me and keep my commandments.

"You shall not take the name of the LORD, your God, in vain. For the LORD will not leave unpunished the one who takes his name in vain.

"Remember to keep holy the sabbath day. Six days you may labor and do all your work, but the seventh day is the sabbath of the LORD, your God. No work may be done then either by you, or your son or daughter, or your male or female slave, or your beast, or by the alien who lives with you. In six days the LORD made the heavens and the earth, the sea and all that is in them; but on the seventh day he rested. That is why the LORD has blessed the sabbath day and made it holy.

"Honor your father and your mother, that you may have a long life in the land which the LORD, your God, is giving you. You shall not kill. You shall not commit adultery. You shall not steal. You shall not bear false witness against your neighbor. You shall not covet your neighbor's house. You shall not covet your neighbor's wife, nor his male or female slave, nor his ox or ass, nor anything else that belongs to him."

Second Reading: *1 Corinthians 1:22-25*

Brothers and sisters: Jews demand signs and Greeks look for wisdom, but we proclaim Christ crucified, a stumbling block to Jews and foolishness to Gentiles, but to those who are called, Jews and Greeks alike, Christ the power of God and the wisdom of God. For the foolishness of God is wiser than human wisdom, and the weakness of God is stronger than human strength.

Gospel Reading: *1 John 2:13-25*

Since the Passover of the Jews was near, Jesus went up to Jerusalem. He found in the temple area those who sold oxen, sheep, and doves, as well as the money changers seated there. He made a whip out of cords and drove them all out of the temple area, with the sheep and oxen, and spilled the coins of the money changers and overturned their tables, and to those who sold doves he said, "Take these out of here, and stop making my Father's house a market-place." His disciples recalled the words of Scripture, Zeal for your house will consume me. At this the Jews answered and said to him, "What sign can you show us for doing this?" Jesus answered and said to them, "Destroy this temple and in three days I will raise it up." The Jews said, "This temple has been under construction for forty-six years, and you will raise it up in three days?" But he was speaking about the temple of his body. Therefore, when he was raised from the dead, his disciples remembered that he had said this, and they came to believe the Scripture and the word Jesus had spoken.

While he was in Jerusalem for the feast of Passover, many began to believe in his name when they saw the signs he was doing. But Jesus would not trust himself to them because he knew them all, and did not need anyone to testify about human nature. He himself understood it well.

Homily Notes:

Third Sunday of Lent

March 3, 2024

Reflection Questions for Each of the Readings:

1. *Based on the First Reading:* This reading presents the Ten Commandments. The first three Commandments apply to our relationship with God; the other seven to our *neighbor.* Why are these commandments still vital today?

2. *Based on the Second Reading:* Why does the crucified Christ still present a stumbling block to Jews and foolishness to Gentiles? What is your testimony with regard to the crucifixion and resurrection of Jesus?

3. *Based on the Gospel Reading:* Define zeal. Why/how was Jesus overcome with *zeal?*

Your Virtue Challenge:

The goal of the virtuous person is to become like God. [CCC 1803] This will require identifying ways to increase this virtue and reduce opposing vice; *fasting [avoiding]* from habits or practices that oppose it; *praying* for God's help; *helping* others; and *doing penance. Based on the Gospel Reading,* your Virtue Challenge for the week is to increase in the virtue of:

ZEAL

My Virtue Goals and Working Plan for the Week:

....

....

....

Daily Mass Readings for the Week:
Monday, March 4: **Saint Casimir** 2 Kings 5:1-15ab; Luke 4:24-30.
Tuesday, March 5: Daniel 3:25, 34-43; Matthew 18:21-35.
Wednesday, March 6: Deuteronomy 4:1, 5-9; Matthew 5:17-19.
Thursday, March 7: **Sts. Perpetua and Felicity** Jeremiah 7:23-28; Luke 11:14-23.
Friday, March 8: **Saint John of God** Hosea 14:2-10; Mark 12:28-34.
Saturday, March 9: **Saint Frances of Rome** Hosea 6:1-6; Luke 18:9-14.

Fourth Sunday of Lent

March 10, 2024

First Reading: *2 Chronicles 36:14-16, 19-23*

In those days, all the princes of Judah, the priests, and the people added infidelity to infidelity, practicing all the abominations of the nations and polluting the LORD's temple which he had consecrated in Jerusalem.

Early and often did the LORD, the God of their fathers, send his messengers to them, for he had compassion on his people and his dwelling place. But they mocked the messengers of God, despised his warnings, and scoffed at his prophets, until the anger of the LORD against his people was so inflamed that there was no remedy. Their enemies burnt the house of God, tore down the walls of Jerusalem, set all its palaces afire, and destroyed all its precious objects. Those who escaped the sword were carried captive to Babylon, where they became servants of the king of the Chaldeans and his sons until the kingdom of the Persians came to power. All this was to fulfill the word of the LORD spoken by Jeremiah: "Until the land has retrieved its lost sabbaths, during all the time it lies waste it shall have rest while seventy years are fulfilled."

In the first year of Cyrus, king of Persia, in order to fulfill the word of the LORD spoken by Jeremiah, the LORD inspired King Cyrus of Persia to issue this proclamation throughout his kingdom, both by word of mouth and in writing: "Thus says Cyrus, king of Persia: All the kingdoms of the earth the LORD, the God of heaven, has given to me, and he has also charged me to build him a house in Jerusalem, which is in Judah. Whoever, therefore, among you belongs to any part of his people, let him go up, and may his God be with him!"

Second Reading: *Ephesians 2:4-10*

Brothers and sisters: God, who is rich in mercy, because of the great love he had for us, even when we were dead in our transgressions, brought us to life with Christ - by grace you have been saved -, raised us up with him, and seated us with him in the heavens in Christ Jesus, that in the ages to come He might show the immeasurable riches of his grace in his kindness to us in Christ Jesus. For by grace you have been saved through faith, and this is not from you; it is the gift of God; it is not from works, so no one may boast. For we are his handiwork, created in Christ Jesus for the good works that God has prepared in advance, that we should live in them.

Gospel Reading: *John 3:14-21*

Jesus said to Nicodemus: "Just as Moses lifted up the serpent in the desert, so must the Son of Man be lifted up, so that everyone who believes in him may have eternal life."

79

Fourth Sunday of Lent

March 10, 2024

For God so loved the world that he gave his only Son, so that everyone who believes in him might not perish but might have eternal life. For God did not send his Son into the world to condemn the world, but that the world might be saved through him. Whoever believes in him will not be condemned, but whoever does not believe has already been condemned, because he has not believed in the name of the only Son of God. And this is the verdict, that the light came into the world, but people preferred darkness to light, because their works were evil. For everyone who does wicked things hates the light and does not come toward the light, so that his works might not be exposed. But whoever lives the truth comes to the light, so that his works may be clearly seen as done in God.

Homily Notes:

....
....
....
....
....
....
....
....
....
....
....
....
....
....
....
....
....
....

80

Reflection Questions for Each of the Readings:

1. Based on the First Reading: Why did God allow foreign nations to conquer the Jewish people and send them into exile? Why did the Jewish people honor King Cyrus?

2. Based on the Second Reading: How does God reveal His Mercy? Explain *mercy* in your own words.

3. Based on the Gospel Reading: What does the Old Testament serpent represent? Explain in your own words why Jesus willingly gave up his life for our sake.

Your Virtue Challenge:

The goal of the virtuous person is to become like God. [CCC 1803] This will require identifying ways to increase this virtue and reduce opposing vice; *fasting [avoiding]* from habits or practices that oppose it; *praying* for God's help; *helping* others; and *doing penance*. *Based on the Gospel Reading,* your Virtue Challenge for the week is to increase in the virtue of:

LOVE / CHARITY

My Virtue Goals and Working Plan for the Week:

....

....

....

....

Daily Mass Readings for the Week:

Monday, March 11: Isaiah 65:17-21; John 4:43-54.
Tuesday, March 12, Ezekiel 47:1-9, 12; John 5:1-16.
Wednesday, March 13: Isaiah 49:8-15; John 5:17-30.
Thursday, March 14: Exodus 32:7-14; John 5:31-47.
Friday, March 15: Wisdom 2:1a, 12-22; John 7:1-2, 10, 25-30.
Saturday, March 16: Jeremiah 11:18-20; John 7:40-53.

First Reading: *Jeremiah 31:31-34*

The days are coming, says the LORD,/ when I will make a new covenant with the house of Israel/ and the house of Judah./ It will not be like the covenant I made with their fathers/ the day I took them by the hand/ to lead them forth from the land of Egypt;/ for they broke my covenant,/ and I had to show myself their master, says the LORD./ But this is the covenant that I will make/ with the house of Israel after those days, says the LORD./ I will place my law within them and write it upon their hearts; / I will be their God, and they shall be my people./ No longer will they have need to teach their friends and relatives how to know the LORD. All, from least to greatest, shall know me, says the LORD,/ for I will forgive their evildoing and remember their sin no more.

Second Reading: *Hebrews 5:7-9*

In the days when Christ Jesus was in the flesh, he offered prayers and supplications with loud cries and tears to the one who was able to save him from death, and he was heard because of his reverence. Son though he was, he learned obedience from what he suffered; and when he was made perfect, he became the source of eternal salvation for all who obey him.

Gospel Reading: *John 12:20-33*

Some Greeks who had come to worship at the Passover Feast came to Philip, who was from Bethsaida in Galilee, and asked him, "Sir, we would like to see Jesus." Philip went and told Andrew; then Andrew and Philip went and told Jesus. Jesus answered them, "The hour has come for the Son of Man to be glorified. Amen, amen, I say to you, unless a grain of wheat falls to the ground and dies, it remains just a grain of wheat; but if it dies, it produces much fruit. Whoever loves his life loses it, and whoever hates his life in this world will  preserve it for eternal life. Whoever serves me must follow me, and where I am, there also will my servant be. The Father will honor whoever serves me.

"I am troubled now. Yet what should I say? 'Father, save me from this hour'? But it was for this purpose that I came to this hour. Father, glorify your name." Then a voice came from heaven, "I have glorified it and will glorify it again." The crowd there heard it and said it was thunder; but others said, "An angel has spoken to him." Jesus answered and said, "This voice did not come for my sake but for yours. Now is the time of judgment on this world; now the ruler of this world will be driven out. And when I am lifted up from the earth, I will draw everyone to myself." He said this indicating the kind of death he would die.

Homily Notes:

....
....
....
....
....
....
....
....
....
....
....
....
....
....
....
....
....
....
....
....
....
....

Reflection Questions for Each of the Readings:

1. Based on the First Reading: Explain the New Covenant - the what, why, when, etc.

2. *Based on the Second Reading*: How does suffering impart obedience? How does obedience impart knowledge? Why is obedience an important virtue?

3. *Based on the Gospel Reading*: Capture Jesus' main teaching points here.

Your Virtue Challenge:

The goal of the virtuous person is to become like God. [CCC 1803] This will require identifying ways to increase this virtue and reduce opposing vice; *fasting [avoiding]* from habits or practices that oppose it; *praying* for God's help; *helping* others; and *doing penance. Based on the Second Reading,* your Virtue Challenge for the week is to increase in the virtue of:

REVERENCE

My Virtue Goals and Working Plan for the Week:

....

....

....

....

Daily Mass Readings for the Week:

Monday, March 18: **Saint Cyril of Jerusalem** Daniel 13:1-9, 15-17, 19-30, 33-62 or 13:41c-62; John 8:1-11.

Tuesday, March 19: **Saint Joseph,** Spouse of the Blessed Virgin Mary 2 Samuel 7:4-5a, 12-14a, 16; Romans 4:13, 16-18, 22; Matthew 1:16, 18-21, 24a or Luke 2:41-51a.

Wednesday, March 20: Daniel 3:14-20, 91-92, 95; John 8:31-42.

Thursday, March 21: Genesis 17:3-9; John 8:51-59.

Friday, March 22: Jeremiah 20:10-13; John 10:31-42.

Saturday, March 23: **Saint Turibius of Mogrovejo** Ezekiel 37:21-28; John 11:45-56.

Palm Sunday of the Passion of the Lord
March 24, 2024

Reading at the Procession of Palms: *Mark 11:1-10* or John 12:12-16

Mark 11:1-10

When Jesus and his disciples drew near to Jerusalem, to Bethphage and Bethany at the Mount of Olives, he sent two of his disciples and said to them, "Go into the village opposite you, and immediately on entering it, you will find a colt tethered on which no one has ever sat. Untie it and bring it here. If anyone should say to you, 'Why are you doing this?' reply, 'The Master has need of it and will send it back here at once.'" So they went off and found a colt tethered at a gate outside on the street, and they untied it. Some of the bystanders said to them, "What are you doing, untying the colt?" They answered them just as Jesus had told them to, and they permitted them to do it. So they brought the colt to Jesus and put their cloaks over it. And he sat on it. Many people spread their cloaks on the road, and others spread leafy branches that they had cut from the fields. Those preceding him as well as those following kept crying out:/ "Hosanna!/ Blessed is he who comes in the name of the Lord!/ Blessed is the kingdom of our father David that is to come! / Hosanna in the highest!'"

John 12:12-16

When the great crowd that had come to the feast heard that Jesus was coming to Jerusalem, they took palm branches and went out to meet him, and cried out:/
"Hosanna!/ "Blessed is he who comes in the name of the Lord, / the king of Israel."
Jesus found an ass and sat upon it, as is written:/ *Fear no more, O daughter Zion;/ see, your king comes, seated upon an ass's colt./* His disciples did not understand this at first, but when Jesus had been glorified they remembered that these things were written about him and that they had done this for him.

At the Mass - First Reading: *Isaiah 50:4-7*

The Lord GOD has given me/ a well-trained tongue,/ that I might know how to speak to the weary/ a word that will rouse them./ Morning after morning/ he opens my ear that I may hear;/ and I have not rebelled,/ have not turned back. / I gave my back to those who beat me,/ my cheeks to those who plucked my beard;/ my face I did not shield/ from buffets and spitting./
The Lord GOD is my help,/ therefore I am not disgraced;/ I have set my face like flint,/ knowing that I shall not be put to shame.

Palm Sunday of the Passion of the Lord
March 24, 2024

Second Reading: *Philippians 2:6-11*

Christ Jesus, though he was in the form of God,/ did not regard equality with God/ something to be grasped./ Rather, he emptied himself,/ taking the form of a slave,/ coming in human likeness;/ and found human in appearance,/ he humbled himself,/ becoming obedient to the point of death,/ even death on a cross./ Because of this, God greatly exalted him/ and bestowed on him the name/ which is above every name,/ that at the name of Jesus/ every knee should bend,/ of those in heaven and on earth and under the earth,/ and every tongue confess that / Jesus Christ is Lord,/ to the glory of God the Father.

Gospel Reading: *Mark 14:1-15:47* or **15:1-39**

The Passover and the Feast of Unleavened Bread were to take place in two days' time. So the chief priests and the scribes were seeking a way to arrest him by treachery and put him to death. They said, "Not during the festival, for fear that there may be a riot among the people."

When he was in Bethany reclining at table in the house of Simon the leper, a woman came with an alabaster jar of perfumed oil, costly genuine spikenard. She broke the alabaster jar and poured it on his head. There were some who were indignant. "Why has there been this waste of perfumed oil? It could have been sold for more than three hundred days' wages and the money given to the poor." They were infuriated with her. Jesus said, "Let her alone. Why do you make trouble for her? She has done a good thing for me. The poor you will always have with you, and whenever you wish you can do good to them, but you will not always have me. She has done what she could. She has anticipated anointing my body for burial. Amen, I say to you, wherever the gospel is proclaimed to the whole world, what she has done will be told in memory of her."

Then Judas Iscariot, one of the Twelve, went off to the chief priests to hand him over to them. When they heard him they were pleased and promised to pay him money. Then he looked for an opportunity to hand him over.

On the first day of the Feast of Unleavened Bread, when they sacrificed the Passover lamb, his disciples said to him, "Where do you want us to go and prepare for you to eat the Passover?" He sent two of his disciples and said to them, "Go into the city and a man will meet you, carrying a jar of water. Follow him. Wherever he enters, say to the master of the house, 'The Teacher says, "Where is my guest room where I may eat the Passover with my disciples?"' Then he will show you a large upper room furnished and ready. Make the preparations for us there." The disciples then went off, entered the city, and found it just as he had told them; and they prepared the Passover.

When it was evening, he came with the Twelve. And as they reclined at table and were eating, Jesus said, "Amen, I say to you, one of you will betray

86

me, one who is eating with me." They began to be distressed and to say to him, one by one, "Surely it is not I?" He said to them, "One of the Twelve, the one who dips with me into the dish. For the Son of Man indeed goes, as it is written of him, but woe to that man by whom the Son of Man is betrayed. It would be better for that man if he had never been born."

While they were eating, he took bread, said the blessing, broke it, and gave it to them, and said, "Take it; this is my body." Then he took a cup, gave thanks, and gave it to them, and they all drank from it. He said to them, "This is my blood of the covenant, which will be shed for many. Amen, I say to you, I shall not drink again the fruit of the vine until the day when I drink it new in the kingdom of God." Then, after singing a hymn, they went out to the Mount of Olives.

Then Jesus said to them, "All of you will have your faith shaken, for it is written:/ I will strike the shepherd,/ and the sheep will be dispersed./ But after I have been raised up, I shall go before you to Galilee." Peter said to him, "Even though all should have their faith shaken, mine will not be." Then Jesus said to him, "Amen, I say to you, this very night before the cock crows twice you will deny me three times." But he vehemently replied, "Even though I should have to die with you, I will not deny you." And they all spoke similarly.

Then they came to a place named Gethsemane, and he said to his disciples, "Sit here while I pray." He took with him Peter, James, and John, and began to be troubled and distressed. Then he said to them, "My soul is sorrowful even to death. Remain here and keep watch." He advanced a little and fell to the ground and prayed that if it were possible the hour might pass by him; he said, "Abba, Father, all things are possible to you. Take this cup away from me, but not what I will but what you will." When he returned he found them asleep. He said to Peter, "Simon, are you asleep? Could you not keep watch for one hour? Watch and pray that you may not undergo the test. The spirit is willing but the flesh is weak." Withdrawing again, he prayed, saying the same thing. Then he returned once more and found them asleep, for they could not keep their eyes open and did not know what to answer him. He returned a third time and said to them, "Are you still sleeping and taking your rest? It is enough. The hour has come. Behold, the Son of Man is to be handed over to sinners. Get up, let us go. See, my betrayer is at hand."

Then, while he was still speaking, Judas, one of the Twelve, arrived, accompanied by a crowd with swords and clubs who had come from the chief priests, the scribes, and the elders. His betrayer had arranged a signal with them, saying, "The man I shall kiss is the one; arrest him and lead him away securely." He came and immediately went over to him and said, "Rabbi." And he kissed him. At this they laid hands on him and arrested him. One of the bystanders drew his sword, struck the high priest's servant, and cut off his ear. Jesus said to them in reply, "Have you come out as against a robber, with swords and clubs, to seize me? Day after day I was with you teaching in the temple area, yet you did not arrest me; but that the Scriptures may be fulfilled." And they all left him and fled. Now a young man followed him wearing nothing but a linen cloth about his body. They seized him, but he left the cloth behind and ran off naked.

They led Jesus away to the high priest, and all the chief priests and the elders and the scribes came together. Peter followed him at a distance into the high priest's courtyard and was seated with the guards, warming himself at the fire. The chief priests and the entire Sanhedrin kept trying to obtain testimony against Jesus in order to put him to death, but they found none. Many gave false witness against him, but their testimony did not agree. Some took the stand and testified falsely against him, alleging, "We heard him say, 'I will destroy this temple made with hands and within three days I will build another not made with hands.'" Even so their testimony did not agree. The high priest rose before the assembly and questioned Jesus, saying, "Have you no answer? What are these men testifying against you?" But he was silent and answered nothing. Again the high priest asked him and said to him, "Are you the Christ, the son of the Blessed One?" Then Jesus answered, "I am;/ and 'you will see the Son of Man seated/ at the right hand of the Power/ and coming with the clouds of heaven.'"/ At that the high priest tore his garments and said, "What further need have we of witnesses? You have heard the blasphemy. What do you think?" They all condemned him as deserving to die. Some began to spit on him. They blindfolded him and struck him and said to him, "Prophesy!" And the guards greeted him with blows.

While Peter was below in the courtyard, one of the high priest's maids came along. Seeing Peter warming himself, she looked intently at him and said, "You too were with the Nazarene, Jesus." But he denied it saying, "I neither know nor understand what you are talking about." So he went out into the outer court. Then the cock crowed. The maid saw him and began again to say to the bystanders, "This man is one of them." Once again he denied it. A little later the bystanders said to Peter once more, "Surely you are one of them; for you too are a Galilean." He began to curse and to swear, "I do not know this man about whom you are talking." And immediately a cock crowed a second time. Then Peter remembered the word that Jesus had said to him, "Before the cock crows twice you will deny me three times." He broke down and wept.

As soon as morning came, the chief priests with the elders and the scribes, that is, the whole Sanhedrin held a council. They bound Jesus, led him away, and handed him over to Pilate. Pilate questioned him, "Are you the king of the Jews?" He said to him in reply, "You say so." The chief priests accused him of many things. Again Pilate questioned him, "Have you no answer? See how many things they accuse you of." Jesus gave him no further answer, so that Pilate was amazed.

Now on the occasion of the feast he used to release to them one prisoner whom they requested. A man called Barabbas was then in prison along with the rebels who had committed murder in a rebellion. The crowd came forward and began to ask him to do for them as he was accustomed. Pilate answered, "Do you want me to release to you the king of the Jews?" For he knew that it was out of envy that the chief priests had handed him over. But the chief priests stirred up the crowd to have him release Barabbas for them instead. Pilate again said to them in reply, "Then what do you want me to do with the man you call the king of the Jews?" They shouted again, "Crucify him." Pilate said to them, "Why? What evil has he done?" They only shouted the louder, "Crucify him." So Pilate, wishing to satisfy the crowd, released Barabbas to them and, after he had Jesus scourged, handed him over to be crucified.

The soldiers led him away inside the palace, that is, the praetorium, and assembled the whole cohort. They clothed him in purple and, weaving a crown of thorns, placed it on him. They began to salute him with, "Hail, King of the Jews!" and kept striking his head with a reed and spitting upon him. They knelt before him in homage. And when they had mocked him, they stripped him of the purple cloak, dressed him in his own clothes, and led him out to crucify him.

They pressed into service a passer-by, Simon, a Cyrenian, who was coming in from the country, the father of Alexander and Rufus, to carry his cross.

They brought him to the place of Golgotha - which is translated Place of the Skull -, They gave him wine drugged with myrrh, but he did not take it. Then they crucified him and divided his garments by casting lots for them to see what each should take. It was nine o'clock in the morning when they crucified him. The inscription of the charge against him read, "The King of the Jews." With him they crucified two revolutionaries, one on his right and one on his left. Those passing by reviled him, shaking their heads and saying, "Aha! You who would destroy the temple and rebuild it in three days, save yourself by coming down from the cross." Likewise the chief priests, with the scribes, mocked him among themselves and said, "He saved others; he cannot save himself. Let the Christ, the King of Israel, come down now from the cross that we may see and believe." Those who were crucified with him also kept abusing him.

At noon darkness came over the whole land until three in the afternoon. And at three o'clock Jesus cried out in a loud voice, *"Eloi, Eloi, lema sabachthani?"* which is translated, "My God, my God, why have you forsaken me?" Some of the bystanders who heard it said, "Look, he is calling Elijah." One of them ran, soaked a sponge with wine, put it on a reed and gave it to him to drink saying, "Wait, let us see if Elijah comes to take him down."

Jesus gave a loud cry and breathed his last.

[Here all kneel and pause for a short time.]

The veil of the sanctuary was torn in two from top to bottom. When the centurion who stood facing him saw how he breathed his last he said, "Truly this man was the Son of God!" There were also women looking on from a distance. Among them were Mary Magdalene, Mary the mother of the younger James and of Joses, and Salome. These women had followed him when he was in Galilee and ministered to him. There were also many other women who had come up with him to Jerusalem.

When it was already evening, since it was the day of preparation, the day before the sabbath, Joseph of Arimathea, a distinguished member of the council, who was himself awaiting the kingdom of God, came and courageously went to Pilate and asked for the body of Jesus. Pilate was amazed that he was already dead. He summoned the centurion and asked him if Jesus had already died. And when he learned of it from the centurion, he gave the body to Joseph. Having bought a linen cloth, he took him down, wrapped him in the linen cloth, and laid him in a tomb that had been hewn out of the rock. Then he rolled a stone against the entrance to the tomb. Mary Magdalene and Mary the mother of Joses watched where he was laid.

Homily Notes:

....
....
....
....
....
....
....
....
....
....
....
....
....
....

Palm Sunday of the Passion of the Lord

March 24, 2024

....
....
....
....
....
....
....
....
....
....

Reflection Questions for Each of the Readings:

1. Based on the First Reading: Name several Old and New Testament prophets. What was their significance in Jewish History? Were they persecuted?

2. Based on the Second Reading: Explain the meaning of the verse, 'Christ Jesus, Who, though he was in the form of God, did not regard equality with God something to be grasped', after studying the image of Jesus riding on the donkey into Jerusalem on Palm Sunday.

3. *Based on the Gospel Reading*: The walk from the Garden to Jerusalem was about two miles. Name the characters mentioned in this reading. Who do you most identify with and why?

Your Virtue Challenge:

The goal of the virtuous person is to become like God. [CCC 1803] This will requires identifying ways to increase this virtue and reduce opposing vice; *fasting [avoiding]* from habits or practices that oppose it; *praying* for God's help; *helping* others; and *doing penance. Based on the First Reading,* your Virtue Challenge for the week is to increase in the virtue of:

PRUDENCE

My Virtue Goals and Working Plan for the Week:

....

....

....

....

Daily Mass Readings for the Week:
Monday, March 25: Isaiah 42:1-7; John 12:1-11.
Tuesday, March 26: Isaiah 49:1-6; John 13:21-33, 36-38.
Wednesday, March 27: Isaiah 50:4-9a; Matthew 26:14-25.
Thursday, March 28: **Evening Mass of the Lord's Supper:** Pages: 93-95.
Friday, March 29: **The Passion of the Lord:** Pages: 95-100.
Saturday, March 30: **Easter Vigil:** Pages: 101-103.

Holy Thursday
Evening Mass of the Lord's Supper   March 28, 2024

First Reading: *Exodus 12:1-8, 11-14*

The LORD said to Moses and Aaron in the land of Egypt, "This month shall stand at the head of your calendar; you shall reckon it the first month of the year. Tell the whole community of Israel: On the tenth of this month every one of your families must procure for itself a lamb, one apiece for each household. If a family is too small for a whole lamb, it shall join the nearest household in procuring one and shall share in the lamb in proportion to the number of persons who partake of it. The lamb must be a year-old male and without blemish. You may take it from either the sheep or the goats. You shall keep it until the fourteenth day of this month, and then, with the whole assembly of Israel present, it shall be slaughtered during the evening twilight. They shall take some of its blood and apply it to the two doorposts and the lintel of every house in which they partake of the lamb. That same night they shall eat its roasted flesh with unleavened bread and bitter herbs.

"This is how you are to eat it: with your loins girt, sandals on your feet and your staff in hand, you shall eat like those who are in flight. It is the Passover of the LORD. For on this same night I will go through Egypt, striking down every firstborn of the land, both man and beast, and executing judgment on all the gods of Egypt—I, the LORD! But the blood will mark the houses where you are. Seeing the blood, I will pass over you; thus, when I strike the land of Egypt, no destructive blow will come upon you.

"This day shall be a memorial feast for you, which all your generations shall celebrate with pilgrimage to the LORD, as a perpetual institution."

Second Reading: *1 Corinthians 11:23-26*

Brothers and sisters: I received from the Lord what I also handed on to you, that the Lord Jesus, on the night he was handed over, took bread, and, after he had given thanks, broke it and said, "This is my body that is for you. Do this in remembrance of me." In the same way also the cup, after supper, saying, "This cup is the new covenant in my blood. Do this, as often as you drink it, in remembrance of me." For as often as you eat this bread and drink the cup, you proclaim the death of the Lord until he comes.

Gospel Reading: *John 13:1-15*

Before the feast of Passover, Jesus knew that his hour had come to pass from this world to the Father. He loved his own in the world and he loved them to the end. The devil had already induced Judas, son of Simon the Iscariot, to hand him over. So, during supper, fully aware that the Father had put everything into his power and that he had come from God and was returning to God, he rose from supper and took off his outer garments. He took a towel and tied it around his waist. Then he poured water into a basin and began to wash the disciples' feet and dry them with the towel around his waist. He came to Simon Peter, who said to him, "Master, are you going to wash my feet?" Jesus answered and said to him, "What I am doing, you do not understand now, but you will understand later." Peter said to him, "You will never wash my feet."

Jesus answered him, "Unless I wash you, you will have no inheritance with me." Simon Peter said to him, "Master, then not only my feet, but my hands and head as well." Jesus said to him, "Whoever has bathed has no need except to have his feet washed, for he is clean all over; so you are clean, but not all." For he knew who would betray him; for this reason, he said, "Not all of you are clean."

So when he had washed their feet and put his garments back on and reclined at table again, he said to them, "Do you realize what I have done for you? You call me 'teacher' and 'master,' and rightly so, for indeed I am. If I, therefore, the master and teacher, have washed your feet, you ought to wash one another's feet. I have given you a model to follow, so that as I have done for you, you should also do."

Homily Notes:

....

....

....

....

....

....

....

....

....

....

....

....

....

....

....

....

....

....

....

....

Reflection Questions for Each of the Readings:

1. Based on the First Reading: Why is the Passover significant - then [for Jews] and now [for Christians]? Compare and contrast the Passover of the Jews with the rituals of the Evening Mass of the Lord's Supper.

2. Based on the Second Reading: What is the New Covenant? Jesus teaches that the bread and wine become His real presence during the Consecration. Do you believe in the Real Presence? Why or Why not?

3. Based on the Gospel Reading: Dr. Leroy Huizenga tells us that Jesus washed the feet of the apostles to demonstrate his love for the apostles and to demonstrate authentic humility. Consider the indignity of washing someone's feet - a task that was normally delegated to slaves or servants in that era. How willingly would you wash someone's feet? Do you possess humility? Explain.

Friday of the Passion of the Lord
Good Friday March 29, 2024

First Reading: *Isaiah 52:13-53:12*

See, my servant shall prosper, / he shall be raised high and greatly exalted./ Even as many were amazed at him-/ so marred was his look beyond human semblance/ and his appearance beyond that of the sons of man/ so shall he startle many nations,/ because of him kings shall stand speechless;/ for those who have not been told shall see,/ those who have not heard shall ponder it./

Who would believe what we have heard? / To whom has the arm of the LORD been revealed?/ He grew up like a sapling before him,/ like a shoot from the parched earth;/ there was in him no stately bearing to make us look at him,/ nor appearance that would attract us to him./ He was spurned and avoided by people, / a man of suffering, / accustomed to infirmity, / one of those from whom people hide their faces,/ spurned, and we held him in no esteem./

Yet it was our infirmities that he bore,/ our sufferings that he endured,/ while we thought of him as stricken, / as one smitten by God and afflicted./ But he was pierced for our offenses,/ crushed for our sins; / upon him was the chastisement that makes us whole, / by his stripes we were healed./ We had all gone astray like sheep,/ each following his own way;/ but the LORD laid upon him/ the guilt of us all. /

Though he was harshly treated,/ he submitted/ and opened not his mouth; / like a lamb led to the slaughter / or a sheep before the shearers,/ he was silent and opened not his mouth./ Oppressed and condemned,/ he was taken away, / and who would have thought any more of his destiny?/ When he was cut off from the land of the living, / and smitten for the sin of his people,/ a grave was assigned him among the wicked / and a burial place with evildoers,/ though he had done no wrong / nor spoken any falsehood./ But the LORD was pleased / to crush him in infirmity./

If he gives his life as an offering for sin,/ he shall see his descendants in a long life, / and the will of the LORD shall be accomplished through him./

Because of his affliction/ he shall see the light in fullness of days;/ through his suffering, my servant shall justify many, / and their guilt he shall bear./ Therefore I will give him his portion among the great,/ and he shall divide the spoils with the mighty,/ because he surrendered himself to death/ and was counted among the wicked;/ and he shall take away the sins of many, / and win pardon for their offenses.

Second Reading: *Hebrews 4:14-16; 5:7-9*

Brothers and sisters: Since we have a great high priest who has passed through the heavens, Jesus, the Son of God, let us hold fast to our confession. For we do not have a high priest who is unable to sympathize with our weaknesses, but one who has similarly been tested in every way, yet without sin. So let us confidently approach the throne of grace to receive mercy and to find grace for timely help.

In the days when Christ was in the flesh, he offered prayers and supplications with loud cries and tears to the one who was able to save him from death, and he was heard because of his reverence. Son though he was, he learned obedience from what he suffered; and when he was made perfect, he became the source of eternal salvation for all who obey him.

Gospel Reading: *John 18:1-19:42*

Jesus went out with his disciples across the Kidron valley to where there was a garden, into which he and his disciples entered. Judas his betrayer also knew the place, because Jesus had often met there with his disciples. So Judas got a band of soldiers and guards from the chief priests and the Pharisees and went there with lanterns, torches, and weapons. Jesus, knowing everything that was going to happen to him, went out and said to them, "Whom are you looking for?" They answered him, "Jesus the Nazorean." He said to them, "I AM." Judas his betrayer was also with them. When he said to them, "I AM, " they turned away and fell to the ground. So he again asked them, "Whom are you looking for?" They said, "Jesus the Nazorean." Jesus answered, "I told you that I AM. So if you are looking for me, let these men go." This was to fulfill what he had said, "I have not lost any of those you gave me." Then Simon Peter, who had a sword, drew it, struck the high priest's slave, and cut off his right ear. The slave's name was Malchus. Jesus said to Peter, "Put your sword into its scabbard. Shall I not drink the cup that the Father gave me?"

So the band of soldiers, the tribune, and the Jewish guards seized Jesus, bound him, and brought him to Annas first. He was the father-in-law of Caiaphas, who was high priest that year. It was Caiaphas who had counseled the Jews that it was better that one man should die rather than the people.

Simon Peter and another disciple followed Jesus. Now the other disciple was known to the high priest, and he entered the courtyard of the high priest with Jesus. But Peter stood at the gate outside. So the other disciple, the acquaintance of the high priest, went out and spoke to the gatekeeper and brought Peter in. Then the maid who was the gatekeeper said to Peter, "You are not one of this man's disciples, are you?" He said, "I am not." Now the slaves and the guards were standing around a charcoal fire that they had made, because it was cold, and were warming themselves. Peter was also standing there keeping warm.

The high priest questioned Jesus about his disciples and about his doctrine. Jesus answered him, "I have spoken publicly to the world. I have always taught in a synagogue or in the temple area where all the Jews gather, and in secret I have said nothing. Why ask me? Ask those who heard me what I said to them. They know what I said." When he had said this, one of the temple guards standing there struck Jesus and said, "Is this the way you answer the high priest?" Jesus answered him, "If I have spoken wrongly, testify to the wrong; but if I have spoken rightly, why do you strike me?" Then Annas sent him bound to Caiaphas the high priest.

Now Simon Peter was standing there keeping warm. And they said to

97

him, "You are not one of his disciples, are you?" He denied it and said, "I am not." One of the slaves of the high priest, a relative of the one whose ear Peter had cut off, said, "Didn't I see you in the garden with him?" Again Peter denied it. And immediately the cock crowed.

Then they brought Jesus from Caiaphas to the praetorium. It was morning. And they themselves did not enter the praetorium, in order not to be defiled so that they could eat the Passover. So Pilate came out to them and said, "What charge do you bring against this man?" They answered and said to him, "If he were not a criminal, we would not have handed him over to you." At this, Pilate said to them, "Take him yourselves, and judge him according to your law." The Jews answered him, "We do not have the right to execute anyone, " in order that the word of Jesus might be fulfilled that he said indicating the kind of death he would die. So Pilate went back into the praetorium and summoned Jesus and said to him, "Are you the King of the Jews?" Jesus answered, "Do you say this on your own or have others told you about me?" Pilate answered, "I am not a Jew, am I? Your own nation and the chief priests handed you over to me. What have you done?" Jesus answered, "My kingdom does not belong to this world. If my kingdom did belong to this world, my attendants would be fighting to keep me from being handed over to the Jews. But as it is, my kingdom is not here." So Pilate said to him, "Then you are a king?" Jesus answered, "You say I am a king. For this I was born and for this I came into the world, to testify to the truth. Everyone who belongs to the truth listens to my voice." Pilate said to him, "What is truth?"

When he had said this, he again went out to the Jews and said to them, "I find no guilt in him. But you have a custom that I release one prisoner to you at Passover. Do you want me to release to you the King of the Jews?" They cried out again, "Not this one but Barabbas!" Now Barabbas was a revolutionary.

Then Pilate took Jesus and had him scourged. And the soldiers wove a crown out of thorns and placed it on his head, and clothed him in a purple cloak, and they came to him and said, "Hail, King of the Jews!" And they struck him repeatedly. Once more Pilate went out and said to them, "Look, I am bringing him out to you, so that you may know that I find no guilt in him." So Jesus came out, wearing the crown of thorns and the purple cloak. And he said to them, "Behold, the man!" When the chief priests and the guards saw him they cried out, "Crucify him, crucify him!" Pilate said to them, "Take him yourselves and crucify him. I find no guilt in him." The Jews answered, "We have a law, and according to that law he ought to die, because he made himself the Son of God." Now when Pilate heard this statement, he became even more afraid, and went back into the praetorium and said to Jesus, "Where are you from?" Jesus did not answer him. So Pilate said to him, "Do you not speak to me? Do you not know that I have power to release you and I have power to crucify you?" Jesus answered him, "You would have no power over me if it had not been given to you from above. For this reason the one who handed me over to you has the greater sin." Consequently, Pilate tried to release him; but the Jews cried out, "If you release him, you are not a Friend of Caesar. Everyone who makes himself a king opposes Caesar."

When Pilate heard these words he brought Jesus out and seated him on the judge's bench in the place called Stone Pavement, in Hebrew, Gabbatha. It was preparation day for Passover, and it was about noon. And he said to the Jews, "Behold, your king!" They cried out, "Take him away, take him away! Crucify him!" Pilate said to them, "Shall I crucify your king?" The chief priests answered, "We have no king but Caesar." Then he handed him over to them to be crucified.

So they took Jesus, and, carrying the cross himself, he went out to what is called the Place of the Skull, in Hebrew, Golgotha. There they crucified him, and with him two others, one on either side, with Jesus in the middle. Pilate also had an inscription written and put on the cross. It read, "Jesus the Nazorean, the King of the Jews." Now many of the Jews read this inscription, because the place where Jesus was crucified was near the city; and it was written in Hebrew, Latin, and Greek. So the chief priests of the Jews said to Pilate, "Do not write 'The King of the Jews,' but that he said, 'I am the King of the Jews'." Pilate answered, "What I have written, I have written."

When the soldiers had crucified Jesus, they took his clothes and divided them into four shares, a share for each soldier. They also took his tunic, but the tunic was seamless, woven in one piece from the top down. So they said to one another, "Let's not tear it, but cast lots for it to see whose it will be, " in order that the passage of Scripture might be fulfilled that says: *They divided my garments among them,/ and for my vesture they cast lots./* This is what the soldiers did. Standing by the cross of Jesus were his mother and his mother's sister, Mary the wife of Clopas, and Mary of Magdala. When Jesus saw his mother and the disciple there whom he loved he said to his mother, "Woman, behold, your son." Then he said to the disciple, "Behold, your mother." And from that hour the disciple took her into his home.

After this, aware that everything was now finished, in order that the Scripture might be fulfilled, Jesus said, "I thirst." There was a vessel filled with common wine. So they put a sponge soaked in wine on a sprig of hyssop and put it up to his mouth. When Jesus had taken the wine, he said, "It is finished." And bowing his head, he handed over the spirit.

Here all kneel and pause for a short time.

Now since it was preparation day, in orde Jews asked Pilate that their legs be broken and that they be taken down. So the soldiers came and broke the legs of the first and then of the other one who was crucified with Jesus. But when they came to Jesus and saw that he was already dead, they did not break his legs, but

one soldier thrust his lance into his side, and immediately blood and water flowed out. An eyewitness has testified, and his testimony is true; he knows that he is speaking the truth, so that you also may come to believe. For this happened so that the Scripture passage might be fulfilled: / *Not a bone of it will be broken.*/ And again another passage says:/ *They will look upon him whom they have pierced.*

After this, Joseph of Arimathea, secretly a disciple of Jesus for fear of the Jews, asked Pilate if he could remove the body of Jesus. And Pilate permitted it. So he came and took his body. Nicodemus, the one who had first come to him at night, also came bringing a mixture of myrrh and aloes weighing about one hundred pounds. They took the body of Jesus and bound it with burial cloths along with the spices, according to the Jewish burial custom. Now in the place where he had been crucified there was a garden, and in the garden a new tomb, in which no one had yet been buried. So they laid Jesus there because of the Jewish preparation day; for the tomb was close by.

Homily Notes:

....
....
....
....
....
....
....
....
....
....
....
....
....
....

Reflection Questions for Each of the Readings:

1. *Based on the First Reading*: What and who was Isaiah foretelling?

2. *Based on the Second Reading*: What were the duties of the High Priest for the Jewish Passover? Explain how Jesus perfected and fulfilled the duties of the Great High Priest - then and now?

3. *Based on the Gospel Reading*: Who are Nicodemus and Joseph of Arimethea? List the humiliations that the Lord of Lords [Jesus Christ] endured for our sake.

First Reading: *Genesis 1:1-2:2* or **1:1, 26-31a**

In the beginning, when God created the heavens and the earth, the earth was a formless wasteland, and darkness covered the abyss, while a mighty wind swept over the waters.

Then God said, "Let there be light,'" and there was light. God saw how good the light was. God then separated the light from the darkness. God called the light "day," and the darkness he called "night." Thus evening came, and morning followed—the first day.

Then God said, "Let there be a dome in the middle of the waters, to separate one body of water from the other." And so it happened: God made the dome, and it separated the water above the dome from the water below it. God called the dome "the sky." Evening came, and morning followed—the second day.

Then God said, "Let the water under the sky be gathered into a single basin, so that the dry land may appear." And so it happened: the water under the sky was gathered into its basin, and the dry land appeared. God called the dry land "the earth, " and the basin of the water he called "the sea." God saw how good it was.

Then God said, "Let the earth bring forth vegetation: every kind of plant that bears seed and every kind of fruit tree on earth that bears fruit with its seed in it." And so it happened: the earth brought forth every kind of plant that bears seed and every kind of fruit tree on earth that bears fruit with its seed in it. God saw how good it was. Evening came, and morning followed—the third day.

Then God said: "Let there be lights in the dome of the sky, to separate day from night. Let them mark the fixed times, the days and the years, and serve as luminaries in the dome of the sky, to shed light upon the earth." And so it happened: God made the two great lights, the greater one to govern the day, and the lesser one to govern the night; and he made the stars. God set them in the dome of the sky, to shed light upon the earth, to govern the day and the night, and to separate the light from the darkness. God saw how good it was. Evening came, and morning followed—the fourth day.

Then God said, "Let the water teem with an abundance of living creatures, and on the earth let birds fly beneath the dome of the sky." And so it happened: God created the great sea monsters and all kinds of swimming creatures with which the water teems, and all kinds of winged birds. God saw how good it was, and God blessed them, saying, "Be fertile, multiply, and fill the water of the seas; and let the birds multiply on the earth." Evening came, and morning followed—the fifth day.

Then God said, "Let the earth bring forth all kinds of living creatures: cattle, creeping things, and wild animals of all kinds." And so it happened: God made all kinds of wild animals, all kinds of cattle, and all kinds of creeping things of the earth. God saw how good it was.

Then God said: "Let us make man in our image, after our likeness. Let them have dominion over the fish of the sea, the birds of the air, and the cattle, and over all the wild animals and all the creatures that crawl on the ground."/ God created man in his image;/ in the image of God he created him;/ male and female he created them./ God blessed them, saying: "Be fertile and multiply; fill the earth and subdue it. Have dominion over the fish of the sea, the birds of the air, and all the living things that move on the earth." God also said: "See, I give you every seed-bearing plant all over the earth and every tree that has seed-bearing fruit on it to be your food; and to all the animals of the land, all the birds of the air, and all the living creatures that crawl on the ground, I give all the green plants for food." And so it happened. God looked at everything he had made, and he found it very good. Evening came, and morning followed — the sixth day.

Thus the heavens and the earth and all their array were completed. Since on the seventh day God was finished with the work he had been doing, he rested on the seventh day from all the work he had undertaken.

Second Reading: *Genesis 22:1-18 or* **22:1-2, 9a, 10-13, 15-18**

God put Abraham to the test. He called to him, "Abraham!" "Here I am," he replied. Then God said: "Take your son Isaac, your only one, whom you love, and go to the land of Moriah. There you shall offer him up as a holocaust on a height that I will point out to you." Early the next morning Abraham saddled his donkey, took with him his son Isaac and two of his servants as well, and with the wood that he had cut for the holocaust, set out for the place of which God had told him.

On the third day Abraham got sight of the place from afar. Then he said to his servants: "Both of you stay here with the donkey, while the boy and I go on over yonder. We will worship and then come back to you." Thereupon Abraham took the wood for the holocaust and laid it on his son Isaac's shoulders, while he himself carried the fire and the knife. As the two walked on together, Isaac spoke to his father Abraham: "Father!" Isaac said. "Yes, son," he replied. Isaac continued, "Here are the fire and the wood, but where is the sheep for the holocaust?" "Son," Abraham answered, "God himself will provide the sheep for the holocaust." Then the two continued going forward.

When they came to the place of which God had told him, Abraham built an altar there and arranged the wood on it. Next he tied up his son Isaac, and put him on top of the wood on the altar. **Then he reached out and took the knife to slaughter his son. But the LORD's messenger called to him from heaven, "Abraham, Abraham!" "Here I am!" he answered.**

"Do not lay your hand on the boy," said the messenger. "Do not do the least thing to him. I know now how devoted you are to God, since you did not withhold from me your own beloved son." As Abraham looked about, he spied a ram caught by its horns in the thicket. So he went and took the ram and offered it up as a holocaust in place of his son. Abraham named the site Yahweh-yireh; hence people now say, "On the mountain the LORD will see."

Again the LORD's messenger called to Abraham from heaven and said: "I swear by myself, declares the LORD, that because you acted as you did in not withholding from me your beloved son, I will bless you abundantly and make your descendants as countless as the stars of the sky and the sands of the seashore; your descendants shall take possession of the gates of their enemies, and in your descendants all the nations of the earth shall find blessing--all this because you obeyed my command."

Third Reading: *Exodus 14:15-15:1*

The LORD said to Moses, "Why are you crying out to me? Tell the Israelites to go forward. And you, lift up your staff and, with hand outstretched over the sea, split the sea in two, that the Israelites may pass through it on dry land. But I will make the Egyptians so obstinate that they will go in after them. Then I will receive glory through Pharaoh and all his army, his chariots and charioteers. The Egyptians shall know that I am the LORD, when I receive glory through Pharaoh and his chariots and charioteers."

The angel of God, who had been leading Israel's camp, now moved and went around behind them. The column of cloud also, leaving the front, took up its place behind them, so that it came between the camp of the Egyptians and that of Israel. But the cloud now became dark, and thus the night passed without the rival camps coming any closer together all night long. Then Moses stretched out his hand over the sea, and the LORD swept the sea with a strong east wind throughout the night and so turned it into dry land. When the water was thus divided, the Israelites marched into the midst of the sea on dry land, with the water like a wall to their right and to their left.

The Egyptians followed in pursuit; all Pharaoh's horses and chariots and charioteers went after them right into the midst of the sea. In the night watch just before dawn the LORD cast through the column of the fiery cloud upon the Egyptian force a glance that threw it into a panic; and he so clogged their chariot wheels that they could hardly drive. With that the Egyptians sounded the retreat before Israel, because the LORD was fighting for them against the Egyptians.

Then the LORD told Moses, "Stretch out your hand over the sea, that the water may flow back upon the Egyptians, upon their chariots and their charioteers." So Moses stretched out his hand over the sea, and at dawn the sea flowed back to its normal depth. The Egyptians were fleeing head on toward the sea, when the LORD hurled them into its midst. As the water flowed back, it covered the chariots and the charioteers of Pharaoh's whole army which had followed the Israelites into the sea. Not a single one of them escaped. But the Israelites had marched on dry land through the midst of the sea, with the water like a wall to their right and to their left. Thus the LORD saved Israel on that day from the power of the Egyptians. When Israel saw the Egyptians lying dead on the seashore and beheld the great power that the LORD had shown against the Egyptians, they feared the LORD and believed in him and in his servant Moses.

Then Moses and the Israelites sang this song to the LORD:/   I will sing to the LORD, for he is gloriously triumphant;/   horse and chariot he has cast into the sea."

Fourth Reading: *Isaiah 54:5-14*

The One who has become your husband is your Maker,/his name is the LORD of hosts;/. your redeemer is the Holy One of Israel,/ called God of all the earth./ The LORD calls you back,/ like a wife forsaken and grieved in spirit, a wife married in youth and then cast off,/ says your God./. For a brief moment I abandoned you,/. but with great tenderness I will take you back./ In an outburst of wrath, for a moment/ I hid my face from you;/ but with enduring/ love I take pity on you,/ says the LORD, your redeemer./. This is for me like the days of Noah,/ when I swore that the waters of Noah/ should never again deluge the earth;/ so I have sworn not to be angry with you,/ or to rebuke you./ Though the mountains leave their place/ and the hills be shaken,/ my love shall never leave you/ nor my covenant of peace be shaken,/ says the LORD, who has mercy on you./ O afflicted one, storm-battered and unconsoled,/ I lay your pavements in carnelians,/ and your foundations in sapphires;/ I will make your battlements of rubies,/. your gates of carbuncles,/ and all your walls of precious stones./ All your children shall be taught by the LORD,/ and great shall be the peace of your children./ In justice shall you be established,/ far from the fear of oppression,/ where destruction cannot come near you.

Fifth Reading: Isaiah 55:1-11

Thus says the LORD:/. All you who are thirsty,/ come to the water!/ You who have no money,/ come, receive grain and eat;/ come, without paying and without cost,/ drink wine and milk!/ Why spend your money for what is not bread,/ your wages for what fails to satisfy?/ Heed me, and you shall eat well,/ you shall delight in rich fare./ Come to me heedfully,/ listen, that you may have life./ I will renew with you the everlasting covenant,/ the benefits assured to David./ As I made him a witness to the peoples,/ a leader and commander of nations,/ so shall you summon a nation you knew not,/ and nations that knew you not shall run to you,/ because of the LORD, your God,/ the Holy One of Israel, who has glorified you./

Seek the LORD while he may be found,/ call him while he is near./ Let the scoundrel forsake his way,/ and the wicked man his thoughts;/ let him turn to the LORD for mercy;/ to our God, who is generous in forgiving./For my thoughts are not your thoughts,/ nor are your ways my ways,/ says the LORD./ As high as the heavens are above the earth,/ so high are my ways above your ways/ and my thoughts above your thoughts./

For just as from the heavens/ the rain and snow come down/ and do not return there/ till they have watered the earth,/ making it fertile and fruitful,/ giving seed to the one who sows/ and bread to the one who eats,/ so shall my word be/ that goes forth from my mouth;/ my word shall not return to me void,/ but shall do my will,/ achieving the end for which I sent it./

Sixth Reading: *Baruch 3:9-15, 32—4:4*

Hear, O Israel, the commandments of life:/ listen, and know prudence!/ How is it, Israel,/ that you are in the land of your foes,/ grown old in a foreign land,/ defiled with the dead,/ accounted with those destined for the netherworld?/ You have forsaken the fountain of wisdom!/ Had you walked in the way of God,/ you would have dwelt in enduring peace./ Learn where prudence is,/ where strength, where understanding;/ that you may know also/ where are length of days, and life,/ where light of the eyes, and peace./ Who has found the place of wisdom,/ who has entered into her treasuries?

The One who knows all things knows her;/ he has probed her by his knowledge -/ The One who established the earth for all time,/ and filled it with four-footed beasts;/ he who dismisses the light, and it departs,/ calls it, and it obeys him trembling;/ before whom the stars at their posts/ shine and rejoice;/ when he calls them, they answer, "Here we are!"/ shining with joy for their Maker./ Such is our God;/ no other is to be compared to him:/ he has traced out the whole way of understanding,/ and has given her to Jacob, his servant,/ to Israel, his beloved son./

Since then she has appeared on earth,/ and moved among people./ She is the book of the precepts of God,/ the law that endures forever;/ all who cling to her will live,/ but those will die who forsake her./ Turn, O Jacob, and receive her:/ walk by her light toward splendor./ Give not your glory to another,/ your privileges to an alien race./ Blessed are we, O Israel;/ for what pleases God is known to us!/

Seventh Reading: *Ezekiel 36:16-17a, 18-28*

The word of the LORD came to me, saying: Son of man, when the house of Israel lived in their land, they defiled it by their conduct and deeds. Therefore I poured out my fury upon them because of the blood that they poured out on the ground, and because they defiled it with idols. I scattered them among the nations, dispersing them over foreign lands; according to their conduct and deeds I judged them. But when they came among the nations wherever they came, they served to profane my holy name, because it was said of them: "These are the people of the LORD, yet they had to leave their land." So I have relented because of my holy name which the house of Israel profaned among the nations where they came. Therefore say to the house of Israel: Thus says the Lord GOD: Not for your sakes do I act, house of Israel, but for the sake of my holy name, which you profaned among the nations to which you came. I will prove the holiness of my great name, profaned among the nations, in whose midst you have profaned it. Thus the nations shall know that I am the LORD, says the Lord GOD, when in their sight I prove my holiness through you. For I will take you away from among the nations, gather you from all the foreign lands, and bring you back to your own land. I will sprinkle clean water upon you to cleanse you from all your impurities, and from all your idols I will cleanse you. I will give you a new heart and place a new spirit within you, taking from your bodies your stony hearts and giving you natural hearts. I will put my spirit within you and make you live by my statutes, careful to observe my decrees. You shall live in the land I gave your fathers; you shall be my people, and I will be your God.

Epistle Reading: *Romans 6:3-11*

Brothers and sisters: Are you unaware that we who were baptized into Christ Jesus were baptized into his death? We were indeed buried with him through baptism into death, so that, just as Christ was raised from the dead by the glory of the Father, we too might live in newness of life.

For if we have grown into union with him through a death like his, we shall also be united with him in the resurrection. We know that our old self was crucified with him, so that our sinful body might be done away with, that we might no longer be in slavery to sin. For a dead person has been absolved from sin. If, then, we have died with Christ, we believe that we shall also live with him. We know that Christ, raised from the dead, dies no more; death no longer has power over him. As to his death, he died to sin once and for all; as to his life, he lives for God. Consequently, you too must think of yourselves as being dead to sin and living for God in Christ Jesus.

Gospel Reading: *Mark 16:1-7*

When the sabbath was over, Mary Magdalene, Mary, the mother of James, and Salome bought spices so that they might go and anoint him. Very early when the sun had risen, on the first day of the week, they came to the tomb. They were saying to one another, "Who will roll back the stone for us from the entrance to the tomb?" When they looked up, they saw that the stone had been rolled back; it was very large. On entering the tomb they saw a young man sitting on the right side, clothed in a white robe, and they were utterly amazed. He said to them, "Do not be amazed! You seek Jesus of Nazareth, the crucified. He has been raised; he is not here. Behold the place where they laid him. But go and tell his disciples and Peter, 'He is going before you to Galilee; there you will see him, as he told you.'"

Homily Notes:

....
....
....
....
....
....
....
....
....
....
....
....
....
....
....
....

....
....
....
....
....
....
....
....
....
....
....
....
....
....

Reflection Questions for the Readings:

1. *Based on one of the Seven Readings*: What did you learn from this reading?

2. *Based on the Epistle Reading*: What did you learn from this reading?

3. *Based on the Gospel Reading*: Describe the sights and sounds heard by those arriving at the empty tomb. Put yourself in the scene. What are you thinking about?

URBI ET ORBI

by Pope John Paul II; Easter Sunday, 11 April 2004

"Why do you seek the living among the dead? He is not here, but has risen" (Lk 24:5-6). Thus the angel encourages the women who have hastened to the tomb. Thus the Easter liturgy repeats to us, the men and women of the third millennium: Christ is risen, Christ is alive among us! His name now is "the Living One" death has no more power over him (cf. Rom 6:9).

Resurrexit! Today you, O Redeemer of mankind, rise victoriously from the tomb to offer to us, troubled by many threatening shadows, your wish for joy and peace. Those who are tempted by anxiety and desperation turn to you, O Christ, our life and our guide, to hear the proclamation of the hope that does not disappoint. On this day of your victory over death, may humanity find in you, O Lord, the courage to oppose in solidarity the many evils that afflict it. In particular, may it find the strength to face the inhuman, and unfortunately growing, phenomenon of terrorism, which rejects life and brings anguish and uncertainty to the daily lives of so many hard-working and peaceful people. May your wisdom enlighten men and women of good will in the required commitment against this scourge.

Take heed all of you who have at heart mankind's future! Take heed men and women of good will! May the temptation to seek revenge give way to the courage to forgive; may the culture of life and love render vain the logic of death; may trust once more give breath to the lives of peoples. If our future is one, it is the task and duty of all to build it with patient and painstaking far-sightedness.

"Lord, to whom shall we go?" You who have conquered death, you alone "have the words of eternal life" (Jn 6:68). To you we raise with confidence our prayer which becomes an invocation of comfort for the families of the many victims of violence. Help us to work ceaselessly for the coming of that more just and united world that you have inaugurated with your resurrection. Accompanying us in this task is "she who believed that there would be a fulfilment of what was spoken to her from the Lord" (Lk 1:45). Blessed are you, O Mary, silent witness of Easter! You, O Mother of the Crucified One now risen,who at the hour of pain and death kept the flame of hope burning, teach us also to be, amongst the incongruities of passing time, convinced and joyful witnesses of the eternal message of life and love brought to the world by the Risen Redeemer.

EASTER

Key Theological Teachings about Easter

Easter is the *greatest and oldest* of all Christian Feast Days.

Easter is called the "*feasts of feasts, the solemnities of solemnities.*"[1]

If Christ has not been raised, then our preaching is in vain and your faith is in vain."[2]

"Christ's Resurrection is the *fulfillment of the promises of the Old Testament* and of Jesus himself during his earthly life."[3]

"Lord, to whom shall we go? You who have conquered death, you alone have the words of eternal life."[4]

Although not given the title of Solemnity, "the first eight days of Easter Time constitute the Octave of Easter and are celebrated as Solemnities of the Lord.

The Easter Window

The Stained Glass image depicts key Easter images and colors. What images and colors can you identify?. ....
....
....
....
....
....

References:

[1] CCC 1169

[2] 1 Corinthians 15:14

[3] CCC 652

[4] John 6:68

Solemnity of the Resurrection of the Lord
Easter Sunday March 31, 2024

First Reading: *Acts of the Apostles 10:34a, 37-43*

Peter proceeded to speak and said: "You know what has happened all over Judea, beginning in Galilee after the baptism that John preached, how God anointed Jesus of Nazareth with the Holy Spirit and power. He went about doing good and healing all those oppressed by the devil, for God was with him. We are witnesses of all that he did both in the country of the Jews and in Jerusalem. They put him to death by hanging him on a tree. This man God raised on the third day and granted that he be visible, not to all the people, but to us, the witnesses chosen by God in advance, who ate and drank with him after he rose from the dead. He commissioned us to preach to the people and testify that he is the one appointed by God as judge of the living and the dead. To him all the prophets bear witness, that everyone who believes in him will receive forgiveness of sins through his name."

Second Reading: *Colossians 3:1-4* **or** *1 Corinthians 5:6b-8*

Colossians 3:1-4

Brothers and sisters: If then you were raised with Christ, seek what is above, where Christ is seated at the right hand of God. Think of what is above, not of what is on earth. For you have died, and your life is hidden with Christ in God. When Christ your life appears, then you too will appear with him in glory.

1 Corinthians 5:6b-8

Brothers and sisters: Do you not know that a little yeast leavens all the dough? Clear out the old yeast, so that you may become a fresh batch of dough, inasmuch as you are unleavened. For our paschal lamb, Christ, has been sacrificed. Therefore, let us celebrate the feast, not with the old yeast, the yeast of malice and wickedness, but with the unleavened bread of sincerity and truth.

Sequence - Victimae Paschali Laudes

Christians, to the Paschal Victim/ Offer your thankful praises!/ A Lamb the sheep redeems;/ Christ, who only is sinless,/ Reconciles sinners to the Father./ Death and life have contended in that combat stupendous:/ The Prince of life, who died, reigns immortal./ Speak, Mary, declaring/ What you saw, wayfaring./ "The tomb of Christ, who is living,/ The glory of Jesus' resurrection;/. bright angels attesting,/ The shroud and napkin resting./ Yes, Christ my hope is arisen;/ to Galilee he goes before you."/ Christ indeed from death is risen, our new life obtaining./ Have mercy, victor King, ever reigning! Amen. Alleluia.

Solemnity of the Resurrection of the Lord
Easter Sunday   March 31, 2024

Gospel Reading: *John 20:1-9*

On the first day of the week, Mary of Magdala came to the tomb early in the morning, while it was still dark, and saw the stone removed from the tomb. So she ran and went to Simon Peter and to the other disciple whom Jesus loved, and told them, "They have taken the Lord from the tomb, and we don't know where they put him." So Peter and the other disciple went out and came to the tomb. They both ran, but the other disciple ran faster than Peter and arrived at the tomb first; he bent down and saw the burial cloths there, but did not go in. When Simon Peter arrived after him, he went into the tomb and saw the burial cloths there, and the cloth that had covered his head, not with the burial cloths but rolled up in a separate place. Then the other disciple also went in, the one who had arrived at the tomb first, and he saw and believed. For they did not yet understand the Scripture that he had to rise from the dead.

Homily Notes:

....

....

....

....

....

....

....

....

....

....

....

....

....

....

....

....

....

....

....

....

....

....

....

....

....

Reflection Questions for Each of the Readings:

1. *Based on the First Reading*: Summarize the main points of the First Reading.

2. *Based on the Second Reading*: Summarize the main points of the Second Reading [that was read at Mass.]

3. *Based on the Gospel Reading*: Who arrived at the tomb first? Is there any significance in when the apostles arrived and who entered the tomb first? What did the witnesses conclude about the empty tomb? How does Easter *perfect* the theological virtues of Faith, Hope & Charity?

Your Virtue Challenge:

The goal of the virtuous person is to become like God. [CCC 1803] This will require identifying ways to increase this virtue and reduce opposing vice; *fasting [avoiding]* from habits or practices that oppose it; *praying* for God's help; *helping* others; and *doing penance. Based on the Second Reading,* your Virtue Challenge for the week is to increase in the virtue of:

AUTHENTICITY

My Virtue Goals and Working Plan for the Week:

....

....

....

....

Daily Mass Readings for the Week:

Monday, April 1: Acts 2:14, 22-33; Matthew 28:8-15.
Tuesday, April 2: Acts 2:36-41; John 20:11-18.
Wednesday, April 3: Acts 3:1-10; Luke 24:13-35.
Thursday, April 4: Acts 3:11-26; Luke 24:35-48.
Friday, April 5: Acts 4:1-12; John 21:1-14.
Saturday, April 6: Acts 4:13-21; Mark 16:9-15.

Second Sunday of Easter
Sunday of Divine Mercy

April 7, 2024

First Reading: *Acts of the Apostles 14:32-35*

  The community of believers was of one heart and mind, and no one claimed that any of his possessions was his own, but they had everything in common. With great power the apostles bore witness to the resurrection of the Lord Jesus, and great favor was accorded them all. There was no needy person among them, for those who owned property or houses would sell them, bring the proceeds of the sale, and put them at the feet of the apostles, and they were distributed to each according to need.

Second Reading: *1 John 5:1-6*

  Beloved: Everyone who believes that Jesus is the Christ is begotten by God, and everyone who loves the Father loves also the one begotten by him. In this way we know that we love the children of God when we love God and obey his commandments. For the love of God is this, that we keep his commandments. And his commandments are not burdensome, for whoever is begotten by God conquers the world. And the victory that conquers the world is our faith. Who indeed is the victor over the world but the one who believes that Jesus is the Son of God?

  This is the one who came through water and blood, Jesus Christ, not by water alone, but by water and blood. The Spirit is the one that testifies, and the Spirit is truth.

Gospel Reading: *John 20:19-31*

  On the evening of that first day of the week, when the doors were locked, where the disciples were, for fear of the Jews, Jesus came and stood in their midst and said to them, "Peace be with you." When he had said this, he showed them his hands and his side. The disciples rejoiced when they saw the Lord. Jesus said to them again, "Peace be with you. As the Father has sent me, so I send you." And when he had said this, he breathed on them and said to them, "Receive the Holy Spirit. Whose sins you forgive are forgiven them, and whose sins you retain are retained."

  Thomas, called Didymus, one of the Twelve, was not with them when Jesus came. So the other disciples said to him, "We have seen the Lord." But he said to them, "Unless I see the mark of the nails in his hands and put my finger into the nail marks and put my hand into his side, I will not believe."

  Now a week later his disciples were again inside and Thomas was with

117

them. Jesus came, although the doors were locked, and stood in their midst and said, "Peace be with you." Then he said to Thomas, "Put your finger here and see my hands, and bring your hand and put it into my side, and do not be unbelieving, but believe." Thomas answered and said to him, "My Lord and my God!" Jesus said to him, "Have you come to believe because you have seen me? Blessed are those who have not seen and have believed."

Now Jesus did many other signs in the presence of his disciples that are not written in this book. But these are written that you may come to believe that Jesus is the Christ, the Son of God,

Homily Notes:

....
....
....
....
....
....
....
....
....
....
....
....
....
....
....
....
....
....
....
....
....
....

Reflection Questions for each of the Readings:

1. *Based on the First Reading*: Describe the attitudes and beliefs of the early believers. Compare and contrast these attitudes and beliefs to today.

2. *Based on the Second Reading*: How do we *prove* that we love the Trinitarian God? Why do many people reject God's commandments?

3. *Based on the Gospel Reading*: *"Blessed are those who believe but have not seen."* Explain how that verse applies to you personally.

Your Virtue Challenge:

The goal of the virtuous person is to become like God. [CCC 1803] This will require identifying ways to increase this virtue and reduce opposing vice; *fasting [avoiding]* from habits or practices that oppose it; *praying* for God's help; *helping* others; and *doing penance*. Based on the Gospel Reading, your Virtue Challenge for the week is to increase in the virtue of:

CONFIDENCE

My Virtue Goals and Working Plan for the Week:

....
....
....
....

Daily Mass Readings for the Week:

Monday, April 8: **Solemnity of the Annunciation of the Lord Solemnity** Isaiah 7:10-14; 8:10; Hebrews 10:4-10; Luke 1:26-38.
Tuesday, April 9: Acts 4:32-37; John 3:7b-15.
Wednesday, April 10: Acts 5:17-26; John 3:16-21.
Thursday, April 11: **Saint Stanislaus** Acts 5:27-33; John 3:31-36.
Friday, April 12: Acts 5:34-42; John 6:1-15.
Saturday, April 13: **Saint Martin I** Acts 6:1-7; John 6:16-21.

Third Sunday of Easter

April 14, 2024

First Reading: *Acts of the Apostles 3:13-15, 17-19*

Peter said to the people: "The God of Abraham, the God of Isaac, and the God of Jacob, the God of our fathers, has glorified his servant Jesus, whom you handed over and denied in Pilate's presence when he had decided to release him. You denied the Holy and Righteous One and asked that a murderer be released to you. The author of life you put to death, but God raised him from the dead; of this we are witnesses. Now I know, brothers, that you acted out of ignorance, just as your leaders did; but God has thus brought to fulfillment what he had announced beforehand through the mouth of all the prophets, that his Christ would suffer. Repent, therefore, and be converted, that your sins may be wiped away."

Second Reading: *1 John 2:1-5a*

My children, I am writing this to you so that you may not commit sin. But if anyone does sin, we have an Advocate with the Father, Jesus Christ the righteous one. He is expiation for our sins, and not for our sins only but for those of the whole world. The way we may be sure that we know him is to keep his commandments. Those who say, "I know him," but do not keep his commandments are liars, and the truth is not in them. But whoever keeps his word, the love of God is truly perfected in him.

Gospel Reading: *Luke 24:35-48*

The two disciples recounted what had taken place on the way, and how Jesus was made known to them in the breaking of bread.

While they were still speaking about this, he stood in their midst and said to them, "Peace be with you." But they were startled and terrified and thought that they were seeing a ghost. Then he said to them, "Why are you troubled? And why do questions arise in your hearts? Look at my hands and my feet, that it is I myself. Touch me and see, because a ghost does not have flesh and bones as you can see I have." And as he said this, he showed them his hands and his feet. While they were still incredulous for joy and were amazed, he asked them, "Have you anything here to eat?" They gave him a piece of baked fish; he took it and ate it in front of them.

He said to them, "These are my words that I spoke to you while I was still with you, that everything written about me in the law of Moses and in the prophets and psalms must be fulfilled." Then he opened their minds to understand the Scriptures. And he said to them, "Thus it is written that the Christ would suffer and rise from the dead on the third day and that repentance, for the forgiveness of sins, would be preached in his name to all the nations, beginning from Jerusalem. You are witnesses of these things."

Third Sunday of Easter

Homily Notes:

....
....
....
....
....
....
....
....
....
....
....
....
....
....
....
....
....
....
....
....
....
....
....
....

Reflection Questions for each of the Readings:
1. *Based on the First Reading*: The first reading discusses repentance. What does *repentance* mean to you?

2. *Based on the Second Reading*: Explain verse four: "'I know him,' but do not keep his commandments ... they are liars, and the truth is not in them."

3. *Based on the Gospel Reading*: How can we be effective witnesses about Jesus; His Resurrection; the Eucharist; and the Trinity?

Your Virtue Challenge:

The goal of the virtuous person is to become like God. [CCC 1803] This will require identifying ways to increase this virtue and reduce opposing vice; *fasting [avoiding]* from habits or practices that oppose it; *praying* for God's help; *helping* others; and *doing penance*. Based on the Gospel Reading, your Virtue Challenge for the week is to increase in the virtue of:

HUMILITY

My Virtue Goals and Working Plan for the Week:

....

....

....

....

Daily Mass Readings for the Week:
Monday, April 15: Acts 6:8-15; Jon 6:22-29.
Tuesday, April 16, Acts 7:51—8:1a; John 6:30-35.
Wednesday, April 17: Acts 8:1b-8; John 6:35-40.
Thursday, April 18: Acts 8:26-40; John 6:44-51.
Friday, April 19: Acts 9:1-20; John 6:52-59.
Saturday, April 20: Acts 9:31-42; John 6:60-69.

Fourth Sunday of Easter

First Reading: *Acts of the Apostles 4:8-12*

Peter, filled with the Holy Spirit, said: "Leaders of the people and elders: If we are being examined today about a good deed done to a cripple, namely, by what means he was saved, then all of you and all the people of Israel should know that it was in the name of Jesus Christ the Nazorean whom you crucified, whom God raised from the dead; in his name this man stands before you healed. He is *the stone rejected by you, the builders, which has become the cornerstone.* There is no salvation through anyone else, nor is there any other name under heaven given to the human race by which we are to be saved."

Second Reading: *1 John 3:1-2*

Beloved: See what love the Father has bestowed on us that we may be called the children of God. Yet so we are. The reason the world does not know us is that it did not know him. Beloved, we are God's children now; what we shall be has not yet been revealed. We do know that when it is revealed we shall be like him, for we shall see him as he is.

Gospel Reading: *John 10:11-18*

Jesus said: "I am the good shepherd. A good shepherd lays down his life for the sheep. A hired man, who is not a shepherd and whose sheep are not his own, sees a wolf coming and leaves the sheep and runs away, and the wolf catches and scatters them. This is because he works for pay and has no concern for the sheep. I am the good shepherd, and I know mine and mine know me, just as the Father knows me and I know the Father; and I will lay down my life for the sheep. I have other sheep that do not belong to this fold. These also I must lead, and they will hear my voice, and there will be one flock, one shepherd. This is why the Father loves me, because I lay down my life in order to take it up again. No one takes it from me, but I lay it down on my own. I have power to lay it down, and power to take it up again. This command I have received from my Father."

Fourth Sunday of Easter

April 21, 2024

Homily Notes:

....
....
....
....
....
....
....
....
....
....
....
....
....
....
....
....
....
....
....
....
....
....
....
....

Reflection Questions for each of the Readings:

1. *Based on the First Reading:* Explain how verse 12 applies to each of us. "There is no salvation through anyone else, nor is there any other name under heaven given to the human race by which we are to be saved."

.

2. Based on the Second Reading: Why did so many people fail to recognize or understand Christ and His Church - then and now?

3. Based on the Gospel Reading: List the qualities of a good shepherd. Why is Jesus **the** ultimate Good Shepherd?

Your Virtue Challenge:

The goal of the virtuous person is to become like God. [CCC 1803] This will requires identifying ways to increase this virtue and reduce opposing vice; *fasting [avoiding]* from habits or practices that oppose it; *praying* for God's help; *helping* others; and *doing penance*. Based on the Gospel Reading, your Virtue Challenge for the week is to increase in the virtue of:

UNDERSTANDING

My Virtue Goals and Working Plan for the Week:

....

....

....

....

Daily Mass Readings for the Week:

Monday, April 22: Acts 11:1-18; John 10:1-10.
Tuesday, April 23: **Sts. George & Adalbert** Acts 11:19-26; John 10:22-30.
Wednesday, April 24: **Saint Fidelis of Sigmaringen** Acts 12:24—13:5a; John 12:44-50.
Thursday, April 25: **Saint Mark** 1 Peter 5:5b-14; Mark 16:15-20.
Friday, April 26: Acts 13:26-33; John 14:1-6.
Saturday, April 27: Acts 13:44-52; John 14:7-14.

Fifth Sunday of Easter

April 28, 2024

First Reading: *Acts of the Apostles 9:26-31*

When Saul arrived in Jerusalem he tried to join the disciples, but they were all afraid of him, not believing that he was a disciple. Then Barnabas took charge of him and brought him to the apostles, and he reported to them how he had seen the Lord, and that he had spoken to him, and how in Damascus he had spoken out boldly in the name of Jesus. He moved about freely with them in Jerusalem, and spoke out boldly in the name of the Lord. He also spoke and debated with the Hellenists, but they tried to kill him. And when the brothers learned of this, they took him down to Caesarea and sent him on his way to Tarsus.

The church throughout all Judea, Galilee, and Samaria was at peace. It was being built up and walked in the fear of the Lord, and with the consolation of the Holy Spirit it grew in numbers.

Second Reading: *I John 3:18-24*

Children, let us love not in word or speech but in deed and truth.

Now this is how we shall know that we belong to the truth and reassure our hearts before him in whatever our hearts condemn, for God is greater than our hearts and knows everything. Beloved, if our hearts do not condemn us, we have confidence in God and receive from him whatever we ask, because we keep his commandments and do what pleases him. And his commandment is this: we should believe in the name of his Son, Jesus Christ, and love one another just as he commanded us. Those who keep his commandments remain in him, and he in them, and the way we know that he remains in us is from the Spirit he gave us.

Gospel Reading: *John 15:1-8*

Jesus said to his disciples: "I am the true vine, and my Father is the vine grower. He takes away every branch in me that does not bear fruit, and every one that does he prunes so that it bears more fruit. You are already pruned because of the word that I spoke to you. Remain in me, as I remain in you. Just as a branch cannot bear fruit on its own unless it remains on the vine, so neither can you unless you remain in me. I am the vine, you are the branches. Whoever remains in me and I in him will bear much fruit, because without me you can do nothing. Anyone who does not remain in me will be thrown out like a branch and wither; people will gather them and throw them into a fire and they will be burned. If you remain in me and my words remain in you, ask for whatever you want and it will be done for you. By this is my Father glorified, that you bear much fruit and become my disciples."

126

Fifth Sunday of Easter

Homily Notes:

....
....
....
....
....
....
....
....
....
....
....
....
....
....
....
....
....
....
....
....
....
....
....
....
....

Reflection Questions for each of the Readings:

1. *Based on the First Reading*: Why were the early apostles and disciples afraid of Paul? When and why did their fears dissipate?

.

2. Based on the Second Reading: Who truly knows our hearts? Who can we trust? What commandment is explained in this reading?

3. Based on the Gospel Reading: Who is the true vine? How have you been pruned by the Vine Grower?

Your Virtue Challenge:

The goal of the virtuous person is to become like God. [CCC 1803] This will require identifying ways to increase this virtue and reduce opposing vice; *fasting [avoiding]* from habits or practices that oppose it; *praying* for God's help; *helping* others; and *doing penance. Based on the Second Reading,* your Virtue Challenge for the week is to increase in the virtue of:

CONFIDENCE

My Virtue Goals and Working Plan for the Week:

....

....

....

....

Daily Mass Readings for the Week:

Monday, April 29: **Saint Catherine of Siena** Acts 14:5-18; John 14:21-26.
Tuesday, April 30: **Saint Pius V** Acts 14:19-28; John 14:27-31a.
Wednesday, May 1: **Saint Joseph the Worker** Acts 15:1-6; John 15:1-8.
or Genesis 1:26—2:3 or Colossians 3:14-15, 17, 23-24/Matthew 13:54-58.
Thursday, May 2: **Saint Athanasius** Acts 15:7-21; John 15:9-11.
Friday, May 3: **Feast of Saints Philip and James** 1 Corinthians 15:1-8; John 14:6-14.
Saturday, May 4: Acts 16:1-10; John 15:18-21.

Sixth Sunday of Easter

First Reading: *Acts of the Apostles 10:25-26; 34-35;44-48*

When Peter entered, Cornelius met him and, falling at his feet, paid him homage. Peter, however, raised him up, saying, "Get up. I myself am also a human being."

Then Peter proceeded to speak and said, "In truth, I see that God shows no partiality. Rather, in every nation whoever fears him and acts uprightly is acceptable to him."

While Peter was still speaking these things, the Holy Spirit fell upon all who were listening to the word. The circumcised believers who had accompanied Peter were astounded that the gift of the Holy Spirit should have been poured out on the Gentiles also, for they could hear them speaking in tongues and glorifying God. Then Peter responded, "Can anyone withhold the water for baptizing these people, who have received the Holy Spirit even as we have?" He ordered them to be baptized in the name of Jesus Christ.

Second Reading: *1 John 4:7-10*

Beloved, let us love one another, because love is of God; everyone who loves is begotten by God and knows God. Whoever is without love does not know God, for God is love. In this way the love of God was revealed to us: God sent his only Son into the world so that we might have life through him. In this is love: not that we have loved God, but that he loved us and sent his Son as expiation for our sins.

Gospel Reading: *John 15:9-17*

Jesus said to his disciples: "As the Father loves me, so I also love you. Remain in my love. If you keep my commandments, you will remain in my love, just as I have kept my Father's commandments and remain in his love.

"I have told you this so that my joy may be in you and your joy might be complete. This is my commandment: love one another as I love you. No one  has greater love than this, to lay down one's life for one's friends. You are my friends if you do what I command you. I no longer call you slaves, because a slave does not know what his master is doing. I have called you friends, because I have told you everything I have heard from my Father. It was not you who chose me, but I who chose you and appointed you to go and bear fruit that will remain, so that whatever you ask the Father in my name he may give you. This I command you: love one another."

129

Homily Notes:

....
....
....
....
....
....
....
....
....
....
....
....
....
....
....
....
....
....
....
....
....
....
....
....

Reflection Questions for Each of the Readings:
1. *Based on the First Reading*: Define partiality. How/why is it destructive to society and our faith?

2. *Based on the Second Reading*: Explain this verse in your own words: *"In this is love: not that we have loved God, but that he loved us and sent his Son as expiation for our sins."* Also, explain the meaning *of the expiation of sins.*

3. *Based on the Gospel Reading*: Describe God's love. How are we to love others?

Your Virtue Challenge:

The goal of the virtuous person is to become like God. [CCC 1803] This will require identifying ways to increase this virtue and reduce opposing vice; *fasting [avoiding]* from habits or practices that oppose it; *praying* for God's help; *helping* others; and *doing penance*. Based on the First Reading, your Virtue Challenge for the week is to increase in the virtue of:

IMPARTIALITY

My Virtue Goals and Working Plan for the Week:

....

....

....

Daily Mass Readings for the Week:
Monday, May 6: Acts 16:11-15; John 15:26—16:4a.
Tuesday, May 7: Acts 16:22-34; John 16:5-11.
Wednesday, May 8: Acts 17:15, 22—18:1; John 16:12-15.
Thursday, May 9: **The Solemnity of the Ascension of the Lord is a HolyDay of Obligation** in the Ecclesiastical Provinces of Boston, Hartford, New York, Omaha, & Philadelphia: Acts 1:1-11; Ephesians 1:17-23 or Ephesians 4:1-13 or 4:1-7, 11-13; Mark 16:15-20. See pages 125 - 127. For all other U.S. Dioceses and Provinces, the Mass readings for Thursday are: Acts 18:1-8; John 16:16-20.
Friday, May 10: **Sts. John of Avila & Damien de Veuster**. Acts 18:9-18; John 16:20-23.
Saturday, May 11: Acts 18:23-28; John 16:23b-28.

The Solemnity of the Ascension of Our Lord
Thursday, May 9, 2024   or   Sunday, May 12, 2024

Note: The Feast of the Ascension of the Lord is celebrated as a Holy Day of Obligation on **May 9, 2024:** the 40th day [Thursday in the sixth week of Easter] for the Ecclesiastical Provinces of **Boston, Hartford, New York, Newark, Omaha, and Philadelphia.** These select provinces will celebrate the *Seventh Sunday of Easter* on **May 12, 2024.** All other US provinces or dioceses will celebrate the **Feast of the Ascension** on May 12. 2024. The Solemnity of the Ascension of the Lord Mass Readings: current page The Seventh Sunday of Easter Mass Readings [May 12]: Page 135.

First Reading: *Acts of the Apostles 1:1–11*

In the first book, Theophilus, I dealt with all that Jesus did and taught until the day he was taken up, after giving instructions through the Holy Spirit to the apostles whom he had chosen. He presented himself alive to them by many proofs after he had suffered, appearing to them during forty days and speaking about the kingdom of God. While meeting with them, he enjoined them not to depart from Jerusalem, but to wait for "the promise of the Father about which you have heard me speak; for John baptized with water, but in a few days you will be baptized with the Holy Spirit."

When they had gathered together they asked him, "Lord, are you at this time going to restore the kingdom to Israel?" He answered them, "It is not for you to know the times or seasons that the Father has established by his own authority. But you will receive power when the Holy Spirit comes upon you, and you will be my witnesses in Jerusalem, throughout Judea and Samaria, and to the ends of the earth." When he had said this, as they were looking on, he was lifted up, and a cloud took him from their sight. While they were looking intently at the sky as he was going, suddenly two men dressed in white garments stood beside them. They said, "Men of Galilee, why are you standing there looking at the sky? This Jesus who has been taken up from you into heaven will return in the same way as you have seen him going into heaven."

Second Reading: *Ephesians 1:17–23* **or Ephesians 4: 4:1-13**

Ephesians 1:17–23

Brothers and sisters: May the God of our Lord Jesus Christ, the Father of glory, give you a Spirit of wisdom and revelation resulting in knowledge of him. May the eyes of your hearts be enlightened, that you may know what is the hope that belongs to his call, what are the riches of glory in his inheritance among the holy ones, and what is the surpassing greatness of his power for us who believe, in accord with the exercise of his great might, which he worked in Christ, raising him from the dead and seating him at his right hand in the heavens, far above every principality, authority, power, and dominion, and every name that is named not only in this age but also in the one to come. And he put
132

all things beneath his feet and gave him as head over all things to the church, which is his body, the fullness of the one who fills all things in every way.

Ephesians 4:1-13 or *4:1-7, 11-13*

Brothers and sisters, I, a prisoner for the Lord, urge you to live in a manner worthy of the call you have received, with all humility and gentleness, with patience, bearing with one another through love, striving to preserve the unity of the spirit through the bond of peace: one body and one Spirit, as you were also called to the one hope of your call; one Lord, one faith, one baptism; one God and Father of all, who is over all and through all and in all.

But grace was given to each of us according to the measure of Christ's gift. Therefore, it says:

He ascended on high and took prisoners captive; he gave gifts to men.

What does "he ascended" mean except that he also descended into the lower regions of the earth? The one who descended is also the one who ascended far above all the heavens, that he might fill all things.

And he gave some as apostles, others as prophets, others as evangelists, others as pastors and teachers, to equip the holy ones for the work of ministry, for building up the body of Christ, until we all attain to the unity of faith and knowledge of the Son of God, to mature to manhood, to the extent of the full stature of Christ.

Gospel Reading: *Mark 16:15-20*

Jesus said to his disciples, "Go into the whole world and proclaim the gospel to every creature. Whoever believes and is baptized will be saved; whoever does not believe will be condemned. These signs will accompany those who believe: in my name they will drive out demons, they will speak new languages. They will pick up serpents with their hands, and if they drink any deadly thing, it will not harm them. They will lay hands on the sick, and they will recover."

So then the Lord Jesus, after he spoke to them, was taken up into heaven and took his seat at the right hand of God. But they went forth and preached everywhere, while the Lord worked with them and confirmed the word through accompanying signs.

The Solemnity of the Ascension of Our Lord
Thursday, May 9, 2024   or   Sunday, May 12, 2024

Homily Notes:

....

....

....

....

....

....

....

....

....

....

....

....

....

....

....

....

....

....

....

....

....

....

....

Reflection Questions for Each of the Readings:

1. Based on the First Reading: What did Jesus teach the disciples between the Resurrection and the Ascension? What sights and sounds were present at the Ascension based on eye witness testimony?

2. Based on the Second Reading: What did you learn from the Second Reading?

3. Based on the Gospel Reading: What signs confirmed the disciples newfound zeal and desire to preach about the risen Lord? What seemed to be their state of mind/attitude/feelings at this time?

Your Virtue Challenge:

The goal of the virtuous person is to become like God. [CCC 1803] This will require identifying ways to increase this virtue and reduce opposing vice; *fasting [avoiding]* from habits or practices that oppose it; *praying* for God's help; *helping* others; and *doing penance. Based on the Second Reading,* your Virtue Challenge for the week is to increase in the virtue of:

GENTLENESS

My Virtue Goals and Working Plan for the Week:

....

....

....

Daily Mass Readings for the Week:
Monday, May 13: **Our Lady of Fatima** Acts 19:1-8; John 16:29-33.
Tuesday, May 14: **Saint Matthias** Acts 1:15-17, 20-26; John 15:9-17.
Wednesday, May 15: **Saint Isidore** Acts 20:28-38; John 17:11b-19.
Thursday, May 16: Acts 22:30; 23:6-11; John 17:20-26.
Friday, May 17: Acts 25:13b-21; John 21:15-19.
Saturday, May 18: **Saint John I** Morning: Acts 28:16-20, 30-31; John 21:20-25.
Pentecost Vigil - See page 141.

Seventh Sunday of Easter

May 12, 2024

Ecclesiastical Provinces of Boston, Hartford, New York, Omaha, Philadelphia Only

First Reading: *Acts of the Apostles 1:15-17, 20a, 20c-26*

Peter stood up in the midst of the brothers —there was a group of about one hundred and twenty persons in the one place. He said, "My brothers, the Scripture had to be fulfilled which the Holy Spirit spoke beforehand through the mouth of David, concerning Judas, who was the guide for those who arrested Jesus. He was numbered among us and was allotted a share in this ministry.

"For it is written in the Book of Psalms: *May another take his office."*

"Therefore, it is necessary that one of the men who accompanied us the whole time the Lord Jesus came and went among us, beginning from the baptism of John until the day on which he was taken up from us, become with us a witness to his resurrection." So they proposed two, Judas called Barsabbas, who was also known as Justus, and Matthias. Then they prayed, "You, Lord, who know the hearts of all, show which one of these two you have chosen to take the place in this apostolic ministry from which Judas turned away to go to his own place." Then they gave lots to them, and the lot fell upon Matthias, and he was counted with the eleven apostles.

Second Reading: *1 John 4:11-16*

Beloved, if God so loved us, we also must love one another. No one has ever seen God. Yet, if we love one another, God remains in us, and his love is brought to perfection in us.

This is how we know that we remain in him and he in us, that he has given us of his Spirit. Moreover, we have seen and testify that the Father sent his Son as savior of the world. Whoever acknowledges that Jesus is the Son of God, God remains in him and he in God. We have come to know and to believe in the love God has for us.

God is love, and whoever remains in love remains in God and God in him.

Gospel Reading: *John 17:11b-19*

Lifting up his eyes to heaven, Jesus prayed saying: "Holy Father, keep them in your name that you have given me, so that they may be one just as we are one. When I was with them I protected them in your name that you gave me, and I guarded them, and none of them was lost except the son of destruction, in order that the Scripture might be fulfilled. But now I am coming to you. I speak this in the world so that they may share my joy completely. I gave them your word, and the world hated them, because they do not belong to the world any more than I belong to the world. I do not ask that you take them out of the world but that you keep them from the evil one. They do not belong to the world any more than I belong to the world. Consecrate them in the truth. Your word is truth. As you sent me into the world, so I sent them into the world. And I consecrate myself for them, so that they also may be consecrated in truth."

Homily Notes:

....
....
....
....
....
....
....
....
....
....
....
....
....
....
....
....
....
....
....
....

Reflection Questions for Each of the Readings:

1. *Based on the First Reading*: Who replaced Judas? How did his selection occur?

2. *Based on the Second Reading*: Many Confirmation students are encouraged to memorize 1 John: 4:11-16. Re-write it here. Try and memorize it! Pray it.

3. *Based on the Gospel Reading*: Who is the son of destruction? Are believers hated today? Explain your answer. What has been your personal experience with non-believers?

Your Virtue Challenge:

       The goal of the virtuous person is to become like God. [CCC 1803] This will require identifying ways to increase this virtue and reduce opposing vice; *fasting [avoiding]* from habits or practices that oppose it; *praying* for God's help; *helping* others; and *doing penance*. Based on the Gospel Reading, your Virtue Challenge for the week is to increase in the virtue of:

FORTITUDE

My Virtue Goals and Working Plan for the Week:

....

....

....

Daily Mass Readings for the Week:
Monday, May 13: **Our Lady of Fatima** Acts 19:1-8; John 16:29-33.
Tuesday, May 14: **Saint Matthias** Acts 1:15-17, 20-26; John 15:9-17.
Wednesday, May 15: **Saint Isidore** Acts 20:28-38; John 17:11b-19.
Thursday, May 16: Acts 22:30; 23:6-11; John 17:20-26.
Friday, May 17: Acts 25:13b-21; John 21:15-19.
Saturday, May 18: Saint John I [Morning] Acts 28:16-20, 30-31; John 21:20-25.
Pentecost Vigil: Genesis 11:1-9 or Exodus 19:3-8a, 16-20b or Ezekiel 37:1-14 or Joel 3:1-5; Romans 8:22-27; John 7:37-39.

Our Lord Jesus Christ, King of the Universe

Pope Francis, Saint Peter's Basilica, Sunday, 21 November 2021

Jesus' freedom draws us in. Let us allow it to resonate within us, to challenge us, to awaken in us the courage born of truth. Let us ask ourselves this: Were I in Pilate's place, looking Jesus in the eye, what would I be ashamed of? Faced with the truth of Jesus, the truth that is Jesus, what are the ways I am deceitful or duplicitous, the ways I displease him? Each of us will find such ways. Look for them, seek them out. We all have these duplicities, these compromises, this "arranging things" so that the cross will go away. It is good to stand before Jesus, who is truth, in order to be set free from our illusions. It is good to worship Jesus, and as a result, to be inwardly free, to see life as it really is, and not be deceived by the fashions of the moment and the displays of consumerism that dazzle but also deaden. Friends, we are not here to be enchanted by the sirens of the world, but to take our lives in hand, to "take a bite out of life", in order to live it to the full!

In this way, with the freedom of Jesus, we find the courage we need to *swim against the current.* I would like to emphasize this: swimming against the current, having the courage to swim against the current. Not the daily temptation to swim against other people, like those perpetual victims and conspiracy theorists who are always casting blame on others; but rather against the unhealthy current of our own selfishness, closed-mindedness and rigidity, that often seeks like-minded groups to survive. Not this, but swimming against the tide so as to become more like Jesus. For he teaches us to meet evil only with the mild and lowly force of good. Without shortcuts, without deceit, without duplicity. Our world, beset by so many evils, does not need any more ambiguous compromises, people who move back and forth like the tide – wherever the wind blows them, wherever their own interests take them – or swing to the right or left, depending on what is most convenient, those who "sit on the fence".

A Christian like that seems more of an "equilibrist" than a Christian. Those who are always performing a balancing act are looking for ways to avoid getting their hands dirty, so as not to compromise their lives, not to take life seriously. Please, be afraid of being young people like that. Instead, be free and authentic, be the critical conscience of society. Don't be afraid to criticize! We need your criticism. Many of you, for example, are critical of environmental pollution. We need this! Be free in criticism. Be passionate about truth, so that, with your dreams, you can say: "My life is not captive to the mindset of the world: I am free, because I reign with Jesus for justice, love and peace!" Dear young people, it is my hope and prayer that each of you can joyfully say: "With Jesus, I too am a king". I too reign: as a living sign of the love of God, of his compassion and his tenderness. I am a dreamer, dazzled by the light of the Gospel, and I watch with hope in the night visions. And whenever I fall, I discover anew in Jesus the courage to continue fighting and hoping, the courage to keep dreaming. At every stage in life.

The Antidotes for Vice

"Now the works of the flesh are obvious: immorality, impurity, licentiousness, [20] idolatry, sorcery, hatreds, rivalry, jealousy, outbursts of fury, acts of selfishness, dissensions, factions, occasions of envy, drinking bouts, orgies, and the like. I warn you, as I warned you before, that those who do such things will not inherit the kingdom of God. In contrast, the fruit of the Spirit is love, joy, peace, patience, kindness, generosity, faithfulness, [23] gentleness, self-control." **Galatians 5:19-25**

The antidotes against sins of the flesh are the virtues; including the Theological Virtues of Faith, Hope and Love; the **Cardinal Virtues** [Fortitude, Justice, Prudence, and Temperance]; the **Seven Key Moral Virtues** [Chastity, Diligence, Generosity, Humility, Kindness, Obedience, and Patience]; **Natural Virtues** and the **Corporal and Spiritual Works of Mercy.**

"The works of mercy are charitable actions by which we come to the aid of our neighbor in his spiritual and bodily necessities. [CCC 242] Instructing, advising, consoling, comforting are spiritual works of mercy, as are forgiving and bearing wrongs patiently. The corporal works of mercy consist especially in feeding the hungry, sheltering the homeless, clothing the naked, visiting the sick and imprisoned, and burying the dead. [CCC 243] Among all these, giving alms to the poor is one of the chief witnesses to fraternal charity: it is also a work of justice pleasing to God: feeding the hungry, sheltering the homeless, clothing the naked, visiting the sick and imprisoned, and burying the dead. [CCC 244]

"There cannot be two parallel lives in the existence of the faithful: on the one hand, our so-called spiritual life, with its values and demands; and on the other, our so-called secular life, that is, life in a family, at work, in social relationships, in the responsibilities of public life, and in culture. Every area of our lives, as different as they are, enters into the plan of God, who desires that these very areas be the places where the love of Christ is revealed and realized for both the glory of the Father and service of others."

"Our lives are measured by time, in the course of which we change, grow old, and as with all living beings on earth, death seems like the normal end of life. That aspect of death lends urgency to our lives; remembering our mortality helps us to realize that we have only a limited time in which to bring our lives to fulfillment." [CCC #1007]

PENTECOST

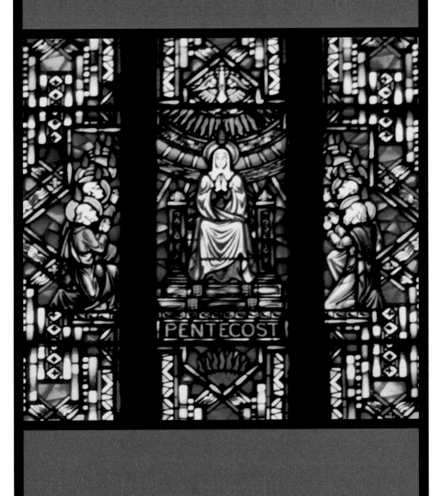

PENTECOST

Key Theological Teachings about Pentecost

The Pentecost occurs seven weeks after the Passion and Resurrection of our Lord. At Pentecost, Jesus completes the pledge that he would send a helper for us. Pentecost provided the opportunity to hear the word of God regardless of culture or language spoken.

At the First Pentecost, the Holy Spirit was manifested, given, and communicated as a divine Person to the Church. Pentecost is the new age of the Church wherein Christ lives and acts in and with his Church." CCC 1076

At the end of every Mass we are told to go out and glorify the Lord with our lives and our whole hearts. Let's do that!

The Holy Spirit wants to unleash energy and empower every person. The gifts of the Holy Spirit include: forgiveness; wisdom; understanding; right judgment; courage; fortitude; knowledge; fear of the Lord; and reverence. We are called to pray for each of these gifts to be manifested in us.

Study the Pentecost Stained Glass Window. What colors and images symbolize Pentecost? List them below; explain why you think they represent the descent of the Holy Spirit on the Apostles.

....

....

....

First Reading: *Genesis 11:1-9* **or** *Exodus 19:3-8a, 16-20b* **or** Ezekiel: 37:1-14 **or** Joel 3:1-5

Genesis 11:1-9

The whole world spoke the same language, using the same words. While the people were migrating in the east, they came upon a valley in the land of Shinar and settled there. They said to one another, "Come, let us mold bricks and harden them with fire." They used bricks for stone, and bitumen for mortar. Then they said, "Come, let us build ourselves a city and a tower with its top in the sky, and so make a name for ourselves; otherwise we shall be scattered all over the earth."

The LORD came down to see the city and the tower that the people had built. Then the LORD said: "If now, while they are one people, all speaking the same language, they have started to do this, nothing will later stop them from doing whatever they presume to do. Let us then go down there and confuse their language, so that one will not understand what another says." Thus the LORD scattered them from there all over the earth, and they stopped building the city. That is why it was called Babel, because there the LORD confused the speech of all the world. It was from that place that he scattered them all over the earth.

Exodus 19:3-8a, 16-20b

Moses went up the mountain to God. Then the LORD called to him and said, "Thus shall you say to the house of Jacob; tell the Israelites: You have seen for yourselves how I treated the Egyptians and how I bore you up on eagle wings and brought you here to myself. Therefore, if you hearken to my voice and keep my covenant, you shall be my special possession, dearer to me than all other people, though all the earth is mine. You shall be to me a kingdom of priests, a holy nation. That is what you must tell the Israelites." So Moses went and summoned the elders of the people. When he set before them all that the LORD had ordered him to tell them, the people all answered together, "Everything the LORD has said, we will do."

On the morning of the third day there were peals of thunder and lightning, and a heavy cloud over the mountain, and a very loud trumpet blast, so that all the people in the camp trembled. But Moses led the people out of the camp to meet God, and they stationed themselves at the foot of the mountain. Mount Sinai was all wrapped in smoke, for the LORD came down upon it in fire. The smoke rose from it as though from a furnace, and the whole mountain trembled violently. The trumpet blast grew louder and louder, while Moses was speaking, and God answering him with thunder.

When the LORD came down to the top of Mount Sinai, he

143

summoned Moses to the top of the mountain.

Ezekiel: 37:1-14

The hand of the LORD came upon me, and he led me out in the spirit of the LORD and set me in the center of the plain, which was now filled with bones. He made me walk among the bones in every direction so that I saw how many they were on the surface of the plain. How dry they were! He asked me: Son of man, can these bones come to life? I answered, "Lord GOD, you alone know that." Then he said to me: Prophesy over these bones, and say to them: Dry bones, hear the word of the LORD! Thus says the Lord GOD to these bones: See! I will bring spirit into you, that you may come to life. I will put sinews upon you, make flesh grow over you, cover you with skin, and put spirit in you so that you may come to life and know that I am the LORD. I, Ezekiel, prophesied as I had been told, and even as I was prophesying I heard a noise; it was a rattling as the bones came together, bone joining bone. I saw the sinews and the flesh come upon them, and the skin cover them, but there was no spirit in them. Then the LORD said to me: Prophesy to the spirit, prophesy, son of man, and say to the spirit: Thus says the Lord GOD: From the four winds come, O spirit, and breathe into these slain that they may come to life. I prophesied as he told me, and the spirit came into them; they came alive and stood upright, a vast army. Then he said to me: Son of man, these bones are the whole house of Israel. They have been saying, "Our bones are dried up, our hope is lost, and we are cut off." Therefore, prophesy and say to them: Thus says the Lord GOD: O my people, I will open your graves and have you rise from them, and bring you back to the land of Israel. Then you shall know that I am the LORD, when I open your graves and have you rise from them, O my people! I will put my spirit in you that you may live, and I will settle you upon your land; thus you shall know that I am the LORD. I have promised, and I will do it, says the LORD.

Joel 3:1-5

Thus says the LORD:/ I will pour out my spirit upon all flesh./ Your sons and daughters shall prophesy,/ your old men shall dream dreams,/ your young men shall see visions;/ even upon the servants and the handmaids,/ in those days, I will pour out my spirit./ And I will work wonders in the heavens and on the earth,/ blood, fire, and columns of smoke;/ the sun will be turned to darkness,/ and the moon to blood,/ at the coming of the day of the LORD,/ the great and terrible day./ Then everyone shall be rescued/ who calls on the name of the LORD;/ for on Mount Zion there shall be a remnant,/ as the LORD has said,/ and in Jerusalem survivors/ whom the LORD shall call.

Second Reading: *1 John 4:11-16*

Brothers and sisters: We know that all creation is groaning in labor pains even until now; and not only that, but we ourselves, who have the first fruits of the Spirit, we also groan within ourselves as we wait for adoption, the redemption of our bodies. For in hope we were saved. Now hope that sees is not hope. For who hopes for what one sees? But if we hope for what we do not see, we wait with endurance.

In the same way, the Spirit too comes to the aid of our weakness; for we do not know how to pray as we ought, but the Spirit himself intercedes with inexpressible groanings. And the one who searches hearts knows what is the intention of the Spirit, because he intercedes for the holy ones according to God's will.

Gospel Reading: *John 7:37-39*

On the last and greatest day of the feast, Jesus stood up and exclaimed, "Let anyone who thirsts come to me and drink. As Scripture says: *Rivers of living water will flow from within him who believes in me.*"

He said this in reference to the Spirit that those who came to believe in him were to receive. There was, of course, no Spirit yet, because Jesus had not yet been glorified.

Mass Readings **During the Day for Pentecost start on page 146.**

Solemnity of the Pentecost
Mass During the Day

May 19, 2024

First Reading: *Acts of the Apostles 2:1-11*

When the time for Pentecost was fulfilled, they were all in one place together. And suddenly there came from the sky a noise like a strong driving wind, and it filled the entire house in which they were. Then there appeared to them tongues as of fire, which parted and came to rest on each one of them. And they were all filled with the Holy Spirit and began to speak in different tongues, as the Spirit enabled them to proclaim.

Now there were devout Jews from every nation under heaven staying in Jerusalem. At this sound, they gathered in a large crowd, but they were confused because each one heard them speaking in his own language. They were astounded, and in amazement they asked, "Are not all these people who are speaking Galileans? Then how does each of us hear them in his native language? We are Parthians, Medes, and Elamites, inhabitants of Mesopotamia, Judea and Cappadocia, Pontus and Asia, Phrygia and Pamphylia, Egypt and the districts of Libya near Cyrene, as well as travelers from Rome, both Jews and converts to Judaism, Cretans and Arabs, yet we hear them speaking in our own tongues of the mighty acts of God."

Second Reading: *1 Corinthians 12:3b-7, 12-13 or **Galatians 5:16-25***

1 Corinthians 12:3b-7, 12-13

Brothers and sisters: No one can say, "Jesus is Lord," except by the Holy Spirit.

There are different kinds of spiritual gifts but the same Spirit; there are different forms of service but the same Lord; there are different workings but the same God who produces all of them in everyone. To each individual the manifestation of the Spirit is given for some benefit.

As a body is one though it has many parts, and all the parts of the body, though many, are one body, so also Christ. For in one Spirit we were all baptized into one body, whether Jews or Greeks, slaves or free persons, and we were all given to drink of one Spirit.

Galatians 5:16-25

Brothers and sisters, live by the Spirit and you will certainly not gratify the desire of the flesh. For the flesh has desires against the Spirit, and the Spirit against the flesh; these are opposed to each other, so that you may not do what you want. But if you are guided by the Spirit, you are not under the law. Now the works of the flesh are obvious: immorality, impurity, lust, idolatry, sorcery, hatreds, rivalry, jealousy, outbursts of fury, acts of selfishness, dissensions, factions, occasions of envy, drinking bouts, orgies, and the like. I warn you, as I warned you before, that those who do such things will not inherit the

146

kingdom of God. In contrast, the fruit of the Spirit is love, joy, peace, patience, kindness, generosity, faithfulness, gentleness, self-control. Against such there is no law. Now those who belong to Christ Jesus have crucified their flesh with its passions and desires. If we live in the Spirit, let us also follow the Spirit.

Sequence: Veni, Sancte Spiritus

Come, Holy Spirit, come!/ And from your celestial home/ Shed a ray of light divine!/ Come, Father of the poor!/ Come, source of all our store!/ Come, within our bosoms shine./ You, of comforters the best;/ You, the soul's most welcome guest;/ Sweet refreshment here below;/ In our labor, rest most sweet;/ Grateful coolness in the heat;/ Solace in the midst of woe./ O most blessed Light divine,/ Shine within these hearts of yours,/ And our inmost being fill!/ Where you are not, we have naught,/ Nothing good in deed or thought,/ Nothing free from taint of ill./ Heal our wounds, our strength renew;/ On our dryness pour your dew;/ Wash the stains of guilt away:/ Bend the stubborn heart and will;/ Melt the frozen, warm the chill;/ Guide the steps that go astray./ On the faithful, who adore/ And confess you, evermore/ In your sevenfold gift descend;/ Give them virtue's sure reward;/ Give them your salvation, Lord;/ Give them joys that never end./ Amen./ Alleluia.

Gospel Reading: *John 20:19-23* or *John 15:26-27; 16:12-15*

John 20:19-23

On the evening of that first day of the week, when the doors were locked, where the disciples were, for fear of the Jews, Jesus came and stood in their midst and said to them, "Peace be with you." When he had said this, he showed them his hands and his side. The disciples rejoiced when they saw the Lord. Jesus said to them again, "Peace be with you. As the Father has sent me, so I send you." And when he had said this, he breathed on them and said to them, "Receive the Holy Spirit. Whose sins you forgive are forgiven them, and whose sins you retain are retained."

John 15:26-27; 16:12-15

Jesus said to his disciples: "When the Advocate comes whom I will send you from the Father, the Spirit of truth that proceeds from the Father, he will testify to me. And you also testify, because you have been with me from the beginning.
"I have much more to tell you, but you cannot bear it now. But when he comes, the Spirit of truth, he will guide you to all truth. He will not speak on his own, but he will speak what he hears, and will declare to you the things that are coming. He will glorify me, because he will take from what is mine and declare it to you. Everything that the Father has is mine; for this reason I told

you that he will take from what is mine and declare it to you."

Homily Notes:

....
....
....
....
....
....
....
....
....
....
....
....
....
....
....
....
....
....
....
....
....
....
....
....
....
....
....
....
....

Reflection Questions for Each of the Readings:

1. *Based on the First Reading*: Imagine you are in the crowd. How many languages do you hear; what do you see?

2. *Based on the Second Reading*: Name the gifts, ministries and works of the Holy Spirit.

3. *Based on the Gospel Reading*: [either reading] In your own words, explain Pentecost. Why did the Church experience exponential growth after Pentecost?

Your Virtue Challenge:

The goal of the virtuous person is to become like God. [CCC 1803] This will requires identifying ways to increase this virtue and reduce opposing vice; *fasting [avoiding]* from habits or practices that oppose it; *praying* for God's help; *helping* others; and *doing penance. Based on the Gospel Reading,* your Virtue Challenge for the week is to increase in the virtue of:

INTEGRITY

My Virtue Goals and Working Plan for the Week:

....

....

....

Daily Mass Readings for the Week:

Monday, May 20: **The Blessed Virgin Mary, Mother of the Church** Genesis 3:9-15, 20 or Acts 1:12-14; John 19:25-34.

Tuesday, May 21: **St. Christopher Magallanes** James 4:1-10; Mark 9:30-37.

Wednesday, May 22: **Saint Rita of Cascia** James 4:13-17; Mark 9:38-40.

Thursday, May 23: James 5:1-6; Mark 9:41-50.

Friday, May 24: James 5:9-12; Mark 10:1-12.

Saturday, May 25: **Sts. Gregory VII; Mary Magdalene de' Pazzi, Bede the Venerable;** and the **The Blessed Virgin Mary** James 5:13-20; Mark 10:13-16.

TIME AFTER EPIPHANY

TIME AFTER EPIPHANY

Did You Know?

The *Holy Trinity Icon* - aka - *The Hospitality of Abraham* - **featured on these two pages** - was created by monk-artist Andrei Rublev in the early 1400's for the Trinity Monastery of St. Sergius [near Moscow, Russia].

"In the icon of the Trinity, we are in the presence of God, but we do not see him; we do not understand him." Rublev based his work on Genesis 18:2-15 which describes the visit of three mysterious travellers to aging Abraham and his wife Sarah during which they announce the couple would soon have a son. The three angels represent the three identities of the Trinity: God the Father, God the Son and God the Holy Spirit. All three figures possess identical features and this is what the artist intended to draw because the three persons of the Trinity are identical, yet each fulfills its own particular role. In Rublev's painting, the angel on the left represents the Father, the middle angel represents the Son and the right angel is the Holy Spirit. The Son and the Holy Spirit turn their heads in the direction of the Father. He remains still since He is the originating principle from whence all derives. All three are blessing the chalice, which contains a sacrificed calf, readied for eating. The calf signifies Christ the Saviour's death on the cross, while its preparation as food represents the sacrament of the Eucharist. Each angel holds a slender staff in a delicate hand as a symbol of their divine power.

The composition of the work is circular - that is, without beginning, without end, without hierarchy." More information about the Holy Trinity Icon can be found at: http://www.visual-arts-cork.com/famous-paintings/trinity-rublev.htm. Is is simply amazing how ancient artisans [sculptors, painters, iconographers, etc.] understood Catholic Theology and were eager to capture it in their artistic expressions!

The Time After Epiphany (Ordinary Time) Window

Study the window. What colors and images symbolize Ordinary Time? List them below; explain why they represent Ordinary Time.

....
....
....
....
....
....

Solemnity of The Most Holy Trinity

First Reading: *Deuteronomy 4:32-34, 39-40*

Moses said to the people: "Ask now of the days of old, before your time, ever since God created man upon the earth; ask from one end of the sky to the other: Did anything so great ever happen before? Was it ever heard of? Did a people ever hear the voice of God speaking from the midst of fire, as you did, and live? Or did any god venture to go and take a nation for himself from the midst of another nation, by testings, by signs and wonders, by war, with strong hand and outstretched arm, and by great terrors, all of which the LORD, your God, did for you in Egypt before your very eyes This is why you must now know, and fix in your heart, that the LORD is God in the heavens above and on earth below, and that there is no other. You must keep his statutes and commandments that I enjoin on you today, that you and your children after you may prosper, and that you may have long life on the land which the LORD, your God, is giving you forever."

Second Reading: *Romans 8:14-17*

Brothers and sisters: For those who are led by the Spirit of God are sons of God. For you did not receive a spirit of slavery to fall back into fear, but you received a Spirit of adoption, through whom we cry, "Abba, Father!" The Spirit himself bears witness with our spirit that we are children of God, and if children, then heirs, heirs of God and joint heirs with Christ, if only we suffer with him so that we may also be glorified with him.

Gospel Reading: *Matthew 28:16-20*

The eleven disciples went to Galilee, to the mountain to which Jesus had ordered them. When they all saw him, they worshiped, but they doubted. Then Jesus approached and said to them, "All power in heaven and on earth has been given to me. Go, therefore, and make disciples of all nations, baptizing them in the name of the Father, and of the Son, and of the Holy Spirit, teaching them to observe all that I have commanded you. And behold, I am with you always, until the end of the age."

Homily Notes:

....
....
....
....
....
....
....
....
....
....
....
....
....
....
....
....
....
....
....
....
....
....
....

Reflection Questions for Each of the Readings:

1. *Based on the First Reading*: Bishop Robert Barron asks: "Why did God, who is perfect in every way and who stands in need of nothing outside of himself, bother to create at all?" His answer: "If we understand the WHY then we will understand *why we must acknowledge, and fix in our hearts, that the LORD is God in the heavens above and on earth below, and that there is no other.*" What is your answer to Bishop Barron's question?

2. *Based on the Second Reading*: What are the seven gifts of the Holy Spirit and the Twelve fruits of the Holy Spirit?

3. *Based on the Gospel Reading*: What did Jesus commission his disciples to do? What promise did Jesus make? How does that apply to us?.

Your Virtue Challenge:

The goal of the virtuous person is to become like God. [CCC 1803] This will require identifying ways to increase this virtue and reduce opposing vice; *fasting [avoiding]* from habits or practices that oppose it; *praying* for God's help; *helping* others; and *doing penance. Based on the First Reading,* your Virtue Challenge for the week is to increase in the virtue of:

STEADFASTNESS

My Virtue Goals and Working Plan for the Week:

....

....

....

Daily Mass Readings for the Week:

Monday, May 27: Saint Augustine of Canterbury 1 Peter 1:3-9; Mark 10:17-27
28 Tuesday, May 28: 1 Peter 1:10-16; Mark 10:28-31
Wednesday, May 29: Saint Paul VI 1 Peter 1:18-25; Mark 10:32-45
Thursday, May 30: 1 Peter 2:2-5, 9-12; Mark 10:46-52
Friday, May 31: The Visitation of the Blessed Virgin Mary Zephaniah 3:14-18a or Romans 12:9-16; Luke 1:39-56
Saturday, June 1: Saint Justin Jude 17, 20b-25; Mark 11:27-33

First Reading: *Exodus 24:3-8*

When Moses came to the people and related all the words and ordinances of the LORD, they all answered with one voice, "We will do everything that the LORD has told us." Moses then wrote down all the words of the LORD and, rising early the next day, he erected at the foot of the mountain an altar and twelve pillars for the twelve tribes of Israel. Then, having sent certain young men of the Israelites to offer holocausts and sacrifice young bulls as peace offerings to the LORD, Moses took half of the blood and put it in large bowls; the other half he splashed on the altar. Taking the book of the covenant, he read it aloud to the people, who answered, "All that the LORD has said, we will heed and do." Then he took the blood and sprinkled it on the people, saying, "This is the blood of the covenant that the LORD has made with you in accordance with all these words of his."

Second Reading: *Hebrews 9:11-15*

Brothers and sisters: When Christ came as high priest of the good things that have come to be, passing through the greater and more perfect tabernacle not made by hands, that is, not belonging to this creation, he entered once for all into the sanctuary, not with the blood of goats and calves but with his own blood, thus obtaining eternal redemption. For if the blood of goats and bulls and the sprinkling of a heifer's ashes can sanctify those who are defiled so that their flesh is cleansed, how much more will the blood of Christ, who through the eternal Spirit offered himself unblemished to God, cleanse our consciences from dead works to worship the living God.

For this reason he is mediator of a new covenant: since a death has taken place for deliverance from transgressions under the first covenant, those who are called may receive the promised eternal inheritance.

Gospel Reading: *Mark 14:12-16; 22-26*

On the first day of the Feast of Unleavened Bread, when they sacrificed the Passover lamb, Jesus' disciples said to him, "Where do you want us to go and prepare for you to eat the Passover?" He sent two of his disciples and said to them, "Go into the city and a man will meet you, carrying a jar of water. Follow him. Wherever he enters, say to the master of the house, 'The Teacher says, "Where is my guest room where I may eat the Passover with my disciples?"' Then he will show you a large upper room furnished and ready. Make the preparations for us there." The disciples then went off, entered the city, and found it just as he had told them; and they prepared the Passover.

While they were eating, he took bread, said the blessing, broke it, gave it to them, and said, "Take it; this is my body." Then he took a cup, gave thanks, and gave it to them, and they all drank from it. He said to them, "This is my blood of the covenant, which will be shed for many. Amen, I say to you, I shall not drink again the fruit of the vine until the day when I drink it new in the kingdom of God." Then, after singing a hymn, they went out to the Mount of Olives.

Homily Notes:

....
....
....
....
....
....
....
....
....
....
....
....
....
....
....
....
....
....
....

Reflection Questions for Each of the Readings:

1. *Based on the First Reading*: Moses made an oath with the Lord. What did he promise on behalf of all the Israelites? Why didn't the Jewish people keep their promises with the Lord?

2. *Based on the Second Reading*: What is the role of a mediator? Why was Jesus' *bloody* sacrifice necessary?

3. *Based on the Gospel Reading*: What is the New Covenant?

Your Virtue Challenge:

The goal of the virtuous person is to become like God. [CCC 1803] This will require identifying ways to increase this virtue and reduce opposing vice; *fasting [avoiding]* from habits or practices that oppose it; *praying* for God's help; *helping* others; and *doing penance. Based on the First Reading,* your Virtue Challenge for the week is to increase in the virtue of:

LOYALTY

My Virtue Goals and Working Plan for the Week:

....

....

....

Daily Mass Readings for the Week:

Monday, June 3: **St. Charles Lwanga & Companions** 2 Peter 1:2-7; Mark 12:1-12.

Tuesday, June 4: 2 Peter 3:12-15a, 17-18; Mark 12:13-17.

Wednesday, June 5: **Saint Boniface** 2 Timothy 1:1-3, 6-12; Mark 12:18-27.

Thursday, June 6: Saint Norbert 2 Timothy 2:8-15; Mark 12:28-34.

Friday, June 7: **The Most Sacred Heart of Jesus Solemnity** Hosea 11:1, 3-4, 8c-9; Ephesians 3:8-12, 14-19; John 19:31-37.

Saturday, June 8: **The Immaculate Heart of the Blessed Virgin Mary** 2 Timothy 4:1-8; Luke 2:41-51.

158

Tenth Sunday of Ordinary Time

June 9, 2024

First Reading: *Genesis 3:9-15*

After the man, Adam, had eaten of the tree, the LORD God called to the man and asked him, "Where are you?" He answered, "I heard you in the garden; but I was afraid, because I was naked, so I hid myself." Then he asked, "Who told you that you were naked? You have eaten, then, from the tree of which I had forbidden you to eat!" The man replied, "The woman whom you put here with me— she gave me fruit from the tree, and so I ate it." The LORD God then asked the woman, "Why did you do such a thing?" The woman answered, "The serpent tricked me into it, so I ate it."

Then the LORD God said to the serpent:/ "Because you have done this, you shall be banned / from all the animals/ and from all the wild creatures;/ on your belly shall you crawl,/ and dirt shall you eat / all the days of your life./ I will put enmity between you and the woman,/ and between your offspring and hers;/ he will strike at your head,/ while you strike at his heel."

Second Reading: *2 Corinthians 4:13 - 5:1*

Brothers and sisters: Since we have the same spirit of faith, according to what is written, *I believed, therefore I spoke,* we too believe and therefore we speak, knowing that the one who raised the Lord Jesus will raise us also with Jesus and place us with you in his presence. Everything indeed is for you, so that the grace bestowed in abundance on more and more people may cause the thanksgiving to overflow for the glory of God. Therefore, we are not discouraged; rather, although our outer self is wasting away, our inner self is being renewed day by day. For this momentary light affliction is producing for us an eternal weight of glory beyond all comparison, as we look not to what is seen but to what is unseen; for what is seen is transitory, but what is unseen is eternal. For we know that if our earthly dwelling, a tent, should be destroyed, we have a building from God, a dwelling not made with hands, eternal in heaven.

Gospel Reading: *Mark 3:20-35*

Jesus came home with his disciples. Again the crowd gathered, making

159

it impossible for them even to eat. When his relatives heard of this they set out to seize him, for they said, "He is out of his mind." The scribes who had come from Jerusalem said, "He is possessed by Beelzebul," and "By the prince of demons he drives out demons."

Summoning them, he began to speak to them in parables, "How can Satan drive out Satan? If a kingdom is divided against itself, that kingdom cannot stand. And if a house is divided against itself, that house will not be able to stand. And if Satan has risen up against himself and is divided, he cannot stand; that is the end of him. But no one can enter a strong man's house to plunder his property unless he first ties up the strong man. Then he can plunder the house. Amen, I say to you, all sins and all blasphemies that people utter will be forgiven them. But whoever blasphemes against the Holy Spirit will never have forgiveness, but is guilty of an everlasting sin." For they had said, "He has an unclean spirit."

His mother and his brothers arrived. Standing outside they sent word to him and called him. A crowd seated around him told him, "Your mother and your brothers and your sisters are outside asking for you." But he said to them in reply, "Who are my mother and my brothers?" And looking around at those seated in the circle he said, "Here are my mother and my brothers. For whoever does the will of God is my brother and sister and mother."

Homily Notes:

....

. . . .

....

....

....

....

....

....

....

....

....

....

....

....

. . . .

....
....
....
....
....
....
....
....
....
....
....
....
....
....
....
....
....
....

Reflection Questions for Each of the Readings:

1. *Based on the First Reading*: Bishop Robert Barron writes: "Beguiled by the serpent's suggestion that God is secretly jealous of his human creatures, Adam and Eve ate of the fruit. They seized at godliness that they might not be dominated by God and had to face the consequences." Explain how mankind continues to demonstrate that we seize *at godliness* so *that we might not be dominated by God*? Use specific examples.

2. *Based on the Second Reading*: What *afflictions* have you had to bear? Did you get bogged down by negative feelings or discouragement? What can we all learn from this reading when we feel discouraged; sick; depressed; tired?

3. *Based on the Gospel Reading*: How does a person blaspheme against the Holy Spirit? How should we discern the will of God?

Your Virtue Challenge:

The goal of the virtuous person is to become like God. [CCC 1803] This will require identifying ways to increase this virtue and reduce opposing vice; *fasting [avoiding]* from habits or practices that oppose it; *praying* for God's help; *helping* others; and *doing penance*. Based on the Second Reading, your Virtue Challenge for the week is to increase in the virtue of:

REVERENCE

My Virtue Goals and Working Plan for the Week:

....
....
....
....

Daily Mass Readings for the Week:

Monday, June 10: 1 Kings 17:1-6; Matthew 5:1-12.
Tuesday, June 11: **Saint Barnabas** Acts 11:21b-26;13:1-3; Matthew 5:13-16.
Wednesday, June 12: 1 Kings 18:20-39; Matthew 5:17-19.
Thursday, June 13: **Saint Anthony of Padua** 1 Kings 18:41-46; Matthew 5:20-26.
Friday, June 14: 1 Kings 19:9a, 11-16; Matthew 5:27-32.
Saturday, June 15: 1 Kings 19:19-21; Matthew 5:33-37.

First Reading: *Ezekiel 17:22-24*

Thus says the Lord GOD:/ I, too, will take from the crest of the cedar,/ from its top-most branches tear off a tender shoot,/ and plant it on a high and lofty mountain;/ on the mountain heights of Israel I will plant it./ It shall put forth branches and bear fruit,/ and become a majestic cedar./ Birds of every kind shall dwell beneath it,/ every winged thing in the shade of its boughs./ And all the trees of the field shall know / that I, the LORD, / bring low the high tree,/ lift high the lowly tree,/ wither up the green tree,/ and make the withered tree bloom./ As I, the LORD, have spoken, so will I do.

Second Reading: *2 Corinthians 5:6-10*

Brothers and sisters: We are always courageous, although we know that while we are at home in the body we are away from the Lord, for we walk by faith, not by sight. Yet we are courageous, and we would rather leave the body and go home to the Lord. Therefore, we aspire to please him, whether we are at home or away. For we must all appear before the judgment seat of Christ, so that each may receive recompense, according to what he did in the body, whether good or evil.

Gospel Reading: *Mark 4:26-34*

Jesus said to the crowds: "This is how it is with the kingdom of God; it is as if a man were to scatter seed on the land and would sleep and rise night and day and through it all the seed would sprout and grow, he knows not how. Of its own accord the land yields fruit, first the blade, then the ear, then the full grain in the ear. And when the grain is ripe, he  wields the sickle at once, for the harvest has come."

He said, "To what shall we compare the kingdom of God, or what parable can we use for it? It is like a mustard seed that, when it is sown in the ground, is the smallest of all the seeds on the earth. But once it is sown, it springs up and becomes the largest of plants and puts forth large branches, so that the birds of the sky can dwell in its shade." With many such parables he spoke the word to them as they were able to understand it. Without parables

Eleventh Sunday of Ordinary Time

he did not speak to them, but to his own disciples he explained everything in private.

Homily Notes:

....
....
....
....
....
....
....
....
....
....
....
....
....
....
....
....
....
....
....
....
....
....
....

Reflection Questions for Each of the Readings:
1. *Based on the First Reading*: Who/what does the cedar represent? Explain the parable in your own words.

2. *Based on the Second Reading*: Explain the meaning of verse seven: *to walk by faith and not by sight*: in your own words.

3. *Based on the Gospel Reading*: Mustard seeds are roughly the size of a pencil point or a new crayon tip - just 1-2 mm! Why/how does Jesus use this seed to teach about the Kingdom of God?

Your Virtue Challenge:

The goal of the virtuous person is to become like God. [CCC 1803] This will require identifying ways to increase this virtue and reduce opposing vice; *fasting [avoiding]* from habits or practices that oppose it; *praying* for God's help; *helping* others; and *doing penance*. *Based on the Second Reading*, your Virtue Challenge for the week is to increase in the virtue of:

FAITHFULNESS

My Virtue Goals and Working Plan for the Week:

....

....

....

....

Daily Mass Readings for the Week:

Monday, June 17: 1 Kings 21:1-16; Matthew 5:38-42.
Tuesday, June 18: 1 Kings 21:17-29; Matthew 5:43-48.
Wednesday, June 19: **Saint Romuald** 2 Kings 2:1, 6-14: Matthew 6:1-6, 16-18.
Thursday, June 20: Sirach 48:1-14; Matthew 6:7-15.
Friday, June 21: **Saint Aloysius Gonzaga** 2 Kings 11:1-4, 9-18, 20; Matthew 6:19-23.
Saturday, June 22: **Sts. Paulinus of Nola, John Fisher, & Thomas More** 2 Chronicles 24:17-25; Matthew 6:24-34.

165

Twelfth Sunday of Ordinary Time

June 23, 2024

First Reading: *Job 38:1, 8-11*

The Lord addressed Job out of the storm and said:/ Who shut within doors the sea,/ when it burst forth from the womb;/ when I made the clouds its garment/ and thick darkness its swaddling bands?/ When I set limits for it/ and fastened the bar of its door,/ and said:/ Thus far shall you come but no farther,/ and here shall your proud waves be stilled!

Second Reading: *2 Corinthians 5:14-17*

Brothers and sisters: The love of Christ impels us, once we have come to the conviction that one died for all; therefore, all have died. He indeed died for all, so that those who live might no longer live for themselves but for him who for their sake died and was raised.

Consequently, from now on we regard no one according to the flesh; even if we once knew Christ according to the flesh, yet now we know him so no longer. So whoever is in Christ is a new creation: the old things have passed away; behold, new things have come.

Gospel Reading: *Mark 4:35-41*

On that day, as evening drew on, Jesus said to his disciples: "Let us cross to the other side." Leaving the crowd, they took Jesus with them in the boat just as he was. And other boats were with him. A violent squall came up and waves were breaking over the boat, so that it was already filling up. Jesus was in the stern, asleep on a cushion. They woke him and said to him, "Teacher, do you not care that we are perishing?" He woke up, rebuked the wind, and said to the sea, "Quiet! Be still!" The wind ceased and there was great calm. Then he asked them, "Why are you terrified? Do you not yet have faith?" They were filled with great awe and said to one another, "Who then is this whom even wind and sea obey?"

Twelfth Sunday of Ordinary Time

Homily Notes:

....
....
....
....
....
....
....
....
....
....
....
....
....
....
....
....
....
....
....
....
....
....
....
....

Reflection Questions for Each of the Readings:

1. *Based on the First Reading*: What does God expect from Job?

2. *Based on the Second Reading*: What did you learn from this reading?

3. *Based on the Gospel Reading*: "Who then is this... even the wind and sea obey him?" What is your answer to the apostle's question? Who do you say Jesus is?

Your Virtue Challenge:

The goal of the virtuous person is to become like God. [CCC 1803] This will require identifying ways to increase this virtue and reduce opposing vice; *fasting [avoiding]* from habits or practices that oppose it; *praying* for God's help; *helping* others; and *doing penance*. Based on the Second Reading, your Virtue Challenge for the week is to increase in the virtue of:

FAITHFULNESS

My Virtue Goals and Working Plan for the Week:

....

....

....

....

Daily Mass Readings for the Week:

Monday, June 24: **Nativity of St. John the Baptist** Solemnity. Isaiah 49:1-6; Acts 13:22-26; Luke 1:57-66, 80.

Tuesday, June 25: 2 Kings 19:9b-11, 14-21, 31-35a, 36; Matthew 7:6, 12-14.

Wednesday, June 26: 2 Kings 22:8-13; 23:1-3; Matthew 7:15-20.

Thursday, June 27: **Saint Cyril of Alexandria** 2 Kings 24:8-17; Matthew 7:21-29.

Friday, June 28: **Saint Irenaeus** 2 Kings 25:1-12; Matthew 8:1-4.

Saturday, June 29: **Sts. Peter and Paul Solemnity**

Vigil: Acts 3:1-10; Galatians 1:11-20; John 21:15-19.

Day: Acts 12:1-11; 2 Timothy 4:6-8, 17-18; Matthew 16:13-19.

Thirteenth Sunday of Ordinary Time

June 30, 2024

First Reading: *Wisdom 1:13-15; 2:23-24*

God did not make death,/ nor does he rejoice in the destruction of the living./ For he fashioned all things that they/ might have being;/ and the creatures of the world are wholesome,/ and there is not a destructive drug among them/ nor any domain of the netherworld on earth,/ for justice is undying./ For God formed man to be imperishable;/ the image of his own nature he made him./ But by the envy of the devil, death entered the world,/ and they who belong to his company experience it.

Second Reading: *2 Corinthians 8:7, 9, 13-15*

Brothers and sisters: As you excel in every respect, in faith, discourse, knowledge, all earnestness, and in the love we have for you, may you excel in this gracious act also.

For you know the gracious act of our Lord Jesus Christ, that though he was rich, for your sake he became poor, so that by his poverty you might become rich. Not that others should have relief while you are burdened, but that as a matter of equality your abundance at the present time should supply their needs, so that their abundance may also supply your needs, that there may be equality. As it is written: / *Whoever had much did not have more,/ and whoever had little did not have less.*

Gospel Reading: *Mark 5:21-43* or *5:21-24, 35b-43*

When Jesus had crossed again in the boat to the other side, a large crowd gathered around him, and he stayed close to the sea. One of the synagogue officials, named Jairus, came forward. Seeing him he fell at his feet and pleaded earnestly with him, saying, "My daughter is at the point of death. Please, come lay your hands on her* that she may get well and live." He went off with him, and a large crowd followed him and pressed upon him.

There was a woman afflicted with hemorrhages for twelve years. She had suffered greatly at the hands of many doctors and had spent all that she had. Yet she was not helped but only grew worse. She had heard about Jesus and came up behind him in the crowd and touched his cloak. She said, "If I but touch his clothes, I shall be cured." Immediately her flow of blood dried up. She felt in her body that she was healed of her affliction. Jesus, aware at once that power had gone out from him, turned around in the crowd and asked, "Who has touched my clothes?" But his disciples said to Jesus, "You see how the crowd is pressing upon you, and yet you ask, 'Who touched me?'" And he looked around to see who had done it. The woman, realizing what had happened to her, approached in fear and trembling. She fell down before Jesus and told him the whole truth. He said to her, "Daughter, your faith has saved you. Go in peace and be cured of your affliction."

   While he was still speaking, people from the synagogue official's house arrived and said, "Your daughter has died; why trouble the teacher any longer?" Disregarding the message that was reported, Jesus said to the synagogue official, "Do not be afraid; just have faith." He did not allow anyone to accompany him inside except Peter, James, and John, the brother of James. When they arrived at the house of the synagogue official, he caught sight of a commotion, people weeping and wailing loudly. So he went in and said to them, "Why this commotion and weeping? The child is not dead but asleep." And they ridiculed him. Then he put them all out. He took along the child's father and mother and those who were with him and entered the room where the child was. He took the child by the hand and said to her, "*Talitha koum,*" which means, "Little girl, I say to you, arise!" The girl, a child of twelve, arose immediately and walked around. At that they were utterly astounded. He gave strict orders that no one should know this and said that she should be given something to eat.

Homily Notes:

....

....

....

....

....

....

....

....

....

....

....

....

....

_____ ....
....
....
....
....
....
....
....
....
....
....
....
....
....
....
....
....
....

Reflection Questions for Each of the Readings:

1. *Based on the First Reading*: Bishop Robert Barron in *This is My Body* [2023 edition] writes: "God did not make death. Since the Garden of Eden experience, He has been on a rescue mission!" Explain God's rescue mission for you.

2. *Based on the Second Reading*: Capture Paul's main points here.

3. *Based on the Gospel Reading*: Jesus had three main goals: to speak the truth; heal people; and deliver them from evil or illness. What elements are showcased in today's Gospel reading?

Your Virtue Challenge:

      The goal of the virtuous person is to become like God. [CCC 1803] This will require identifying ways to increase this virtue and reduce opposing vice; *fasting [avoiding]* from habits or practices that oppose it; *praying* for God's help; *helping* others; and *doing penance*. *Based on the Second Reading,* your Virtue Challenge for the week is to increase in the virtue of:

GRACIOUSNESS

My Virtue Goals and Working Plan for the Week:

....

....

....

....

Daily Mass Readings for the Week:

Monday, July 1: **Saint Junípero Serra** Amos 2:6-10, 13-16; Matthew 8:18-22.

Tuesday, July 2: Amos 3:1-8; 4:11-12; Matthew 8:23-27.

Wednesday, July 3: **Saint Thomas the Apostle** Ephesians 2:19-22; John 20:24-29.

Thursday, July 4: **Independence Day** Amos 7:10-17; Matthew 9:1-8.

Friday, July 5: **Sts. Anthony Zaccaria & Elizabeth of Portuga**l; Amos 8:4-6, 9-12; Matthew 9:9-13.

Saturday, July 6: **Saint Maria Goretti** Amos 9:11-15; Matthew 9:14-17.

First Reading: *Ezekiel 2:2-5*

As the LORD spoke to me, the spirit entered into me and set me on my feet, and I heard the one who was speaking say to me: Son of man,/ I am sending you to the Israelites,/ rebels who have rebelled against me;/ they and their ancestors have revolted against me to this very day./ Hard of face and obstinate of heart/ are they to whom I am sending you. / But you shall say to them: Thus says the LORD GOD! / And whether they heed or resist—for they are a rebellious house/ they shall know that a prophet has been among them.

Second Reading: *2 Corinthians 12:7-10*

Brothers and sisters: That I, Paul, might not become too elated, because of the abundance of the revelations, a thorn in the flesh was given to me, an angel of Satan, to beat me, to keep me from being too elated. Three times I begged the Lord about this, that it might leave me, but he said to me, "My grace is sufficient for you, for power is made perfect in weakness." I will rather boast most gladly of my weaknesses, in order that the power of Christ may dwell with me. Therefore, I am content with weaknesses, insults, hardships, persecutions, and constraints, for the sake of Christ;
for when I am weak, then I am strong.

Gospel Reading: *Mark 6:1-6a*

Jesus departed from there and came to his native place, accompanied by his disciples. When the sabbath came he began to teach in the synagogue, and many who heard him were astonished. They said, "Where did this man get all this? What kind of wisdom has been given him? What mighty deeds are wrought by his hands! Is he not the carpenter, the son of Mary, and the brother of James and Joses and Judas and Simon? And are not his sisters here with us?" And they took offense at him. Jesus said to them, "A prophet is not without honor except in his native place and among his own kin and in his own house." So he was not able to perform any mighty deed there, apart from curing a few sick people by laying his hands on them. He was amazed at their lack of faith.

Fourteenth Sunday of Ordinary Time

Homily Notes:

....
....
....
....
....
....
....
....
....
....
....
....
....
....
....
....
....
....
....
....
....
....

Reflection Questions for Each of the Readings:
1. *Based on the First Reading:* Who is Ezekiel? What era did he live in? What was his mission?

2. *Based on the Second Reading:* What does St. Paul teach us about personal thorns? When and why are they often very good for us? Give personal examples.

3. *Based on the Gospel Reading:* Who is Jesus? What do we know about Jesus from the eye witness accounts?

Your Virtue Challenge:

The goal of the virtuous person is to become like God. [CCC 1803] This will require identifying ways to increase this virtue and reduce opposing vice; *fasting [avoiding]* from habits or practices that oppose it; *praying* for God's help; *helping* others; and *doing penance.* Based on the Second Reading, your Virtue Challenge for the week is to increase in the virtue of:

PERSEVERANCE

My Virtue Goals and Working Plan for the Week:

....

....

....

....

Daily Mass Readings for the Week:
Monday, July 8: Hosea 2:16, 17c-18, 21-22; Matthew 9:18-26.
Tuesday, July 9: **Saint Augustine Zhao Rong** Hosea 8:4-7, 11-13; Matthew 9:32-38.
Wednesday, July 10: Hosea 10:1-3, 7-8, 12; Matthew 10:1-7.
Thursday, July 11: **Saint Benedict** Hosea 11:1-4, 8e-9; Matthew 10:7-15.
Friday, July 12: Hosea 14:2-10; Matthew 10:16-23.
Saturday, July 13: **Saint Henry** Isaiah 6:1-8; Matthew 10:24-33.

First Reading: *Amos 7:12-15*

Amaziah, priest of Bethel, said to Amos, "Off with you, visionary, flee to the land of Judah! There earn your bread by prophesying, but never again prophesy in Bethel; for it is the king's sanctuary and a royal temple." Amos answered Amaziah, "I was no prophet, nor have I belonged to a company of prophets; I was a shepherd and a dresser of sycamores. The LORD took me from following the flock, and said to me, Go, prophesy to my people Israel."

Second Reading: *Ephesians 1:3-14 or* **1:3-10**

Blessed be the God and Father of our Lord Jesus Christ, who has blessed us in Christ with every spiritual blessing in the heavens, as he chose us in him, before the foundation of the world, to be holy and without blemish before him. In love he destined us for adoption to himself through Jesus Christ, in accord with the favor of his will, for the praise of the glory of his grace that he granted us in the beloved.

In him we have redemption by his blood, the forgiveness of trans-gressions, in accord with the riches of his grace that he lavished upon us. In all wisdom and insight, he has made known to us the mystery of his will in accord with his favor that he set forth in him as a plan for the fullness of times, to sum up all things in Christ, in heaven and on earth.

In him we were also chosen, destined in accord with the purpose of the One who accomplishes all things according to the intention of his will, so that we might exist for the praise of his glory, we who first hoped in Christ. In him you also, who have heard the word of truth, the gospel of your salvation, and have believed in him, were sealed with the promised holy Spirit, which is the first installment of our inheritance toward redemption as God's possession, to the praise of his glory.

Gospel Reading: *Mark 6:7-13*

Jesus summoned the Twelve and began to send them out two by two and gave them authority over unclean spirits. He instructed them to take nothing for the journey but a walking stick— no food, no sack, no money in their belts. They were, however, to wear sandals but not a second tunic. He said to them, "Wherever you enter a house, stay there until you leave. What-ever place does not welcome you or listen to you, leave there and shake the dust off your feet in testimony against them." So they went off and preached repentance. The Twelve drove out many demons, and they anointed with oil many who were sick and cured them.

Fifteenth Sunday of Ordinary Time

Homily Notes:

....
....
....
....
....
....
....
....
....
....
....
....
....
....
....
....
....
....
....
....
....
....
....

Reflection Questions for Each of the Readings:

1. *Based on the First Reading*: Who is Amaziah? Why did he prohibit Amos from prophesying during Jeroboam's reign? What was Amos' response? What is your response when people reject you for discussing matters of faith?

2. *Based on the Second Reading*: List the spiritual gifts available to us.

3. *Based on the Gospel Reading*: Like Jesus, the apostles had three main goals. What were they? Why did Jesus instruct the disciples to wear sandals and not bring with them money, bread, or traveling bags? What did this request imply?

Your Virtue Challenge:

The goal of the virtuous person is to become like God. [CCC 1803] This will require identifying ways to increase this virtue and reduce opposing vice; *fasting [avoiding]* from habits or practices that oppose it; *praying* for God's help; *helping* others; and *doing penance*. Based on the Second Reading, your Virtue Challenge for the week is to increase in the virtue of:

FORGIVENESS

My Virtue Goals and Working Plan for the Week:

....

....

....

....

Daily Mass Readings for the Week:

Monday, July 15: **Saint Bonaventure** Isaiah 1:10-17; Matthew 10:34—11:1.

Tuesday, July 16: **Our Lady of Mount Carmel** Isaiah 7:1-9; Matthew 11:20-24.

Wednesday, July 17: Isaiah 10:5-7, 13b-16; Matthew 11:25-27.

Thursday, July 18: **Saint Camillus de Lellis** Isaiah 26:7-9, 12, 16-19; Matthew 11:28-30.

Friday, July 19: Isaiah 38:1-6, 21-22, 7-8; Matthew 12:1-8.

Saturday, July 20: **Saint Apollinaris** Micah 2:1-5; Matthew 12:14-21.

Sixteenth Sunday of Ordinary Time

First Reading: *Jeremiah 23:1-6*

Woe to the shepherds who mislead and scatter the flock of my pasture, says the LORD. / Therefore, thus says the LORD, the God of Israel,/ against the shepherds who shepherd my people:/ You have scattered my sheep and driven them away. / You have not cared for them,/ but I will take care to punish your evil deeds. / I myself will gather the remnant of my flock from all the lands to which I have driven them and bring them back to their meadow;/ there they shall increase and multiply. / I will appoint shepherds for them who will shepherd them/ so that they need no longer fear and tremble; and none shall be missing, says the LORD.

Behold, the days are coming, says the LORD,/ when I will raise up a righteous shoot to David;/ as king he shall reign and govern wisely,/ he shall do what is just and right in the land./ In his days Judah shall be saved,/ Israel shall dwell in security. / This is the name they give him:/ "The LORD our justice."

Second Reading: *Ephesians 2:13-18*

Brothers and sisters: In Christ Jesus you who once were far off have become near by the blood of Christ.

For he is our peace, he who made both one and broke down the dividing wall of enmity, through his flesh, abolishing the law with its commandments and legal claims, that he might create in himself one new person in place of the two, thus establishing peace, and might reconcile both with God, in one body, through the cross, putting that enmity to death by it. He came and preached peace to you who were far off and peace to those who were near, for through him we both have access in one Spirit to the Father.

Gospel Reading: *Mark 6:30-34*

The apostles gathered together with Jesus and reported all they had done and taught. He said to them, "Come away by yourselves to a deserted place and rest a while." People were coming and going in great numbers, and they had no opportunity even to eat. So they went off in the boat by themselves to a deserted place. People saw them leaving and many came to know about it. They hastened there on foot from all the towns and arrived at the place before them.

When he disembarked and saw the

vast crowd, his heart was moved with pity for them, for they were like sheep without a shepherd; and he began to teach them many things.

Homily Notes:

....
....
....
....
....
....
....
....
....
....
....
....
....
....
....
....
....
....
....
....
....
....
....

Reflection Questions for Each of the Readings:
1. *Based on the First Reading*: What is the role of a shepherd? Why does God refer to the Jewish people as sheep? Who is the Good Shepherd?

2. *Based on the Second Reading:* Explain verse 18: *"for through him we both have access in one Spirit to the Father,"* in your own words.

3. *Based on the Gospel Reading:* Why does Jesus take pity on the crowds? What do they need?

Your Virtue Challenge:

The goal of the virtuous person is to become like God. [CCC 1803] This will require identifying ways to increase this virtue and reduce opposing vice; *fasting [avoiding]* from habits or practices that oppose it; *praying* for God's help; *helping* others; and *doing penance. Based on the Gospel Reading,* your Virtue Challenge for the week is to increase in the virtue of:

SYMPATHY

My Virtue Goals and Working Plan for the Week:

....
....
....
....

Daily Mass Readings for the Week:

Monday, July 22: **Saint Mary Magdalene** Song of Songs 3:1-4b or 2 Corinthians 5:14-17; John 20:1-2, 11-18.
Tuesday, July 23: **Saint Bridget** Micah 7:14-15, 18-20; Matthew 12:46-50.
Wednesday, July 24: **Saint Sharbel Makhlūf** Jeremiah 1:1, 4-10; Matthew 13:1-9.
Thursday, July 25: **Saint James, Apostle** 2 Corinthians 4:7-15; Matthew 20:20-28.
Friday, July 26: **Sts. Joachim and Anne** Jeremiah 3:14-17; Matthew 13:18-23.
Saturday, July 27: Jeremiah 7:1-11; Matthew 13:24-30.

Seventeenth Sunday of Ordinary Time

First Reading: *2 Kings 4:42-44*

A man came from Baal-shalishah bringing to Elisha, the man of God, twenty barley loaves made from the firstfruits, and fresh grain in the ear. Elisha said, "Give it to the people to eat." But his servant objected, "How can I set this before a hundred people?" Elisha insisted, "Give it to the people to eat." "For thus says the LORD, 'They shall eat and there shall be some left over.'" And when they had eaten, there was some left over, as the LORD had said.

Second Reading: *Ephesians 4:1-6*

Brothers and sisters: I, a prisoner for the Lord, urge you to live in a manner worthy of the call you have received, with all humility and gentleness, with patience, bearing with one another through love, striving to preserve the unity of the spirit through the bond of peace: one body and one Spirit, as you were also called to the one hope of your call; one Lord, one faith, one baptism; one God and Father of all, who is over all and through all and in all.

Gospel Reading: *John 6:1-15*

Jesus went across the Sea of Galilee. A large crowd followed him, because they saw the signs he was performing on the sick. Jesus went up on the mountain, and there he sat down with his disciples. The Jewish feast of Passover was near. When Jesus raised his eyes and saw that a large crowd was coming to him, he said to Philip, "Where can we buy enough food for them to eat?" He said this to test him, because he himself knew what he was going to do. Philip answered him, "Two hundred days' wages worth of food would not be enough for each of them to have a little." One of his disciples, Andrew, the brother of Simon Peter, said to him, "There is a boy here who has five barley loaves and two fish; but what good are these for so many?" Jesus said, "Have the people recline." Now there was a great deal of grass in that place. So the men reclined, about five thousand in number. Then Jesus took the loaves, gave thanks, and distributed them to those who were reclining, and also as much of the fish as they wanted. When they had had their fill, he said to his disciples, "Gather the fragments left over, so that nothing will be wasted." So they collected them, and filled twelve wicker baskets with frag-

Seventeenth Sunday of Ordinary Time

July 28, 2024

ments from the five barley loaves that had been more than they could eat. When the people saw the sign he had done, they said, "This is truly the Prophet, the one who is to come into the world." Since Jesus knew that they were going to come and carry him off to make him king, he withdrew again to the mountain alone.

Homily Notes:

....
....
....
....
....
....
....
....
....
....
....
....
....
....
....
....
....
....
....
....

Reflection Questions for Each of the Readings:

1. *Based on the First Reading*: What other New Testament readings come to mind as you read this passage from 2 Kings?

2. *Based on the Second Reading*: What do we need in order to *live in a manner worthy of the call we have received?*

3. *Based on the Gospel Reading*: What sights and sounds come to mind as you read the Gospel? What is the significance of the number of bread loaves; the fish; or the people present?

Your Virtue Challenge:

      The goal of the virtuous person is to become like God. [CCC 1803] This will require identifying ways to increase this virtue and reduce opposing vice; *fasting [avoiding]* from habits or practices that oppose it; *praying* for God's help; *helping* others; and *doing penance. Based on the Gospel Reading,* your Virtue Challenge for the week is to increase in the virtue of:

GENEROSITY

My Virtue Goals and Working Plan for the Week:

....
....
....
....

Daily Mass Readings for the Week:

Monday, July 29: **Sts. Martha, Mary & Lazarus** Jeremiah 13:1-11; John 11:19-27 or Luke 10:38-42.

Tuesday, July 30: **Saint Peter Chrysologus** Jeremiah 14:17-22; Matthew 13:36-43.

Wednesday, July 31: **Saint Ignatius of Loyola** Jeremiah 15:10, 16-21; Matthew 13:44-46.

Thursday, August 1: **Saint Alphonsus Liguori** Jeremiah 18:1-6; Matthew 13:47-53.

Friday, August 2: **Sts. Eusebius of Vercelli & Peter Julian Eymard** Jeremiah 26:1-9; Matthew 13:54-58.

Saturday, August 3: Jeremiah 26:11-16, 24; Matthew 14:1-12.

Eighteenth Sunday of Ordinary Time

August 4, 2024

First Reading: Exodus 16:2-4, 12-15

The whole Israelite community grumbled against Moses and Aaron. The Israelites said to them, "Would that we had died at the LORD's hand in the land of Egypt, as we sat by our fleshpots and ate our fill of bread! But you had to lead us into this desert to make the whole community die of famine!"

Then the LORD said to Moses, "I will now rain down bread from heaven for you. Each day the people are to go out and gather their daily portion; thus will I test them, to see whether they follow my instructions or not.

"I have heard the grumbling of the Israelites. Tell them: In the evening twilight you shall eat flesh, and in the morning you shall have your fill of bread, so that you may know that I, the LORD, am your God."

In the evening quail came up and covered the camp. In the morning a dew lay all about the camp, and when the dew evaporated, there on the surface of the desert were fine flakes like hoarfrost on the ground. On seeing it, the Israelites asked one another, "What is this?" for they did not know what it was. But Moses told them, "This is the bread that the LORD has given you to eat."

Second Reading: *Ephesians 4:17, 20-24*

Brothers and sisters: I declare and testify in the Lord that you must no longer live as the Gentiles do, in the futility of their minds; that is not how you learned Christ, assuming that you have heard of him and were taught in him, as truth is in Jesus, that you should put away the old self of your former way of life, corrupted through deceitful desires, and be renewed in the spirit of your minds, and put on the new self, created in God's way in righteousness and holiness of truth.

Gospel Reading: *John 6:24-35*

When the crowd saw that neither Jesus nor his disciples were there, they themselves got into boats and came to Capernaum looking for Jesus. And when they found him across the sea they said to him, "Rabbi, when did you get here?" Jesus answered them and said, "Amen, amen, I say to you, you are looking for me not because you saw signs but because you ate the loaves and were filled. Do not work for food that perishes but for the food that endures for eternal life, which the Son of Man will give you. For on him the Father, God, has set his seal." So they said to him, "What can we do to accomplish the works of God?" Jesus answered and said to them, "This is the work of God, that you believe in the one he sent." So they said to him, "What sign can you do, that we may see and believe in you? What can you do? Our ancestors ate manna in the desert, as it is written:/ *He gave them bread from heaven to eat." /* So Jesus said to them, "Amen, amen, I say to you, it was not Moses who gave the bread

185

from heaven; my Father gives you the true bread from heaven. For the bread of God is that which comes down from heaven and gives life to the world."

So they said to him, "Sir, give us this bread always." Jesus said to them, "I am the bread of life; whoever comes to me will never hunger, and whoever believes in me will never thirst."

Homily Notes:

....

....

....

....

....

....

....

....

....

....

....

....

....

....

....

....

....

....

....

Reflection Questions for Each of the Readings:

1. *Based on the First Reading:* The Israelites grumble 'if only...' Have you grumbled against God? How does society grumble? What virtues hold grumbling in check?

2. Based on the Second Reading: How does the verse: '*You must no longer live as the Gentiles do, in the futility of their minds,*' apply today for you and me? Give examples.

3. Based on the Gospel Reading: "What can you do to accomplish the works of God?" Answer this question from a personal perspective.

Your Virtue Challenge:

The goal of the virtuous person is to become like God. [CCC 1803] This will require identifying ways to increase this virtue and reduce opposing vice; *fasting [avoiding]* from habits or practices that oppose it; *praying* for God's help; *helping* others; and *doing penance. Based on the First Reading,* your Virtue Challenge for the week is to increase in the virtue of:

GRATITUDE

My Virtue Goals and Working Plan for the Week:

....

....

....

....

Daily Mass Readings for the Week:

Monday, August 5: **The Dedication of the Basilica of Saint Mary Major** Jeremiah 28:1-17; Matthew 14:13-21.

Tuesday, August 6: **The Transfiguration of the Lord** Daniel 7:9-10, 13-14; 2 Peter 1:16-19; Mark 9:2-10.

Wednesday, August 7: **Sts. Sixtus II & Cajetan** Jeremiah 31:1-7; Matthew 15:21-28.

Thursday, August 8: **Saint Dominic** Jeremiah 31:31-34; Matthew 16:13-23.

Friday, August 9: **Saint Teresa Benedicta of the Cross** Nahum 2:1, 3; 3:1-3, 6-7; Matthew 16:24-28.

Saturday, August 10: **Saint Lawrence** 2 Corinthians 9:6-10; John 12:24-26.

Nineteenth Sunday of Ordinary Time

August 11, 2024

First Reading: *1 Kings 19:4-8*

Elijah went a day's journey into the desert, until he came to a broom tree and sat beneath it. He prayed for death saying: "This is enough, O LORD! Take my life, for I am no better than my fathers." He lay down and fell asleep under the broom tree, but then an angel touched him and ordered him to get up and eat. Elijah looked and there at his head was a hearth cake and a jug of water. After he ate and drank, he lay down again, but the angel of the LORD came back a second time, touched him, and ordered, "Get up and eat, else the journey will be too long for you!" He got up, ate, and drank; then strengthened by that food, he walked forty days and forty nights to the mountain of God, Horeb.

Second Reading: *Ephesians 4:30 - 5:2*

Brothers and sisters: Do not grieve the Holy Spirit of God, with which you were sealed for the day of redemption. All bitterness, fury, anger, shouting, and reviling must be removed from you, along with all malice. And be kind to one another, compassionate, forgiving one another as God has forgiven you in Christ.

So be imitators of God, as beloved children, and live in love, as Christ loved us and handed himself over for us as a sacrificial offering to God for a fragrant aroma.

Gospel Reading: *John 6:41 - 51*

The Jews murmured about Jesus because he said, "I am the bread that came down from heaven, " and they said, "Is this not Jesus, the son of Joseph? Do we not know his father and mother? Then how can he say, 'I have come down from heaven'?" Jesus answered and said to them, "Stop murmuring among yourselves. No one can come to me unless the Father who sent me draw him, and I will raise him on the last day. It is written in the prophets:/ *They shall all be taught by God.* / Everyone who listens to my Father and learns from him comes to me. Not that anyone has seen the Father except the one who is from God; he has seen the Father. Amen, amen, I say to you, whoever believes has eternal life. I am the bread of life. Your ancestors ate the manna in the desert, but they died; this is the bread that comes down from heaven so that one may eat it and not die. I am the living bread that came down from heaven; whoever eats this bread will live forever; and the bread that I will give is my flesh for the life of the world."

Homily Notes:

....
....
....
....
....
....
....
....
....
....
....
....
....
....
....
....
....
....
....
....
....
....
....
....

Reflection Questions for Each of the Readings:

1. *Based on the First Reading*: What other New Testament parables come to mind after reading that Elijah walked for forty days and forty nights? Explain the significance of the number *forty*.

2. *Based on the Second Reading*: How do we grieve the Holy Spirit? What virtues are necessary to live as imitators of God? Are you an imitator of God?

3. *Based on the Gospel Reading*: What *stumbling block*s prevent you from recognizing Jesus as the Messiah? What does Jesus proclaim about himself?

Your Virtue Challenge:

The goal of the virtuous person is to become like God. [CCC 1803] This will require identifying ways to increase this virtue and reduce opposing vice; *fasting [avoiding]* from habits or practices that oppose it; *praying* for God's help; *helping* others; and *doing penance*. *Based on the Second Reading,* your Virtue Challenge for the week is to increase in the virtue of:

SELF CONTROL

My Virtue Goals and Working Plan for the Week:

....

....

....

Daily Mass Readings for the Week:

Monday, August 12: **Saint Jane Frances de Chantal** Ezekiel 1:2-5, 24-28c; Matthew 17:22-27.

Tuesday, August 13: **Sts. Pontian & Hippolytus** Ezekiel 2:8—3:4; Matthew 18:1-5, 10, 12-14.

Wednesday, August 14: **Saint Maximilian Kolbe** Ezekiel 9:1-7; 10:18-22; Matthew 18:15-20.

Thursday, August 15: **The Assumption of the Blessed Virgin Mary, Holyday of Obligation** - pages 180 - 183.

Friday, August 16: **Saint Stephen of Hungary** Ezekiel 16:1-15, 60, 63 or 16:59-63; Matthew 19:3-12.

Saturday, August 17: Ezekiel 18:1-10, 13b, 30-32; Matthew 19:13-15.

Solemnity of the Assumption of the Blessed Virgin Mary
Vigil August 15, 2024

First Reading: *1 Chronicles 15:3-4, 15-16; 16:1-2*

David assembled all Israel in Jerusalem to bring the ark of the LORD to the place which he had prepared for it. David also called together the sons of Aaron and the Levites.

The Levites bore the ark of God on their shoulders with poles, as Moses had ordained according to the word of the LORD.

David commanded the chiefs of the Levites to appoint their kinsmen as chanters, to play on musical instruments, harps, lyres, and cymbals, to make a loud sound of rejoicing.

They brought in the ark of God and set it within the tent which David had pitched for it. Then they offered up burnt offerings and peace offerings to God. When David had finished offering up the burnt offerings and peace offerings, he blessed the people in the name of the LORD.

Second Reading: *1 Corinthians 15:54b-57*

Brothers and sisters: When that which is mortal clothes itself with immortality, then the word that is written shall come about:
Death is swallowed up in victory./ Where, O death,/ is your victory?/ Where, O death,/ is your sting?/ The sting of death is sin, and the power of sin is the law. But thanks be to God who gives us the victory through our Lord Jesus Christ.

Gospel Reading: *Luke 11:27-28*

While Jesus was speaking, a woman from the crowd called out and said to him, "Blessed is the womb that carried you and the breasts at which you nursed." He replied, "Rather, blessed are those who hear the word of God and observe it."

Solemnity of the Assumption of the Blessed Virgin Mary
Day   August 15, 2024

First Reading: *Revelation 11:19a, 12:1-6a, 10ab*

God's temple in heaven was opened, and the ark of his covenant could be seen in the temple.

A great sign appeared in the sky, a woman clothed with the sun, with the moon under her feet, and on her head a crown of twelve stars. She was with child and wailed aloud in pain as she labored to give birth. Then another sign appeared in the sky; it was a huge red dragon, with seven heads and ten horns, and on its heads were seven diadems. Its tail swept away a third of the stars in the sky and hurled them down to the earth. Then the dragon stood before the woman about to give birth, to devour her child when she gave birth. She gave birth to a son, a male child, destined to rule all the nations with an iron rod. Her child was caught up to God and his throne. The woman herself fled into the desert where she had a place prepared by God.

Then I heard a loud voice in heaven say:/   "Now have salvation/ and power come,/ and the Kingdom of our God/   and the authority of his Anointed One."/

Second Reading: *1 Corinthians 15:20-27*

Brothers and sisters: Christ has been raised from the dead, the firstfruits of those who have fallen asleep. For since death came through man, the resurrection of the dead came also through man. For just as in Adam all die, so too in Christ shall all be brought to life, but each one in proper order: Christ the firstfruits; then, at his coming, those who belong to Christ; then comes the end, when he hands over the Kingdom to his God and Father, when he has destroyed every sovereignty and every authority and power. For he must reign until he has put all his enemies under his feet. The last enemy to be destroyed is death, for "he subjected everything under his feet."

Gospel Reading: *Luke1:39-56*

Mary set out and traveled to the hill country in haste to a town of Judah, where she entered the house of Zechariah and greeted Elizabeth. When Elizabeth heard Mary's greeting, the infant leaped in her womb, and Elizabeth, filled with the Holy Spirit, cried out in a loud voice and said, "Blessed are you among women, and blessed is the fruit of your womb. And how does this happen to me, that the mother of my Lord should come to me? For at the moment the sound of your greeting reached my ears, the infant in my womb leaped for joy. Blessed are you who believed that what was spoken to you by the Lord would be fulfilled."

And Mary said: "My soul proclaims the greatness of the Lord;/   my spirit rejoices in God my Savior/   for he has looked with favor on his lowly servant./ From this day all generations will call me blessed:/ the Almighty has done great things for me/ and holy is his Name./ He has mercy on those who fear him/ in every generation. / He has shown the strength of his arm,/ and has scattered the proud in their conceit./ He has cast down the mighty from their thrones,/ and has lifted up the lowly./ He has filled the hungry with good things,/ and the rich he has sent away empty./ He has come to the help of his servant Israel/ for he has remembered his promise of mercy,/ the promise he made to our fathers, / to Abraham and his children forever."

Mary remained with her about three months and then returned to her home.

Homily Notes:

....
....
....
....
....
....
....
....
....
....
....
....
....
....
....
....
....
....
....
....
....

Solemnity of the Assumption of the Blessed Virgin Mary
August 15, 2024

Reflection Questions for Each of the Readings:

1. *Based on the First Reading*: Who is the woman described in this reading?

2. *Based on the Second Reading*: Who is Jesus? Who do you say Jesus is?

3. *Based on the Gospel Reading*: List Mary's virtues. List your own virtues.

Twentieth Sunday of Ordinary Time
August 18, 2024

First Reading: *Proverbs 9:1-6*

Wisdom has built her house,/   she has set up her seven columns;/ she has dressed her meat, mixed her wine,/   yes, she has spread her table./ She has sent out her maidens; she calls/   from the heights out over the city: / "Let whoever is simple turn in here;/   To the one who lacks understanding, she says,/   Come, eat of my food,/   and drink of the wine I have mixed!/   Forsake foolishness that you may live;/   advance in the way of understanding."

Second Reading: *Ephesians 5:15-20*

Brothers and sisters: Watch carefully how you live, not as foolish persons but as wise, making the most of the opportunity, because the days are evil. Therefore, do not continue in ignorance, but try to understand what is the will of the Lord. And do not get drunk on wine, in which lies debauchery, but be filled with the Spirit, addressing one another in psalms and hymns and spiritual songs, singing and playing to the Lord in your hearts, giving thanks always and for everything in the name of our Lord Jesus Christ to God the Father.

Gospel Reading: *John 6:51-58*

Jesus said to the crowds: "I am the living bread that came down from heaven; whoever eats this bread will live forever; and the bread that I will give is my flesh for the life of the world."

The Jews quarreled among themselves, saying, "How can this man give us his flesh to eat?" Jesus said to them, "Amen, amen, I say to you, unless you eat the flesh of the Son of Man and drink his blood, you do not have life within you. Whoever eats my flesh and drinks my blood has eternal life, and I will raise him on the last day. For my flesh is true food, and my blood is true drink. Whoever eats my flesh and drinks my blood remains in me and I in him. Just as the living Father sent me and I have life because of the Father, so also the one who feeds on me will have life because of me. This is the bread that came down from heaven. Unlike your ancestors who ate and still died, whoever eats this bread will live forever."

Homily Notes:

....
....
....
....
....

....
....
....
....
....
....
....
....
....
....
....
....

Reflection Questions for Each of the Readings:

1. *Based on the First Reading*: What advice does this reading from the Book of Wisdom provide for us? Who/what is Wisdom?

2. *Based on the Second Reading*: How are you heeding the advice of this verse: 'Watch carefully then how you live..."

3. *Based on the Gospel Reading*: Jesus speaks about eating his body and drinking his blood. How do we honor His *command* today?

Prior to his death, Blessed Carlos Acutis created a website listing the Eucharistic miracles [by countries and dates]. Independent research has confirmed that the Eurcharistic host changed from wheat to flesh and blood in many of these miracles. Turn the page to read about the *Eucharistic Miracles of the World*.

Your Virtue Challenge:

The goal of the virtuous person is to become like God. [CCC 1803] This will require identifying ways to increase this virtue and reduce opposing vice; *fasting [avoiding]* from habits or practices that oppose it; *praying* for God's help; *helping* others; and *doing penance*. *Based on the First Reading*, your Virtue Challenge for the week is to increase in the virtue of:

UNDERSTANDING

My Virtue Goals and Working Plan for the Week:

....

....

....

Daily Mass Readings for the Week:

Monday, August 19: **Saint John Eudes** Ezekiel 24:15-23; Matthew 19:16-22.
Tuesday, August 20: **Saint Bernard** Ezekiel 28:1-10; Matthew 19:23-30.
Wednesday, August 21: **Saint Pius X** Ezekiel 34:1-11; Matthew 20:1-16.
Thursday, August 22: **The Queenship of the Blessed Virgin Mary** Ezekiel 36:23-28; Matthew 22:1-14.
Friday, August 23: **Saint Rose of Lima** Ezekiel 37:1-14; Matthew 22:34-40.
Saturday, August 24: **Saint Bartholomew** Revelation 21:9b-14; John 1:45-51; John 1:45-51.

The Eucharistic Miracles

Fr. Roberto Coggi, O.P.

Eucharistic miracles are God's extraordinary interventions, which are meant to confirm the faith in the presence of the body and blood of the Lord in the Eucharist. We know the Catholic teaching on the real presence. With the words of consecration: "This is my body," "This is my blood," the substance of bread becomes the body of Christ and the substance of wine His blood. This marvelous change is called *transubstantiation,* that is to say, the passage of substance. There remain only the appearance or species of the bread and wine, which, using a philosophical term, are called accidents. In other words, only the dimensions, color, taste, smell and even the nutritive capacity remain. But the substance, or the true reality, does not remain, for it has become the body and blood of the Lord. *Transubstantiation cannot be experienced by the senses; only faith assures us of this marvelous change.*

The Eucharistic miracles confirm this faith, which is based on Jesus's words according to what which seems to be like bread is no longer bread, and what seems to be wine is no longer wine. In the Eucharistic miracles the flesh and blood, or one or the other, appear, depending on the situation. These miracles show that we must not look at *external appearances (bread and wine)* but at the *substance, or the true reality of the thing, which is flesh and blood.* Medieval theologians carefully examined the issue of Eucharistic Miracles (which were frequent in their day) and have given various interpretations; but the best founded and most reasonable seems to be that of St. Thomas Aquinas, the "Eucharistic Doctor" par excellence (Summa Theolgica III, q. 76, a. 8). He said that the body and blood which appear after a miracle are due to the transformation of the Eucharistic species, namely, of the accidents, and do not touch the true substance of the body and blood of Christ. In other words, the species of bread and wine are miraculously changed into the species of flesh and blood; but not the true body and true blood of Jesus but those which, even before the miracle, were hidden beneath the species of flesh and blood. If the flesh and blood were truly the flesh and blood of Christ, we would have to say that the risen Jesus, who reigns impassibly at the right hand of the Father, loses a part of his flesh and blood, something which cannot be accepted. We must say that the flesh and blood which appear in the miracles are species or appearances, neither more nor less than the species of bread and wine. *The Lord performs these miracles to give us a sign, easy and visible to all, that in the Eucharist there is the true body and true blood of the Lord.* But this true body and this true blood are not those that appear, but rather those that are substantially *contained* under the species or appearances, species and appearances that, before the miracle, were those of bread and wine, and after the miracle are those of flesh and blood. Under the appearances of flesh and blood Jesus is truly and substantially contained as he was before the miracle. For this reason we can adore Jesus truly present under the species of flesh and blood.

Twenty-First Sunday of Ordinary Time

August 25, 2024

First Reading: *Joshua 24:1-2a, 15-17, 18b*

Joshua gathered together all the tribes of Israel at Shechem, summoning their elders, their leaders, their judges, and their officers. When they stood in ranks before God, Joshua addressed all the people:"If it does not please you to serve the LORD, decide today whom you will serve, the gods your fathers served beyond the River or the gods of the Amorites in whose country you are now dwelling. As for me and my household, we will serve the LORD."

But the people answered, "Far be it from us to forsake the LORD for the service of other gods. For it was the LORD, our God, who brought us and our fathers up out of the land of Egypt, out of a state of slavery. He performed those great miracles before our very eyes and protected us along our entire journey and among the peoples through whom we passed. Therefore we also will serve the LORD, for he is our God."

Second Reading: *Ephesians 5:21-32* or **5:2a, 25-32**

Brothers and sisters: Be subordinate to one another out of reverence for Christ. Wives should be subordinate to their husbands as to the Lord. For the husband is head of his wife just as Christ is head of the church, he himself the savior of the body. As the church is subordinate to Christ, so wives should be subordinate to their husbands in everything. [**Live in love, as Christ loved us.**] **Husbands, love your wives, even as Christ loved the church and handed himself over for her to sanctify her, cleansing her by the bath of water with the word, that he might present to himself the church in splendor, without spot or wrinkle or any such thing,that she might be holy and without blemish. So also husbands should love their wives as their own bodies. He who loves his wife loves himself. For no one hates his own flesh but rather nourishes and cherishes it, even as Christ does the church, because we are members of his body./** *For this reason a man shall leave his father and his mother/ and be joined to his wife,/ and the two shall become one flesh./* **This is a great mystery, but I speak in reference to Christ and the church.**

Gospel Reading: *John 6:60-69*

Many of Jesus' disciples who were listening said, "This saying is hard; who can accept it?" Since Jesus knew that his disciples were murmuring about this, he said to them, "Does this shock you? What if you were to see the Son of Man ascending to where he was before? It is the spirit that gives life, while the flesh is of no avail. The words I have spoken to you are Spirit and life. But there are some of you who do not believe." Jesus knew from the beginning the ones who would not believe and the one who would betray him. And he said, "For this reason I have told you that no one can come to me unless it is granted him by my Father."

As a result of this, many of his disciples returned to their former way of life and no longer accompanied him. Jesus then said to the Twelve, "Do you also want to leave?" Simon Peter answered him, "Master, to whom shall we go? You have the words of eternal life. We have come to believe and are convinced that you are the Holy One of God."

Homily Notes:

....
....
....
....
....
....
....
....
....
....
....
....
....
....
....
....
....
....
....
....
....
....
....

Twenty-First Sunday of Ordinary Time

August 25, 2024

Reflection Questions for Each of the Readings:

1. *Based on the First Reading*: The Israelites re-commit themselves to serving the Lord in the First Reading. Why and how do you serve the Lord?

2. *Based on the Second Reading*: How are we to love each other? How are husbands and wives to love each other?

3. *Based on the Gospel Reading*: If asked, how would you respond to: *do you also want to leave*? What does *staying with Jesus* look like? Why do people leave?

Your Virtue Challenge:

The goal of the virtuous person is to become like God. [CCC 1803] This will require identifying ways to increase this virtue and reduce opposing vice; *fasting [avoiding]* from habits or practices that oppose it; *praying* for God's help; *helping* others; and *doing penance*. Based on the Second Reading, your Virtue Challenge for the week is to increase in the virtue of:

SUBORDINATION

My Virtue Goals and Working Plan for the Week:

....

....

....

Daily Mass Readings for the Week:

Monday, August 26: 2 Thessalonians 1:1-5, 11-12; Matthew 23:13-22.
Tuesday, August 27: **Saint Monica** 2 Thessalonians 2:1-3a, 14-17; Matthew 23:23-26.
Wednesday, August 28: **Saint Augustine** 2 Thessalonians 3:6-10, 16-18; Matthew 23:27-32.
Thursday, August 29: **The Passion of Saint John the Baptist** 1 Corinthians 1:1-9; Mark 6:17-29.
Friday, August 30: 1 Corinthians 1:17-25; Matthew 25:1-13.
Saturday, August 31: 1 Corinthians 1:26-31; Matthew 25:14-30.

Twenty-Second Sunday of Ordinary Time
September 1, 2024

First Reading: *Deuteronomy 4:1-2, 6-8*

Moses said to the people: "Now, Israel, hear the statutes and decrees which I am teaching you to observe, that you may live, and may enter in and take possession of the land which the LORD, the God of your fathers, is giving you. In your observance of the commandments of the LORD, your God, which I enjoin upon you, you shall not add to what I command you nor subtract from it. Observe them carefully, for thus will you give evidence of your wisdom and intelligence to the nations, who will hear of all these statutes and say, 'This great nation is truly a wise and intelligent people.' For what great nation is there that has gods so close to it as the LORD, our God, is to us whenever we call upon him? Or what great nation has statutes and decrees that are as just as this whole law which I am setting before you today?"

Second Reading: *James 1:17-18, 21b-22, 27*

Dearest brothers and sisters: All good giving and every perfect gift is from above, coming down from the Father of lights, with whom there is no alteration or shadow caused by change. He willed to give us birth by the word of truth that we may be a kind of firstfruits of his creatures.

Humbly welcome the word that has been planted in you and is able to save your souls.

Be doers of the word and not hearers only, deluding yourselves.

Religion that is pure and undefiled before God and the Father is this: to care for orphans and widows in their affliction and to keep oneself unstained by the world.

Gospel Reading: *Mark 7:1-8, 14-15, 21-23*

When the Pharisees with some scribes who had come from Jerusalem gathered around Jesus, they observed that some of his disciples ate their meals with unclean, that is, unwashed, hands. -- For the Pharisees and, in fact, all Jews, do not eat without carefully washing their hands, keeping the tradition of the elders. And on coming from the marketplace they do not eat without purifying themselves. And there are many other things that they have traditionally observed, the purification of cups and jugs and kettles and beds.-- So the Pharisees and scribes questioned him, "Why do your disciples not follow the tradition of the elders but instead eat a meal with unclean hands?" He responded, "Well did Isaiah prophesy about you hypocrites, as it is written:/ *This people honors me with their lips,/ but their hearts are far from me;/ in vain do they worship me,/ teaching as doctrines human precepts./* You disregard God's commandment but cling to human tradition." He summoned the crowd again and said to them, "Hear me, all of you, and understand. Nothing that enters one from outside can defile that person; but the things that come out from within are what defile.

"From within people, from their hearts,/ come evil thoughts, unchastity, theft, murder, adultery, greed, malice, deceit, licentiousness, envy, blasphemy, arrogance, folly. All these evils come from within and they defile."

Homily Notes:

....
....
....
....
....
....
....
....
....
....
....
....
....
....
....
....
....
....
....
....
....
....
....
....

Reflection Questions for Each of the Readings:

1. *Based on the First Reading:* What blessings are promised [to Israel] if they heed God's commandments?

2. *Based on the Second Reading:* What/who is a *doer* of the Word? Today, we have largely assigned the responsibility of taking care of the needy to *agencies.* Does this meet Jesus' command to take care of the needy?

3. *Based on the Gospel Reading:* "*They honor God with their lips but their hearts are far from me.*" How is this evidenced today among believers?

Your Virtue Challenge:

      The goal of the virtuous person is to become like God. [CCC 1803] This will require identifying ways to increase this virtue and reduce opposing vice; *fasting [avoiding]* from habits or practices that oppose it; *praying* for God's help; *helping* others; and *doing penance. Based on the Gospel Reading,* your Virtue Challenge for the week is to increase in the virtue of:

HONORABLE

My Virtue Goals and Working Plan for the Week:

....

....

....

Daily Mass Readings for the Week:

Monday, September 2: 1 Corinthians 2:1-5; Luke 4:16-30.

Tuesday, September **Saint Gregory the Great** 1 Corinthians 2:10b-16; Luke 4:31-37.

Wednesday, September 4: 1 Corinthians 3:1-9; Luke 4:38-44.

Thursday, September 5: 1 Corinthians 3:18-23; Luke 5:1-11.

Friday, September 6: 1 Corinthians 4:1-5; Luke 5:33-39.

Saturday, September 7: 1 Corinthians 4:6b-15; Luke 6:1-5.

Twenty-Third Sunday of Ordinary Time
September 8, 2024

First Reading: *Isaiah 35:4-7a*

Thus says the LORD:/ Say to those whose hearts are frightened:/ Be strong, fear not!/ Here is your God,/ he comes with vindication;/ with divine recompense/ he comes to save you./ Then will the eyes of the blind be opened,/ the ears of the deaf be cleared/ then will the lame leap like a stag,/ then the tongue of the mute will sing./ Streams will burst forth in the desert,/ and rivers in the steppe./ The burning sands will become pools, / and the thirsty ground, springs of water.

Second Reading: *James 2:1-5*

My brothers and sisters, show no partiality as you adhere to the faith in our glorious Lord Jesus Christ. For if a man with gold rings and fine clothes comes into your assembly, and a poor person in shabby clothes also comes in, and you pay attention to the one wearing the fine clothes and say, "Sit here, please, " while you say to the poor one, "Stand there, " or "Sit at my feet, " have you not made distinctions among yourselves and become judges with evil designs?

Listen, my beloved brothers and sisters. Did not God choose those who are poor in the world to be rich in faith and heirs of the kingdom that he promised to those who love him?

Gospel Reading: *Mark 7:31-37*

Again Jesus left the district of Tyre and went by way of Sidon to the Sea of Galilee, into the district of the Decapolis. And people brought to him a deaf man who had a speech impediment and begged him to lay his hand on him. He took him off by himself away from the crowd. He put his finger into the man's ears and, spitting, touched his tongue; then he looked up to heaven and groaned, and said to him, "*Ephphatha!*" -- that is, "Be opened!" And immediately the man's ears were opened, his speech impediment was removed, and he spoke plainly. He ordered them not to tell anyone. But the more he ordered them not to, the more they  proclaimed it. They were exceedingly astonished and they said, "He has done all things well. He makes the deaf hear and the mute speak"

Twenty Third Sunday of Ordinary Time
September 8, 2024

Homily Notes:

....
....
....
....
....
....
....
....
....
....
....
....
....
....
....
....
....
....
....
....
....
....
....
....

Reflection Questions for Each of the Readings:
1. *Based on the First Reading*: Explain Isaiah's prophecy in your own words.

2. *Based on the Second Reading*: What gifts and opportunites do the poor and needy provide to us? Who represent the poor and weak in your community?

3. *Based on the Gospel Reading*: Why does Jesus heal the blind man? Who asks Jesus to heal the man? Why did they ask for the healing? What could the man's sight and speech represent?

Your Virtue Challenge:

The goal of the virtuous person is to become like God. [CCC 1803] This will require identifying ways to increase this virtue and reduce opposing vice; *fasting [avoiding]* from habits or practices that oppose it; *praying* for God's help; *helping* others; and *doing penance*. *Based on the Gospel Reading*, your Virtue Challenge for the week is to increase in the virtue of:

HELPFUL

My Virtue Goals and Working Plan for the Week:

....

....

....

Daily Mass Readings for the Week:
Monday, September 9: **Saint Peter Claver** 1 Corinthians 5:1-8; Luke 6:6-11.
Tuesday, September 10: 1 Corinthians 6:1-11/Lk 6:12-19.
Wednesday, September 11: 1 Corinthians 7:25-31; Luke 6:20-26.
Thursday, September 12: **The Most Holy Name of Mary** 1 Corinthians 8:1b-7, 11-13; Luke 6:27-38.
Friday, September 13: **Saint John Chrysostom** 1 Corinthians 9:16-19, 22b-27; Luke 6:39-42.
Saturday, September 14 **The Exaltation of the Holy Cross** Numbers 21:4b-9; Philippeans 2:6-11; John 3:13-17.

Twenty-Fourth Sunday of Ordinary Time
September 15, 2024

First Reading: *Isaiah 50:5-9a*

The Lord GOD opens my ear that I may hear;/ and I have not rebelled,/ have not turned back./ I gave my back to those who beat me,/ my cheeks to/ those who plucked my beard;/ my face I did not shield/ from buffets and spitting.

The Lord GOD is my help,/ therefore I am not disgraced;/ I have set my face like flint,/ knowing that I shall not be put to shame./ He is near who upholds my right;/ if anyone wishes to oppose me,/let us appear together./ Who disputes my right?/ Let that man confront me./ See, the Lord GOD is my help;/ who will prove me wrong?

Second Reading: *James 2:14-18 a*

What good is it, my brothers and sisters, if someone says he has faith but does not have works? Can that faith save him? If a brother or sister has nothing to wear and has no food for the day, and one of you says to them, "Go in peace, keep warm, and eat well, " but you do not give them the necessities of the body, what good is it? So also faith of itself, if it does not have works, is dead.

Indeed someone might say, "You have faith and I have works." Demonstrate your faith to me without works, and I will demonstrate my faith to you from my works.

Gospel Reading: *Mark 8:27-35*

Jesus and his disciples set out for the villages of Caesarea Philippi. Along the way he asked his disciples, "Who do people say that I am?" They said in reply, "John the Baptist, others Elijah, still others one of the prophets." And he asked them, "But who do you say that I am?" Peter said to him in reply, "You are the Christ." Then he warned them not to tell anyone about him.

He began to teach them that the Son of Man must suffer greatly and be rejected by the elders, the chief priests, and the scribes, and be killed, and rise after three days. He spoke this openly. Then Peter took him aside and began to rebuke him. At this he turned around and, looking at his disciples, rebuked Peter and said, "Get behind me, Satan. You are thinking not as God does, but as human beings do."

He summoned the crowd with his disciples and said to them, "Whoever wishes to come after me must deny himself, take up his cross and

Twenty-Fourth Sunday of Ordinary Time
September 15, 2024

follow me. For whoever wishes to save his life will lose it, but whoever loses his life for my sake and that of the gospel will save it."

Homily Notes:

....
....
....
....
....
....
....
....
....
....
....
....
....
....
....
....
....
....
....
....
....
....
....
....

Reflection Questions for Each of the Readings:
1. *Based on the First Reading*: Who is Isaiah describing?

.

2. *Based on the Second Reading*: Why are faith and works of charity indivisible? Are spirituality and religion-ism separate entities? Explain.

3. *Based on the Gospel Reading*: Capture Jesus' main points about life, faith, and suffering in your own words.

Your Virtue Challenge:
   The goal of the virtuous person is to become like God. [CCC 1803] This will require identifying ways to increase this virtue and reduce opposing vice; *fasting [avoiding]* from habits or practices that oppose it; *praying* for God's help; *helping* others; and *doing penance. Based on the Second Reading,* your Virtue Challenge for the week is to increase in the virtue of:

CHARITY

My Virtue Goals and Working Plan for the Week:

....

....

....

Daily Mass Readings for the Week:
Monday,September 16: **Sts. Cornelius and Cyprian** 1 Corinthians 11:17-26, 33; Luke 7:1-10.
Tuesday, September 17: **Sts. Robert Bellarmine & Hildegard of Bingen** 1 Corinthians 12:12-14, 27-31a; Luke 7:11-17. Wednesday, September 18: 1 Corinthians 12:31—13:13; Luke 7:31-35.
Thursday, September 19: **Saint Januarius** 1 Corinthians 15:1-11: Luke 7:36-50.
Friday, September 20: **Sts. Andrew Kim Tae-gon & Paul Chong Ha-sang, and Companions.** 1 Corinthians 15:12-20; Luke 8:1-3.
Saturday, September 21: Saint Matthew. Ephesians 4:1-7, 11-13; Matthew 9:9-13.

Twenty-Fifth Sunday of Ordinary Time
September 22, 2024

First Reading: *Wisdom 2:12, 17-20*

The wicked say:/ Let us beset the just one, because he is obnoxious to us;/ he sets himself against our doings,/ reproaches us for transgressions of the law/ and charges us with violations of our training./ Let us see whether his words be true; / let us find out what will happen to him./ For if the just one be the son of God, God will defend him and deliver him from the hand of his foes./ With revilement and torture let us put the just one to the test/ that we may have proof of his gentleness/ and try his patience. / Let us condemn him to a shameful death; / for according to his own words, God will take care of him.

Second Reading: *James 3:16-4:3*

Beloved: Where jealousy and selfish ambition exist, there is disorder and every foul practice. But the wisdom from above is first of all pure, then peaceable, gentle, compliant, full of mercy and good fruits, without inconstancy or insincerity. And the fruit of righteousness is sown in peace for those who cultivate peace.

Where do the wars and where do the conflicts among you come from? Is it not from your passions that make war within your members? You covet but do not possess. You kill and envy but you cannot obtain; you fight and wage war. You do not possess because you do not ask. You ask but do not receive, because you ask wrongly, to spend it on your passions.

Gospel Reading: *Mark 9:30-37*

Jesus and his disciples left from there and began a journey through Galilee, but he did not wish anyone to know about it. He was teaching his disciples and telling them, "The Son of Man is to be handed over to men and they will kill him, and three days after his death the Son of Man will rise." But they did not understand the saying, and they were afraid to question him.

They came to Capernaum and, once inside the house, he began to ask them, "What were you arguing about on the way?" But they remained silent. They had been discussing among themselves on the way who was the greatest. Then he sat down, called the Twelve, and said to them, "If anyone wishes to be first, he shall be the last of all and the servant of all." Taking a child, he placed it in their midst, and putting his arms around it, he said to them, "Whoever receives one child such as this in my name, receives me; and whoever receives me, receives not me but the One who sent me."

Homily Notes:

....

....

....

....

....

....

....

....

....

....

....

....

....

....

....

....

....

....

....

....

....

Reflection Questions for Each of the Readings:
1. *Based on the First Reading*: Who or what is Wisdom talking about?

Twenty-Fifth Sunday of Ordinary Time
September 22, 2024

2. Based on the Second Reading: List the vices mentioned in this reading. List the virtues that counteract these vices. How and why should we to ask for God's blessings?

3. Based on the Gospel Reading: The desire to be first (getting to the front of a line, receiving awards, recognition, promotions, etc.] is not the same thing as striving for excellence. What are the differences? Why does Jesus use the example of a child?

Your Virtue Challenge:

The goal of the virtuous person is to become like God. [CCC 1803] This will require identifying ways to increase this virtue and reduce opposing vice; *fasting [avoiding]* from habits or practices that oppose it; *praying* for God's help; *helping* others; and *doing penance. Based on the Second Reading,* your Virtue Challenge for the week is to increase in the virtue of:

RIGHTEOUSNESS

My Virtue Goals and Working Plan for the Week:

....

....

....

Daily Mass Readings for the Week:

Monday, September 23: **Saint Pius of Pietrelcina.** Proverbs 3:27-34; Luke 8:16-18.

Tuesday, September 24: Proverbs 21:1-6, 10-13; Luke 8:19-21.

Wednesday, September 25: Proverbs 30:5-9; Luke 9:1-6.

Thursday, September 26: **Sts. Cosmas and Damian.** Ecclesiastes 1:2-11; Luke 9:7-9.

Friday, September 27: **Saint Vincent de Paul.** Ecclesiastes 3:1-11; Luke 9:18-22.

Saturday, September 28: **Sts. Wenceslaus, Lawrence Ruiz and Companions** Ecclesiastes 11:9—12:8; Luke 9:43b-45.

First Reading: *Numbers 11:25-29*

The LORD came down in the cloud and spoke to Moses. Taking some of the spirit that was on Moses, the LORD bestowed it on the seventy elders; and as the spirit came to rest on them, they prophesied.

Now two men, one named Eldad and the other Medad, were not in the gathering but had been left in the camp. They too had been on the list, but had not gone out to the tent; yet the spirit came to rest on them also, and they prophesied in the camp. So, when a young man quickly told Moses, "Eldad and Medad are prophesying in the camp, " Joshua, son of Nun, who from his youth had been Moses' aide, said, "Moses, my lord, stop them." But Moses answered him, "Are you jealous for my sake? Would that all the people of the LORD were prophets! Would that the LORD might bestow his spirit on them all!"

Second Reading: *James 5:1-6*

Come now, you rich, weep and wail over your impending miseries. Your wealth has rotted away, your clothes have become moth-eaten, your gold and silver have corroded, and that corrosion will be a testimony against you; it will devour your flesh like a fire. You have stored up treasure for the last days. Behold, the wages you withheld from the workers who harvested your fields are crying aloud; and the cries of the harvesters have reached the ears of the Lord of hosts. You have lived on earth in luxury and pleasure; you have fattened your hearts for the day of slaughter. You have condemned; you have murdered the righteous one; he offers you no resistance.

Gospel Reading: *Mark 9:38-43, 45, 47-48*

At that time, John said to Jesus, "Teacher, we saw someone driving out demons in your name, and we tried to prevent him because he does not follow us." Jesus replied, "Do not prevent him. There is no one who performs a mighty deed in my name who can at the same time speak ill of me. For whoever is not against us is for us. Anyone who gives you a cup of water to drink because you belong to Christ, amen, I say to you, will surely not lose his reward.

"Whoever causes one of these little ones who believe in me to sin, it would be better for him if a great millstone were put around his neck and he were thrown into the sea. If your hand causes you to sin, cut it off. It is better for you to enter into life maimed than with two hands to go into Gehenna, into the unquenchable fire. And if your foot causes you to sin, cut it off. It is better

Twenty-Sixth Sunday of Ordinary Time
September 29, 2024

for you to enter into life crippled than with two feet to be thrown into Gehenna. And if your eye causes you to sin, pluck it out. Better for you to enter into the kingdom of God with one eye than with two eyes to be thrown into Gehenna,where 'their worm does not die, and the fire is not quenched.'"

Homily Notes:

....
....
....
....
....
....
....
....
....
....
....
....
....
....
....
....
....
....
....
....
....

Reflection Questions for Each of the Readings:

1. *Based on the First Reading*: The first reading speaks about the Spirit. Who is the Spirit in relationship to God the Father and Son? Name the seven gifts of the Holy Spirit? Name the Twelve Fruits of the Holy Spirit? When do we receive these gifts?

2. Based on the Second Reading: Summarize what the book of James teaches us to do about wealth?

3. Based on the Gospel Reading: Summarize what Jesus teaches about sin, demons, and taking care of the children?

Your Virtue Challenge:
>The goal of the virtuous person is to become like God. [CCC 1803] This will require identifying ways to increase this virtue and reduce opposing vice; *fasting [avoiding]* from habits or practices that oppose it; *praying* for God's help; *helping* others; and *doing penance. Based on the Second Reading,* your Virtue Challenge for the week is to increase in the virtue of:

UNDERSTANDING

My Virtue Goals and Working Plan for the Week:

....

....

....

Daily Mass Readings for the Week:
Monday, September 30: **Saint Jerome** Job 1:6-22; Luke 9:46-50.
Tuesday, October 1: **Saint Thérèse of the Child Jesus** Job 3:1-3, 11-17, 20-23; Luke 9:51-56.
Wednesday, October 2: **The Holy Guardian Angels** Job 9:1-12, 14-16;Matthew 18:1-5, 10.
Thursday, October 3: Job 19:21-27; Luke 10:1-12.
Friday, October 4: **Saint Francis of Assisi** Job 38:1, 12-21; 40:3-5; Luke 10:13-16.
Saturday, October 5: **Saint Faustina Kowalska** & **Blessed Francis Xavier Seelos** Job 42:1-3, 5-6, 12-17; Luke 10:17-24.

216

Twenty-Seventh Sunday of Ordinary Time
October 6, 2024

First Reading: *Genesis 2:18-24*

The LORD God said: "It is not good for the man to be alone. I will make a suitable partner for him." So the LORD God formed out of the ground various wild animals and various birds of the air, and he brought them to the man to see what he would call them; whatever the man called each of them would be its name. The man gave names to all the cattle, all the birds of the air, and all wild animals; but none proved to be the suitable partner for the man.

So the LORD God cast a deep sleep on the man, and while he was asleep, he took out one of his ribs and closed up its place with flesh. The LORD God then built up into a woman the rib that he had taken from the man. When he brought her to the man, the man said:/   "This one, at last, is bone of my bones/   and flesh of my flesh;/   this one shall be called 'woman',/   for out of 'her man'   this one has been taken./"   That is why a man leaves his father and mother and clings to his wife, and the two of them become one flesh.

Second Reading: *Hebrews 2:9-11*

Brothers and sisters: He "for a little while" was made "lower than the angels, " that by the grace of God he might taste death for everyone.

For it was fitting that he, for whom and through whom all things exist, in bringing many children to glory, should make the leader to their salvation perfect through suffering. He who consecrates and those who are being consecrated all have one origin. Therefore, he is not ashamed to call them "brothers."

Gospel Reading: *Mark* **10:2-12** or *10:2-16*

The Pharisees approached Jesus and asked, "Is it lawful for a husband to divorce his wife?" They were testing him. He said to them in reply, "What did Moses command you?" They replied, "Moses permitted a husband to write a bill of divorce and dismiss her." But Jesus told them, "Because of the hardness of your hearts he wrote you this commandment. But from the beginning of creation, *God made them male and female. For this reason a man shall leave his father and mother and be joined to his wife, and the two shall become one flesh.* **So they are no longer two but one flesh. Therefore what God has joined together, no human being must separate." In the house the disciples again questioned Jesus about this. He said to them, "Whoever divorces his wife and marries another commits adultery against her; and if she divorces her husband and marries another, she commits adultery."**

And people were bringing children to him that he might touch them, but the disciples rebuked them. When Jesus saw this he became indignant and

Twenty Seventh Sunday of Ordinary Time
October 6, 2024

said to them, "Let the children come to me; do not prevent them, for the kingdom of God belongs to such as these. Amen, I say to you, whoever does not accept the kingdom of God like a child will not enter it." Then he embraced them and blessed them, placing his hands on them.

Homily Notes:

....
....
....
....
....
....
....
....
....
....
....
....
....
....
....
....
....
....
....
....
....

Reflection Questions for Each of the Readings:

1. *Based on the First Reading*: *"This one, at last, is bone of my bones and flesh of my flesh; This one shall be called 'woman,' for out of man this one has been taken."* Explain how Adam & Eve were *gifts* for each other? Why did God create man and woman? How is marriage and family life under attack today?

2. Based on the Second Reading: Is there a hierarchy in heaven? What is it? Explain your answer.

3. Based on the Gospel Reading: Summarize what Jesus teaches us about marriage and family life today.

Your Virtue Challenge:

The goal of the virtuous person is to become like God. [CCC 1803] This will require identifying ways to increase this virtue and reduce opposing vice; *fasting [avoiding]* from habits or practices that oppose it; *praying* for God's help; *helping* others; and *doing penance. Based on the First Reading,* your Virtue Challenge for the week is to increase in the virtue of:

ACCEPTANCE

My Virtue Goals and Working Plan for the Week:

....

....

....

Daily Mass Readings for the Week:

Monday, October 7: **Our Lady of the Rosary** Galatians 1:6-12; Luke 10:25-37.

Tuesday, October 8: Galatians 1:13-24; Luke 10:38-42.

Wednesday, October 9: **Sts. Denis & John Leonardi** Galatians 2:1-2, 7-14; Luke 11:1-4.

Thursday, October 10: Galatians 3:1-5; Luke 11:5-13.

Friday, October 11: **Saint John XXIII** Galatians 3:7-14; Luke 11:15-26.

Saturday, October 12: Galatians 3:22-29; Luke 11:27-28.

Twenty Eighth Sunday of Ordinary Time
October 13, 2024

First Reading: *Wisdom 7:7-11*

I prayed, and prudence was given me;/ I pleaded, and the spirit of wisdom came to me./ I preferred her to scepter and throne,/ and deemed riches nothing in comparison with her,/ nor did I liken any priceless gem to her;/ because all gold, in view of her, is a little sand,/ and before her, silver is to be accounted mire./ Beyond health and comeliness I loved her,/ and I chose to have her rather than the light,/ because the splendor of her never yields to sleep./ Yet all good things together came to me in her company,/ and countless riches at her hands.

Second Reading: *Hebrews 4:12-13*

Brothers and sisters: Indeed the word of God is living and effective, sharper than any two-edged sword, penetrating even between soul and spirit, joints and marrow, and able to discern reflections and thoughts of the heart. No creature is concealed from him, but everything is naked and exposed to the eyes of him to whom we must render an account.

Gospel Reading: *Mark 10:17-27* or *10:17-30*

As Jesus was setting out on a journey, a man ran up, knelt down before him, and asked him, "Good teacher, what must I do to inherit eternal life?" Jesus answered him, "Why do you call me good? No one is good but God alone. You know the commandments: *You shall not kill; you shall not commit adultery; you shall not steal; you shall not bear false witness; you shall not defraud; honor your father and your mother.*" He replied and said to him, "Teacher, all of these I have observed from my youth." Jesus, looking at him, loved him and said to him, "You are lacking in one thing. Go, sell what you have, and give to the poor and you will have treasure in heaven; then come, follow me." At that statement his face fell, and he went away sad, for he had many possessions.

Jesus looked around and said to his disciples, "How hard it is for those who have wealth to enter the kingdom of God!" The disciples were amazed at his words. So Jesus again said to them in reply, "Children, how hard it is to enter the kingdom of God! It is easier for a camel to pass through the eye of a needle than for one who is rich to enter the kingdom of God." They were exceedingly astonished and said among themselves, "Then who can be saved?" Jesus looked at them and said, "For human beings it is impossible, but not for God. All things are possible for God." Peter began to say to him, "We have given up everything and followed you." Jesus said, "Amen, I say to you, there is no one who has given up house or brothers or sisters or mother or father or children or lands for my sake and

Twenty-Eighth Sunday of Ordinary Time
October 13, 2024

for the sake of the gospel who will not receive a hundred times more now in this present age: houses and brothers and sisters and mothers and children and lands, with persecutions, and eternal life in the age to come."

Homily Notes:

....
....
....
....
....
....
....
....
....
....
....
....
....
....
....
....
....
....
....
....
....

Reflection Questions for Each of the Readings:
1. *Based on the First Reading:* Solomon is awarded Wisdom by God. What is Wisdom? To whom [of the Trinity] should we pray for wisdom?

2. *Based on the Second Reading:* A double-edged sword has two sharp edges. It is also a metaphor for *cutting both ways;* meaning it can hurt the person who is attacked and the attacker at the same time. Why/how is the Word of God more piercing than a double edged sword?

3. *Based on the Gospel Reading:* What was lacking in the young man in today's Gospel? What is the lesson for us? Why are riches & materialism a stumbling block to faith, hope and charity? Explain.

Your Virtue Challenge:

The goal of the virtuous person is to become like God. [CCC 1803] This will require identifying ways to increase this virtue and reduce opposing vice; *fasting [avoiding]* from habits or practices that oppose it; *praying* for God's help; *helping* others; and *doing penance. Based on the First Reading,* your Virtue Challenge for the week is to increase in the virtue of:

WISDOM

My Virtue Goals and Working Plan for the Week:

....

....

....

Daily Mass Readings for the Week:

Monday, October 14: **Saint Callistus I** Galatians 4:22-24, 26-27, 31—5:1; Luke 11:29-32.

Tuesday, October 15: **Saint Teresa of Jesus** Galatians 5:1-6; Luke 11:37-41.

Wednesday, October 16: **Sts. Hedwig & Margaret Mary Alacoque** Galatians 5:18-25; Luke 11:42-46.

Thursday, October 17: **Saint Ignatius of Antioch** Ephesians 1:1-10; Luke 11:47-54.

Friday, October 18: **Saint Luke** 2 Timothy 4:10-17b; Luke 10:1-9.

Saturday, October 19: **Sts. John de Brébeuf & Isaac Jogues.** Ephesians 1:15-23; Luke 12:8-12.

Twenty-Ninth Sunday of Ordinary Time
October 20, 2024

First Reading: *Isaiah 53:10-11*

The LORD was pleased/   to crush him in infirmity./
If he gives his life as an offering for sin,/   he shall see his descendants in a long life,/   and the will of the LORD shall be accomplished through him.

Because of his affliction/   he shall see the light in fullness of days;/ through his suffering, my servant shall justify many,/   and their guilt he shall bear.

Second Reading: *Hebrews 4:14-16*

Brothers and sisters: Since we have a great high priest who has passed through the heavens, **Jesus, the Son of God**,   let us hold fast to our confession. For we do not have a high priest who is unable to sympathize with our weaknesses, but one who has similarly been tested in every way, yet without sin.   So let us confidently approach the throne of grace to receive mercy and to find grace for timely help.

Gospel Reading: *Mark 10:35-45 or* **10:42-45**

James and John, the sons of Zebedee, came to Jesus and said to him, "Teacher, we want you to do for us whatever we ask of you."   He replied, "What do you wish me to do for you?"   They answered him, "Grant that in your glory we may sit one at your right and the other at your left."   Jesus said to them, "You do not know what you are asking.   Can you drink the cup that I drink or be baptized with the baptism with which I am baptized?"   They said to him, "We can."   Jesus said to them, "The cup that I drink, you will drink, and with the baptism with which I am baptized, you will be baptized; but to sit at my right or at my left is not mine to give but is for those for whom it has been prepared."   When the ten heard this, they became indignant at James and John. **Jesus summoned** them **[the Twelve] and said to them, "You know that those who are recognized as rulers over the Gentiles lord it over them, and their great ones make their authority over them felt.   But it shall not be so among you. Rather, whoever wishes to be great among you will be your servant; whoever wishes to be first among**  **you will be the slave of all.   For the Son of Man did not come to be served but to serve and to give his life as a ransom for many."**

Homily Notes:

....

....

....

....

....

....

....

....

....

....

....

....

....

....

....

....

....

....

....

....

....

....

Reflection Questions for Each of the Readings:
1. *Based on the First Reading: Who* is the just servant? What does a just servant do? Who does he serve?

2. *Based on the Second Reading*: What is the role of a High Priest? Who is the greatest High Priest? What is his role?

3. *Based on the Gospel Reading*: What did the Apostles argue about? Why is humility an effective antidote to pride? Why is suffering necessary?

Your Virtue Challenge:

The goal of the virtuous person is to become like God. [CCC 1803] This will require identifying ways to increase this virtue and reduce opposing vice; *fasting [avoiding]* from habits or practices that oppose it; *praying* for God's help; *helping* others; and *doing penance*. *Based on the First Reading,* your Virtue Challenge for the week is to increase in the virtue of:

ALTRUISM

My Virtue Goals and Working Plan for the Week:

....

....

....

Daily Mass Readings for the Week:

Monday, October 21: Ephesians 2:1-10; Luke 12:13-21.
Tuesday, October 22: **Saint John Paul II** Ephesians 2:12-22; Luke 12:35-38.
Wednesday, October 23: **Saint John of Capistrano** Ephesians 3:2-12; Luke 12:39-48.
Thursday, October 24: **Saint Anthony Mary Claret** Ephesians 3:14-21; Luke 12:49-53.
Friday, October 25: Ephesians 4:1-6; Luke 12:54-59.
Saturday, October 26: Ephesians 4:7-16; Luke 13:1-9.

Thirtieth Sunday of Ordinary Time

October 27, 2024

First Reading: *Jeremiah 31:7-9*

Thus says the LORD:/ Shout with joy for Jacob,/ exult at the head of the nations;/ proclaim your praise and say:/ The LORD has delivered his people,/ the remnant of Israel./ Behold, I will bring them back/ from the land of the north;/ I will gather them from the ends of the world,/ with the blind and the lame in their midst,/ the mothers and those with child;/ they shall return as an immense throng./ They departed in tears,/ but I will console them and guide them;/ I will lead them to brooks of water,/ on a level road, so that none shall stumble./ For I am a father to Israel,/ Ephraim is my first-born.

Second Reading: *Hebrews 5:1-6*

Brothers and sisters: Every high priest is taken from among men and made their representative before God, to offer gifts and sacrifices for sins. He is able to deal patiently with the ignorant and erring, for he himself is beset by weakness and so, for this reason, must make sin offerings for himself as well as for the people. No one takes this honor upon himself but only when called by God, just as Aaron was. In the same way, it was not Christ who glorified himself in becoming high priest, but rather the one who said to him:/ *You are my son:/ this day I have begotten you;/* just as he says in another place:/ *You are a priest forever/ according to the order of Melchizedek.*

Gospel Reading: *Mark 10:46-52*

As Jesus was leaving Jericho with his disciples and a sizable crowd, Bartimaeus, a blind man, the son of Timaeus, sat by the roadside begging. On hearing that it was Jesus of Nazareth, he began to cry out and say, "Jesus, son of David, have pity on me." And many rebuked him, telling him to be silent. But he kept calling out all the more, "Son of David, have pity on me." Jesus stopped and said, "Call him." So they called the blind man, saying to him, "Take courage; get up, Jesus is calling you." He threw aside his cloak, sprang up, and came to Jesus. Jesus said to him in reply, "What do you want me to do for you?" The blind man replied to him, "Master, I want to see." Jesus told him, "Go your way; your faith has saved you." Immediately he received his sight and followed him on the way.

Thirtieth Sunday of Ordinary Time

October 27, 2024

Homily Notes:

....
....
....
....
....
....
....
....
....
....
....
....
....
....
....
....
....
....
....
....
....
....
....
....

Reflection Questions for Each of the Readings:

1. *Based on the First Reading:* Explain how we are all like exiles. When will we all rejoice?

2. *Based on the Second Reading*: What is the role of the high priest? Who is the eternal High Priest and what role does he have?

3. *Based on the Gospel Reading*: Parables can have multiple meanings. Explain what *seeing* could mean in the spiritual sense.

Your Virtue Challenge:
      The goal of the virtuous person is to become like God. [CCC 1803] This will require identifying ways to increase this virtue and reduce opposing vice; *fasting [avoiding]* from habits or practices that oppose it; *praying* for God's help; *helping* others; and *doing penance*. Based on the Gospel Reading, your Virtue Challenge for the week is to increase in the virtue of:

HUMILITY

My Virtue Goals and Working Plan for the Week:

....

....

....

Daily Mass Readings for the Week:
Monday, October 28: **Sts. Simon & Jude**. Ephesians 2:19-22; Luke 6:12-16.
Tuesday, October 29: Ephesians 5:21-33; Luke 13:18-21.
Wednesday, October 30: Ephesians 6:1-9; Luke 13:22-30.
Thursday, October 31: Ephesians 6:10-20; Luke 13:31-35.
Friday, November 1: **Solemnity of All Saints; Holyday of Obligation**
Revelation 7:2-4, 9-14; 1 John 3:1-3; Matthew 5:1-12a.
Saturday, November 2: **All Souls' Day** Wisdom 3:1-9; Romans 5:5-11 or
Romans 6:3-9; John 6:37-40.

Solemnity of All Saints

First Reading: *Revelation 7:2-4, 9-14*

I, John, saw another angel come up from the East, holding the seal of the living God. He cried out in a loud voice to the four angels who were given power to damage the land and the sea, "Do not damage the land or the sea or the trees until we put the seal on the foreheads of the servants of our God." I heard the number of those who had been marked with the seal, one hundred and forty-four thousand marked from every tribe of the children of Israel.

After this I had a vision of a great multitude, which no one could count, from every nation, race, people, and tongue. They stood before the throne and before the Lamb, wearing white robes and holding palm branches in their hands. They cried out in a loud voice: "Salvation comes from our God, who is seated on the throne,/ and from the Lamb." All the angels stood around the throne and around the elders and the four living creatures. They prostrated themselves before the throne, worshiped God, and exclaimed:

"Amen. Blessing and glory, wisdom and thanksgiving,/ honor, power, and might / be to our God forever and ever./ Amen." Then one of the elders spoke up and said to me, "Who are these wearing white robes, and where did they come from?" I said to him, "My lord, you are the one who knows." He said to me "These are the ones who have survived the time of great distress; they have washed their robes and made them white in the Blood of the Lamb."

Second Reading: *1 John 3:1-3*

Beloved: See what love the Father has bestowed on us that we may be called the children of God. Yet so we are. The reason the world does not know us is that it did not know him. Beloved, we are God's children now; what we shall be has not yet been revealed. We do know that when it is revealed we shall be like him, for we shall see him as he is. Everyone who has this hope based on him makes himself pure, as he is pure.

Gospel Reading: *Matthew 5:1-12a*

When Jesus saw the crowds, he went up the mountain, and after he had sat down, his disciples came to him. He began to teach them, saying: "Blessed are the poor in spirit,/ for theirs is the Kingdom of heaven./ Blessed are they who mourn,/ for they will be comforted./ Blessed are the meek,/ for they will inherit the land./ Blessed are they who hunger and thirst for righteousness,/ for they will be satisfied./ Blessed are the merciful,/ for they will be shown mercy. / Blessed are the clean of heart, / for they will see God. / Blessed are the peacemakers, / for they will be called children of God. / Blessed are they who are persecuted for the sake of righteousness,/ for

Solemnity of All Saints

November 1, 2024

theirs is the Kingdom of heaven. / Blessed are you when they insult you and persecute you/ and utter every kind of evil against you falsely because of me. / Rejoice and be glad, / for your reward will be great in heaven."

Homily Notes:

....
....
....
....
....
....
....
....
....
....
....
....
....
....
....
....
....
....
....
....
....
....
....
....
....

Reflection Questions for Each of the Readings:

1. *Based on the First Reading:* What did you learn from Revelations?

2. *Based on the Second Reading:* Explain what the following verse means to you: *"Everyone who has this hope based on him makes himself pure, as he is pure."*

3. *Based on the Gospel Reading:* Beatitude means blessings. Which Beatitude is the most difficult for you to practice? Which Beatitude is the easiest one to practice?

Thirty First Sunday in Ordinary Time
November 3, 2024

First Reading: *Deuteronomy 6:2-6*

Moses spoke to the people, saying: "Fear the LORD, your God, and keep, throughout the days of your lives, all his statutes and commandments which I enjoin on you, and thus have long life. Hear then, Israel, and be careful to observe them, that you may grow and prosper the more, in keeping with the promise of the LORD, the God of your fathers, to give you a land flowing with milk and honey.

"Hear, O Israel! The LORD is our God, the LORD alone! Therefore, you shall love the LORD, your God, with all your heart, and with all your soul, and with all your strength. Take to heart these words which I enjoin on you today."

Second Reading: *Hebrews 7:23-28*

Brothers and sisters: The levitical priests were many because they were prevented by death from remaining in office, but Jesus, because he remains forever, has a priesthood that does not pass away. Therefore, he is always able to save those who approach God through him, since he lives forever to make intercession for them.

It was fitting that we should have such a high priest: holy, innocent, undefiled, separated from sinners, higher than the heavens. He has no need, as did the high priests, to offer sacrifice day after day, first for his own sins and then for those of the people; he did that once for all when he offered himself. For the law appoints men subject to weakness to be high priests, but the word of the oath, which was taken after the law, appoints a son, who has been made perfect forever.

Gospel Reading: *Mark 12:28b-34*

One of the scribes came to Jesus and asked him, "Which is the first of all the commandments?" Jesus replied, "The first is this: *Hear, O Israel! The Lord our God is Lord alone! You shall love the Lord your God with all your heart, with all your soul, with all your mind, and with all your strength.* The second is this: *You shall love your neighbor as yourself.* There is no other commandment greater than these." The scribe said to him, "Well said, teacher. You are right in saying, 'He is One and there is no other than he.' And 'to love him with all your heart, with all your understanding, with all your strength, and to love your neighbor as yourself' is worth more than all burnt offerings and sacrifices." And when Jesus saw that he answered with understanding, he said to him, "You are not far from the kingdom of God." And no one dared to ask him any more questions.

Homily Notes:

....

....

....

....

....

....

....

....

....

....

....

....

....

....

....

....

....

....

....

....

....

Reflection Questions for Each of the Readings:
1. *Based on the First Reading:* Write down the Ten Commandments.

2. *Based on the Second Reading*: Who is Jesus? What ultimate sacrifice did Jesus make for us?

3. *Based on the Gospel Reading*: How are we to love God? How are we to love others?

Your Virtue Challenge:

The goal of the virtuous person is to become like God. [CCC 1803] This will require identifying ways to increase this virtue and reduce opposing vice; *fasting [avoiding]* from habits or practices that oppose it; *praying* for God's help; *helping* others; and *doing penance*. Your Virtue Challenge for the week is to increase in the virtue of:

RESPECTFULNESS

My Virtue Goals and Working Plan for the Week:

....

....

....

Daily Mass Readings for the Week:

Monday, November 4: **Saint Charles Borromeo** Philippians 2:1-4; Luke 14:12-14.

Tuesday, November 5: Philippians 2:5-11; Luke 14:15-24.

Wednesday, November 6: Philippians 2:12-18; Luke 14:25-33.

Thursday, November 7: Philippians 3:3-8a; Luke 15:1-10.

Friday, November 8: Philippians 3:17—4:1; Luke 16:1-8.

Saturday, November 9: **The Dedication of the Lateran Basilica** Ezekiel 47:1-2, 8-9, 12; 1 Corinthians 3:9c-11, 16-17; John 2:13-22.

Thirty-Second Sunday in Ordinary Time
November 10, 2024

First Reading: *1 Kings 17:10-16*

In those days, Elijah the prophet went to Zarephath. As he arrived at the entrance of the city, a widow was gathering sticks there; he called out to her, "Please bring me a small cupful of water to drink." She left to get it, and he called out after her, "Please bring along a bit of bread." She answered, "As the LORD, your God, lives, I have nothing baked; there is only a handful of flour in my jar and a little oil in my jug. Just now I was collecting a couple of sticks, to go in and prepare something for myself and my son; when we have eaten it, we shall die." Elijah said to her, "Do not be afraid. Go and do as you propose. But first make me a little cake and bring it to me. Then you can prepare something for yourself and your son. For the LORD, the God of Israel, says, 'The jar of flour shall not go empty, nor the jug of oil run dry, until the day when the LORD sends rain upon the earth.'" She left and did as Elijah had said. She was able to eat for a year, and he and her son as well; the jar of flour did not go empty, nor the jug of oil run dry, as the LORD had foretold through Elijah.

Second Reading: *Hebrews 9:24-28*

Christ did not enter into a sanctuary made by hands, a copy of the true one, but heaven itself, that he might now appear before God on our behalf. Not that he might offer himself repeatedly, as the high priest enters each year into the sanctuary with blood that is not his own; if that were so, he would have had to suffer repeatedly from the foundation of the world. But now once for all he has appeared at the end of the ages to take away sin by his sacrifice. Just as it is appointed that human beings die once, and after this the judgment, so also Christ, offered once to take away the sins of many, will appear a second time, not to take away sin but to bring salvation to those who eagerly await him.

Gospel Reading: *Mark 12:38-44 or* **12:41-44**

In the course of his teaching Jesus said to the crowds, "Beware of the scribes, who like to go around in long robes and accept greetings in the marketplaces, seats of honor in synagogues, and places of honor at banquets. They devour the houses of widows and, as a pretext recite lengthy prayers. They will receive a very severe condemnation."

[He] **Jesus sat down opposite the treasury and observed how the crowd put money into the treasury. Many rich people put in large sums. A poor widow also came and put in two small coins worth a few cents. Calling his disciples to himself, he said to them, "Amen, I say to you, this poor widow put in more than all the other contributors to the treas-**

ury. **For they have all contributed from their surplus wealth, but she, from her poverty, has contributed all she had, her whole livelihood."**

Homily Notes:

. . . .

. . . .

. . . .

. . . .

. . . .

. . . .

. . . .

. . . .

. . . .

. . . .

. . . .

. . . .

. . . .

. . . .

. . . .

. . . .

. . . .

. . . .

. . . .

. . . .

. . . .

Reflection Questions for Each of the Readings:
1. *Based on the First Reading:* What promise did Elijah make to the widow? What would you have done if you didn't have enough flour to feed your family?

2. Based on the Second Reading: What will Jesus do at the final coming?

3. Based on the Gospel Reading: Who & what do we need to beware of today?

Your Virtue Challenge:

The goal of the virtuous person is to become like God. [CCC 1803] This will require identifying ways to increase this virtue and reduce opposing vice; *fasting [avoiding]* from habits or practices that oppose it; *praying* for God's help; *helping* others; and *doing penance.* Based on the Gospel Reading your Virtue Challenge for the week is to increase in the virtue of:

CAREFULNESS

My Virtue Goals and Working Plan for the Week:

....

....

....

Daily Mass Readings for the Week:
Monday, November 11: **Saint Martin of Tours** Titus 1:1-9; Luke 17:1-6.
Tuesday, November 12: **Saint Josaphat** Titus 2:1-8, 11-14; Luke 17:7-10.
Wednesday, November 13: **Saint Frances Xavier Cabrini**. Titus 3:1-7; Luke 17:11-1.
Thursday, November 14: Philemon 7-20; Luke 17:20-25.
Friday, November 15: **Saint Albert the Great** 2 John 4-9; Luke 17:26-37.
Saturday, November 16: **Sts. Margaret of Scotland & Gertrude** 3 John 5-8; Luke 18:1-8.

First Reading: *Daniel 12:1-3*

In those days, I Daniel,/ heard this word of the Lord: "At that time there shall arise/ Michael, the great prince,/ guardian of your people; it shall be a time unsurpassed in distress/ since nations began until that time./ At that time your people shall escape,/ everyone who is found written in the book./

"Many of those who sleep in the dust of the earth shall awake; some shall live forever,/ others shall be an everlasting horror and disgrace./

"But the wise shall shine brightly/ like the splendor of the firmament, and those who lead the many to justice/ shall be like the stars forever."

Second Reading: *Hebrews 10:11-14, 18*

Brothers and sisters: Every priest stands daily at his ministry, offering frequently those same sacrifices that can never take away sins. But this one offered one sacrifice for sins, and took his seat forever at the right hand of God; now he waits until his enemies are made his footstool. For by one offering he has made perfect forever those who are being consecrated.

Where there is forgiveness of these, there is no longer offering for sin.

Gospel Reading: *Mark 13:24-32*

Jesus said to his disciples: "In those days after that tribulation the sun will be darkened, and the moon will not give its light, and the stars will be falling from the sky, and the powers in the heavens will be shaken.

"And then they will see 'the Son of Man coming in the clouds' with great power and glory, and then he will send out the angels and gather his elect from the four winds, from the end of the earth to the end of the sky.

"Learn a lesson from the fig tree. When its branch becomes tender and sprouts leaves, you know that summer is near. In the same way, when you see these things happening, know that he is near, at the gates. Amen, I say to you, this generation will not pass away until all these things have taken place. Heaven and earth will pass away, but my words will not pass away.

"But of that day or hour, no one knows, neither the angels in heaven, nor the Son, but only the Father."

Homily Notes:

....

....

....

....

....

....

....

....

....

....

....

....

....

....

....

....

....

....

....

....

....

Reflection Questions for Each of the Readings:
1. *Based on the First Reading*: Who is Michael? What do these verses from the Book of Daniel teach us?

2. *Based on the Second Reading:* What does the following verse mean: *Where there is forgiveness, there is no longer offering for sin?* Who is this reading describing?

3. *Based on the Gospel:* Describe the end of time based on this reading.

Note: The 2024 Liturgical Year is coming to an end. Order your 2025 edition today. www.fortifyingfamiliesoffaith.com

Your Virtue Challenge:
   The goal of the virtuous person is to become like God. [CCC 1803] This will require identifying ways to increase this virtue and reduce opposing vice; *fasting [avoiding]* from habits or practices that oppose it; *praying* for God's help; *helping* others; and *doing penance.* Based on the *Gospel Reading* your Virtue Challenge for the week is to increase in the virtue of:

PREPAREDNESS

My Virtue Goals and Working Plan for the Week:

....

....

....

Daily Mass Readings for the Week:
Monday November 18: **The Dedication of the Basilicas of Saints Peter and Paul; Saint Rose Philippine Duchesne** Revelation 1:1-4; 2:1-5; Luke 18:35-43 or Acts 28:11-16, 30-31; Matthew 14:22-33.
Tuesday, November19: Revelation 3:1-6, 14-22; Luke 19:1-10.
Wednesday, November 20: Revelation 4:1-11/Lk 19:11-28.
Thursday, November 21: **The Presentation of the Blessed Virgin Mary** Revelation 5:1-10: Luke 19:41-44.
Friday, November 22: **Saint Cecilia** Revelation 10:8-11; Luke 19:45-48.
Saturday, November 23: Sts. Clement I, Columban & Blessed Miguel Agustín. Revelation 11:4-12; Luke 20:27-40.
240

The Solemnity of Our Lord Jesus Christ, King of the Universe

November 24, 2024

First Reading: *Daniel 7:13-14*

As the visions during the night continued, I saw/ one like a Son of man coming,/ on the clouds of heaven; / when he reached the Ancient One/ and was presented before him, / the one like a Son of man received dominion, glory, and kingship; / all peoples, nations, and languages serve him. / His dominion is an everlasting dominion / that shall not be taken away, / his kingship shall not be destroyed.

Second Reading: *Revelation 1:5-8*

Jesus Christ is the faithful witness, the firstborn of the dead and ruler of the kings of the earth. To him who loves us and has freed us from our sins by his blood, who has made us into a kingdom, priests for his God and Father, to him be glory and power forever and ever. Amen.

Behold, he is coming amid the clouds,/ and every eye will see him,/ even those who pierced him./ All the peoples of the earth will lament him./ Yes. Amen.

"I am the Alpha and the Omega," says the Lord God, "the one who is and who was and who is to come, the almighty."

Gospel Reading: *John 18:33b-37*

Pilate said to Jesus, "Are you the King of the Jews?" Jesus answered, "Do you say this on your own or have others told you about me?" Pilate answered, "I am not a Jew, am I? Your own nation and the chief priests handed you over to me. What have you done?" Jesus answered, "My kingdom does not belong to this world. If my kingdom did belong to this world, my attendants would be fighting to keep me from being handed over to the Jews. But as it is, my kingdom is not here." So Pilate said to him, "Then you are a king?" Jesus answered, "You say I am a king. For this I was born and for this I came into the world, to testify to the truth. Everyone who belongs to the truth listens to my voice."

Homily Notes:

....

....

....

....

....

....

....

....

....

....

....

....

....

....

....

....

....

....

....

....

....

....

....

....

....

....

Reflection Questions for Each of the Readings:
1. *Based on the First Reading*: Describe the scene in your own words.

2. *Based on the Second Reading:* Compare and contrast the first and second readings. How are they similar? How are they different? Who is Jesus - based on this reading?

3. *Based on the Gospel:* The last Sunday of the Liturgical Year talks about the judgment of Jesus by Pilate. Why do you think this gospel story is retold here?

Author's Commentary: I hope you found the **Virtue Challenge** challenging and fulfilling. You have read **over 52 times** that the Church teaches us that our ultimate goal is to become like God. [CCC 1803] Do you feel that the Virtue Challenge helped you to grow in Virtue? God bless you for your diligence in using this book and for dedicating yourself to spiritual growth this past year and to continue that growth in 2025! Our faith is never constant; like other personal aspects we are either growing in our faith or losing ground.

Daily Mass Readings for the Week:
Monday, November 25: **Saint Catherine of Alexandria** Revelation 14:1-3, 4b-5; Luke 21:1-4
Tuesday, November 26: Revelation 14:14-19; Luke 21:5-11
Wednesday, November 27: Revelation 15:1-4; Luke 21:12-19
Thursday, November 28: **Thanksgiving Day** Revelation 18:1-2, 21-23; 19:1-3, 9a; Luke 21:20-28
Friday, November 29: Revelation 20:1-4, 11—21:2; Luke 21:29-33
Saturday, November 30: Saint Andrew. Romans 10:9-18; Matthew 4:18-22

The 2025 Liturgical Year Begins Next Sunday With the Start of Advent.

Order your 2025 copy of
Journaling with Sunday Scripture
on
www.FortifyingFamiliesofFaith.com.

This journal makes a wonderful gift for any age birthday, Christmas gift, or Confirmation gift and will be used all year long.

PRAYERS

PRAYERS

PRAYERS

Prayers Said During the Mass

The Sign of the Cross

In the name of the Father, / and of the Son,/ and of the Holy Spirit. Amen.

The Sign of the Cross is a simple prayer that acknowledge the Trinity as three persons in one God; the Father, the Son and the Holy Spirit. It should be prayed as solemnly and reverently as all prayers while signing oneself with the Sign of the Cross:

Penitential Prayer - Confiteor

I confess to almighty God/ and to you, my brothers and sisters, that I have greatly sinned,/ in my thoughts and in my words,/ in what I have done and in what I have failed to do,/ through my fault,/ through my fault,/ through my most grievous fault;/ therefore I ask blessed Mary ever-Virgin/ , all the Angels and Saints,/ and you, my brothers and sisters,/ to pray for me to the Lord our God. Amen   - or -

Kyrie, eleison. Kyrie, eleison. Christe eleison
Lord, have mercy. Lord, have mercy. Christ, have mercy.

Gloria

Glory to God in the highest,/ and on earth peace to people of good will./ We praise you,/ we bless you,/ we adore you,/ we glorify you,/ we give you thanks for your great glory, Lord God, heavenly King,/ O God, almighty Father./ Lord Jesus Christ,/ Only Begotten Son,/ Lord God, Lamb of God, / Son of the Father,/ you take away the sins of the world,/ have mercy on us;/ you take away the sins of the world,/ receive our prayer;/ you are seated at the right hand/ of the Father,/ have mercy on us./ For you alone are the Holy One, you alone are the Lord,/ you alone are the Most High, Jesus Christ, with the Holy Spirit,/ in the glory of God the Father. Amen.

The Apostles Creed

I believe in God, the Father almighty, / Creator of heaven and earth,/ and in Jesus Christ,/ his only Son, our Lord,/ who was conceived by the Holy Spirit,/ born of the Virgin Mary,/ suffered under Pontius Pilate, / was crucified, died and was buried;/ he descended into hell; on the third day he rose again from the dead;/ he ascended into heaven, and is seated at the right hand of God the Father almighty; / from there he will come to judge the living and the dead. / I believe in the Holy Spirit///, the holy catholic Church,/ the communion of saints,/ the forgiveness of sins,/ the resurrection of the body, and life everlasting./ Amen./

The Nicene Creed

I believe in one God,/ the Father almighty,/ maker of heaven and earth, of all things visible and invisible.

I believe in one Lord Jesus Christ,/ the Only Begotten Son of God,/ born of the Father before all ages./ God from God, Light from Light,/ true God from true God,/ begotten, not made, consubstantial with the Father;/ through him all things were made./ For us men and for our salvation/ he came down from heaven,/ and by the Holy Spirit was incarnate of the Virgin Mary,/ and became man./ For our sake he was crucified under Pontius Pilate,/ he suffered death and was buried,/ and rose again on the third day/ in accordance with the Scriptures./ He ascended into heaven/ and is seated at the right hand of the Father./ He will come again in glory/ to judge the living and the dead/ and his kingdom will have no end.

I believe in the Holy Spirit, the Lord, the giver of life,/ who proceeds from the Father and the Son,/ who with the Father and the Son is adored and glorified,/ who has spoken through the prophets.

I believe in one, holy, catholic and apostolic Church./ I confess one Baptism for the forgiveness of sins/ and I look forward to the resurrection of the dead/ and the life of the world to come. Amen.

Holy, Holy, Holy

Holy, Holy, Holy Lord God of hosts./ Heaven and earth are full of your glory./ Hosanna in the highest./ Blessed is he who comes in the name of the Lord./ Hosanna in the highest.

The Mystery of Faith.

We proclaim your Death, O Lord,/ and profess your Resurrection/ until you come again. **Or:**

When we eat this Bread/ and drink this Cup,/ we proclaim your Death, O Lord,/ until you come again. **Or:**

Save us, Saviour of the world,/ for by your Cross and Resurrection/ you have set us free.

Glory Be

Glory be to the Father and to the Son and to the Holy Spirit. As it was in the beginning is now, and ever shall be, world without end. Amen.

Lamb of God

Lamb of God/ who takes away the sins of the world/ have mercy on us./ Lamb of God/ who takes away the sins of the world,/ have mercy on us./ Lamb of God who takes away the sins of the world/, grant us peace.

The Our Father

Our Father,/   who art in heaven, /   hallowed be thy name;/   thy kingdom come,/   thy will be done/   on earth as it is in heaven./   Give us this day our daily bread, /   and forgive us our trespasses,/   as we forgive those who trespass against us;/   and lead us not into temptation,/   but deliver us from evil./   now and at the hour of our death. /   Amen

Prayers Before & After Holy Communion

The Act of Contrition - 1 *[Also said during the Sacrament of Reconciliation]*

Oh my God,/   I am heartily sorry for having offended Thee./   I detest all my sins because I dread the loss of heaven and the pains of hell./   But most of all because they offend Thee,/   my God, /   who art all good and deserving of all my love./   I firmly resolve, /   with the help of Thy sins, to confess my sins,/ to do penance,/   and to amend my life. /   Amen.

The Act of Contrition - 2

O my God,/   I am heartily sorry for having offended Thee,/   and I detest all my sins/   because of thy just punishments,/   but most of all because they offend Thee,/   my God, who art all good and deserving of all my love./   I firmly resolve with the help of Thy grace to sin no more and to avoid the near occasion of sin. Amen {USCCB]

Prayer of St. Thomas Aquinas

O almighty and eternal God, behold, I approach the Sacrament of your only begotten Son, our Lord Jesus Christ. I come as one sick to the Physician of life, as one unclean to the source of all mercy. Please heal my infirmities, cleanse me from my sins, illumine my sinfulness, enrich my faith. Grant that I may receive the Lord of lords with reverence and humility, contrition and devotion, purity and faith, with uprightness of purpose and intention, may this reception be profitable to the salvation of my soul. Grant that I may receive not only the Sacrament of the Lord's Body and Blood but also the grace and virtue of the Sacrament. Grant that I may one day contemplate forever, face to face, the One whose face is now hidden beneath the sacramental veil, who lives and reigns with Thee in the unity of the Holy Spirit, God, world without end. Amen.

Anima Christi

Soul of Christ, sanctify me. /   Body of Christ, save me. /   Blood of Christ, inebriate me. /   Water from the side of Christ, wash me. / Passion of Christ, strengthen me. /   O good Jesus, hear me. /   Within Your wounds, hide me. /   Permit me not to be separated from You./   From the evil enemy defend me. /   In the hour of my death, call me and bid me come to You,/ that I may praise You with Your saints and angels forever and ever. /   Amen
St. Ignatius Loyola

Come, Holy Spirit

Come, Holy Spirit,/   fill the hearts of your faithful and enkindle in them the fire of your divine love./   Send forth your Spirit and they are created, /   and you renew the face of the earth./   Let us pray:/   Lord, by the light of your Holy Spirit/   you have taught the hearts of your faithful/   In that same Spirit give us your right judgment and the joy of your consolation./   We ask this through Christ our Lord. Amen.

Marian Prayers

The Magnificat - The Prayer Of Mary

My soul proclaims the greatness of the Lord,/   my spirit rejoices in God my Savior/   for he has looked with favor on his lowly servant./ From this day all generations will call me blessed:/   the Almighty has done great things for me,/   and holy is his Name./   He has mercy on those who fear him in every generation./   He has shown the strength of his arm,/   he has scattered the proud in their conceit./   He has cast down the mighty from their thrones,/   and has lifted up the lowly./   He has filled the hungry with good things,/   and the rich he has sent away empty./   He has come to the help of his servant Israel for he remembered his promise of mercy,/   the promise he made to our fathers,/   to Abraham and his children forever./   Luke 1: 46-55

The Memorare

Remember, O most gracious Virgin Mary, /   that never was it known/ that anyone who fled to thy protection,/   implored thy help,/   or sought thine intercession was left unaided./   Inspired by this confidence,/   I fly unto thee,/   O Virgin of virgins,/   my mother;/   to thee do I come, /   before thee I stand,/   sinful and sorrowful./   O Mother of the
252

the Word Incarnate,/   despise not my petitions,/   but in thy mercy
hear and answer me./   Amen.

Prayer to Our Lady of Guadalupe

Holy Mary, who under the title of Our Lady of Guadalupe are Invoked as
Mother by the men and women of Mexico and Latin America,/   encouraged
by the love that you inspire in us, /   we once again place our life in your
motherly hands.

Mary, you hold sway in the hearts of all the mothers of the world and in our
own heart. / With great hope, we turn to you and trust in you. Conclude with
the Hail Mary - below] Pope Emeritus Benedict XVI, May 11, 2005

Hail Mary

Hail, Mary, full of grace, / the Lord is with thee./   Blessed art thou among
women/   and blessed is the fruit of thy womb, Jesus./   Holy Mary, Mother
of God,/   pray for us sinners,/   now and at the hour of our death./ Amen.

Prayer to Our Lady of Lourdes

Hail Mary, poor and humble Woman,/   Blessed by the Most High! Virgin of
hope,/   dawn of a new era, / We join in your song of praise, to celebrate the
Lord's mercy, to proclaim the coming of the Kingdom and the full liberation of
humanity./ Hail Mary, / lowly handmaid of the Lord, / Glorious Mother
of Christ! / Faithful Virgin,/   holy dwelling-place of the Word,/ Teach us
to persevere in listening to the Word,/   and to be docile to the voice of the
Spirit,/   attentive to his promptings in the depths of our conscience and to his
manifestations in the events of history./ Hail Mary,/   Woman of sorrows,/
Mother of the living!/   Virgin spouse beneath the Cross,/   the new Eve, /
Be our guide along the paths of the world./   Teach us to experience and to
spread the love of Christ,/   to stand with you before the innumerable crosses
on which your Son is still crucified./ Hail Mary,/ woman of faith,/   First of
the disciples! / Virgin Mother of the Church,/   help us always to account for
the hope that is in us,/   with trust in human goodness and the Father's love.
/ Teach us to build up the world beginning from within:/   in the depths of
silence and prayer,/   in the joy of fraternal love,/   in the unique fruitfulness
of the Cross./ Holy Mary,/   Mother of believers, Our Lady of Lourdes, pray
for us. Amen.
Prayer said by Pope John Paul II, August 15, 2004 at Lourdes, France

Hail, Holy Queen,

Hail, Holy Queen/   Mother of Mercy/ /   our life, our sweetness and our hope./   To you do we cry,/   poor banished children of Eve. /   To you do we send up our sighs, /   mourning and weeping in this valley of tears / Turn then, most gracious advocate,/   your eyes of mercy toward us,/   and after this exile/ show unto us the blessed fruit of thy womb,/ Jesus./   O clement, O loving,/ O sweet Virgin Mary. Pray for us/   O holy Mother of God,/ that we may be made worthy of the promises of Christ. Amen

The Angelus

V/. The Angel of the Lord declared unto Mary,
R/. And she conceived of the Holy Spirit.

Hail Mary, full of grace, the Lord is with you;
blessed are you among women,
and blessed is the fruit of your womb, Jesus.
Holy Mary, Mother of God,
pray for us sinners
now and at the hour of our death.
Amen.

V/. Behold the handmaid of the Lord,
R/. Be it done unto me according to your Word.
Hail Mary…

V/. And the Word was made flesh,
R/. And dwelt among us.
Hail Mary…

V/. Pray for us, O holy Mother of God,
R/. That we may be made worthy of the promises of Christ.

Let us pray. Pour forth, we beseech you, O Lord, your grace into our hearts: that we, to whom the Incarnation of Christ your Son was made known by the message of an Angel, may by his Passion and Cross be brought to the glory of his Resurrection. Through the same Christ our Lord. Amen.

Prayer to God, the Trinity

Heavenly Father,/ I pray that your Holy Spirit may open my eyes,/ my ears/ and my mind to your word O Lord,/ for your words are precious to me. / May your words and the teachings of Jesus the Christ help me to better know./ love/ and serve you in this world / and be happy with You forever in the next.

Morning Offering

O Jesus,/ through the Immaculate Heart of Mary,/ I offer You my prayers, works,/ joys and sufferings/ of this day for all the intentions/ of Your Sacred Heart,/ in union with the Holy Sacrifice of the Mass/ throughout the world,/ in reparation for my sins,/ for the intentions of all my relatives and friends, / and in particular/ for the intentions of the Holy Father.
Amen.

Act of Faith

O my God,/ I firmly believe that Thou art one God,/ in three Divine Persons,/ the Father,/ the Son/ and the Holy Ghost./ I believe that Thy Divine Son became man and died for our sins/ and that He will come to judge the living and the dead./ I believe these and all the truths / which the Holy Catholic Church teaches, because Thou hast revealed them, / Who can neither deceive or be deceived. Amen.

Act of Hope

O my God, relying on Thy almighty power and infinite mercy and promises, I hope to obtain pardon of my sins, the help of Thy grace, and life everlasting, through the merits of Jesus Christ, my Lord and Redeemer. Amen

Act of Love

O my God, I love you above all things, with my whole heart and soul, because you are all good and worthy of all my love. I love my neighbor as myself for the love of you. I forgive all who have injured me and I ask pardon of all whom I have injured.

Prayer to St. Michael the Archangel

Saint Michael the Archangel, defend us in battle, be our protection against the wickedness and snares of the devil. May God rebuke him we humbly pray; and do thou, O Prince of the Heavenly host, by the power of God, cast into hell Satan and all the evil spirits who prowl about the world seeking the ruin of souls. Amen.

Prayer of St. Francis

Lord, make me a channel of thy peace,/ that where there is hatred, I may bring love;/ that where there is wrong,/ I may bring the spirit of forgiveness;/ that where there is discord, I may bring harmony;/ that where there is error, I may bring truth;/ that where there is doubt, I may bring faith;/ that where there is despair, I may bring hope;/ that where there are shadows, I may bring light;/ that where there is sadness, I may bring joy./ Lord, grant that I may seek rather to / comfort than to be comforted;/ to understand, than to be understood;/ to love, than to be loved./ For it is by self-forgetting that one finds./ It is by forgiving that one is forgiven./ It is by dying that one awakens to Eternal Life.

Prayer for St. Joseph's Protection

St. Joseph, whose protection is so great, so prompt, so strong, before the throne of God,/ I place in you all my interests and desires./ St. Joseph, do assist me by your powerful intercession,/ and obtain for me from your Divine Son all spiritual blessings, through Jesus Christ, our Lord./ So that, having engaged here below your heavenly power,/ I may offer my thanksgiving and homage to the most loving of fathers. St. Joseph, I never weary contemplating you and Jesus asleep in your arms;/ I dare not approach while he reposes near your heart./ Press him in my name and kiss his fine head for me and ask him to return the kiss when I draw my dying breath./ St. Joseph, patron of departing souls - pray for me. Amen.

A Prayer to St. Joseph

O blessed Joseph, faithful guardian of my Redeemer, Jesus Christ, protector of thy chaste spouse, the virgin Mother of God, I choose thee this day to be my special patron and advocate and I firmly resolve to honor thee all the days of my life. Therefore I humbly beseech thee to receive me as thy client, to instruct me in every doubt, to comfort me in every affliction, to obtain for me and for all the knowledge and love of the Heart of Jesus, and finally to defend and protect me at the hour of my death. Amen

Devotion to St. Joseph

To you, O blessed Joseph, do we come in our tribulation, and having implored the help of your most holy spouse, we confidently invoke your patronage also. Through that charity which bound you to the Immaculate Virgin Mother of God and through the paternal love with which you embraced the Child Jesus, we humbly beg you graciously to regard the inheritance which Jesus Christ has purchased by his Blood, and with your power and strength to aid us in our necessities. O most watchful Guardian of the Holy Family, defend the chosen children of Jesus Christ; O most loving father, ward off from us every contagion of error and corrupting influence; O our most mighty protector, be propitious to us and from heaven assist us in our struggle with the power of darkness; and, as once you rescued the Child Jesus from deadly peril, so now protect God's Holy Church from the snares of the enemy and from all adversity; shield, too, each one of us by your constant protection, so that, supported by your example and your aid, we may be able to live piously, to die holy, and to obtain eternal happiness in heaven. Amen. Pope Leo XlII

Memorare to St. Joseph

Remember, O most chaste spouse of the Virgin Mary, that never was it known that anyone who implored your help and sought your intercession were left unassisted. Full of confidence in your power I fly unto you and beg your protection. Despise not O Guardian of the Redeemer my humble supplication, but in your bounty, hear and answer me. Amen.

Act of Consecration to St. Joseph

O dearest St. Joseph, I consecrate myself to your honor and give myself to you, that you may always be my father, my protector and my guide in the way of salvation. Obtain for me a greater purity of heart and fervent love of the interior life. After your example may I do all my actions for the greater glory of God, in union with the Divine Heart of Jesus and the Immaculate Heart of Mary. O Blessed St. Joseph, pray for me, that I may share in the peace and joy of your holy death. Amen.

Prayer for Strength by St. Ignatius of Loyola

O Christ Jesus; When all is darkness/ And we feel our weakness and helplessness, / Give us the sense of Your Presence, / Your Love and Your Strength. / Help us to have perfect trust/ In Your protecting love/ And strengthening power, / So that nothing may frighten or worry us, / For, living close to You, / We shall see Your Hand, / Your Purpose,/ Your Will through all things.

Lorica of Saint Patrick

I arise today/ Through a mighty strength, the invocation of the Trinity, / Through a belief in the Threeness, / Through confession of the Oneness / Of the Creator of creation./ I arise today / Through the strength of Christ's birth and His baptism, / Through the strength of His crucifixion and His burial, Through the strength of His resurrection and His ascension, / Through the strength of His descent for the judgment of doom./ I arise today/ Through the strength of the love of cherubim, / In obedience of angels, / In service of archangels, / In the hope of resurrection to meet with reward, / In the prayers of patriarchs, / In preachings of the apostles, / In faiths of confessors, In innocence of virgins, / In deeds of righteous men./ I arise today/ Through the strength of heaven; / Light of the sun, / Splendor of fire, / Speed of lightning, / Swiftness of the wind, Depth of the sea, / Stability of the earth, / Firmness of the rock./ I arise today/ Through God's strength to pilot me; / God's might to uphold me, God's wisdom to guide me, / God's eye to look before me, / God's ear to hear me, / God's word to speak for me, / God's hand to guard me, / God's way to lie before me, / God's shield to protect me, / God's hosts to save me / From snares of the devil, / From temptations of vices, / From every one who desires me ill, / Afar and near, / Alone or in a multitude.

Prayer for Peace - St. Francis of Assisi

Lord, make me a channel of your peace, that where there is hatred, I may bring love; where there is wrong, I may bring the spirit of forgiveness where there is discord, I may bring harmony; where there is error, I may bring truth; where there is doubt, I may bring faith; where there is despair, I may bring hope; where there are shadows, I may bring light; where there is sadness, I may bring joy. Lord, grant that I may seek rather to comfort than to be comforted; to understand than to be understood; to love than to be loved; For it is by forgetting self that one finds; it is by forgiving that one is forgiven; it is by dying that one awakens to eternal life. Amen.

Prayer by St. Mother Teresa of Calcutta

Dear Jesus, help me to spread Thy fragrance everywhere I go. Flood my soul with Thy spirit and love. Penetrate and possess my whole being so utterly that all my life may only be a radiance of Thine. Shine through me and be so in me that every soul I come in contact with may feel Thy presence in my soul. Let them look up and see no longer me but only Jesus. Stay with me and then I shall begin to shine as you shine, so to shine as to be a light to others. Amen.

Prayer for Families by St. Mother Teresa

Heavenly Father, you have given us a model of life in the Holy Family of Nazareth. Help us, O Loving Father, to make our family another Nazareth where love, peace and joy reign. May it be deeply contemplative, intensely Eucharistic and vibrant with joy. Help us to stay together in joy and sorrow through family prayer. Teach us to see Jesus in the members of our family, especially in their distressing disguise. May the Eucharistic Heart of Jesus make our hearts meek and humble like His, and help us to carry out our family duties in a holy way. May we love one another as God loves each one of us, more and more each day, and forgive each others faults as you forgive our sins. Help us, O Loving Father, to take whatever you give and to give whatever you take, with a big smile. Help us, O Holy Father, to make our families one heart, full of love, in the Heart of Jesus through Mary. Immaculate Heart of Mary, cause of our joy, pray for us. St. Joseph, pray for us. Holy Guardian Angels, be always with us, guide and protect us. Amen.

Prayer of St. Faustina before the Eucharist

I adore You, Lord and Creator, hidden in the Most Blessed Sacrament. I adore You for all the works of Your hands, that reveal to me so much wisdom, goodness and mercy, O Lord. You have spread so much beauty over the earth and it tells me about Your beauty, even though these beautiful things are but a faint reflection of You, incomprehensible Beauty. And although You have hidden Yourself and concealed Your beauty, my eye, enlightened by faith, reaches You and my soul recognizes its Creator, its Highest Good, and my heart is completely immersed in prayer of adoration.

My Lord and Creator, Your goodness encourages me to converse with You. Your mercy abolishes the chasm which separates the Creator from the creature. To converse with You, O Lord, is the delight of my heart. In You I find everything that my heart could desire. Here You light illumines my mind, enabling it to know You more and more deeply. Here streams of graces flow down upon my heart. Here my soul draws eternal life. O my Lord and Creator, You alone, beyond all these gifts, give Your own self to me and unite Yourself intimately with Your miserable creature.

O Christ, let my greatest delight be to see You loved and Your praise and glory proclaimed, especially the honor of Your mercy. O Christ, let me glorify Your goodness and mercy to the last moment of my life, with every drop of my blood and every beat of my heart. Would that I be transformed into a hymn of adoration of You. When I find myself on my deathbed, may the last beat of my heart be a loving hymn glorifying Your unfathomable mercy. Amen.

Make Us Worthy, Lord by Pope St. Paul VI

Make us worthy, Lord, to serve our fellow men/ throughout the world who live and die in poverty and hunger./ Give them through our hands, this day their daily bread,/ and by our understanding love, give peace and joy. Amen.

Oh My Jesus

Oh my Jesus, son of God, Son of Man. You came to Earth to be our Saviour and Redeemer. You became one of us; our body, our blood, your soul, your divinity. By your example, you showed us how to live our lives to be pleasing to your Father. Your teachings have taught us God's love, mercy and forgiveness. Through your passion and death, you atoned for the sin of all mankind. Your resurrection and ascension into heaven has shown us your mighty power as God. Thank you for your Holy Eucharist that we may have your true presence with us always, your body and blood, your soul and divinity in the Holy Eucharist.

Glory Be

Glory Be to the Father and to the Son and to the Holy Spirit. As it was in the beginning is now, and ever shall be, world without end. Amen.

Prayer to our Guardian Angels

Angel of God, my guardian dear, to whom God's love commits me here, ever this day be at my side, to light and guard, to rule and guide.

Morning Offering

O Jesus, through the Immaculate Heart of Mary,/ I offer you my prayers, works, joys, and sufferings of this day/ for all the intentions of your Sacred Heart/ in union with the Holy Sacrifice of the Mass throughout the world/, for the salvation of souls, / the reparation of sins,/ the reunion of all Christians,/ and for the intentions [_____ of the Holy Father this month. Amen.

The Morning Offering by St. Patrick

I arise today through God's strength to pilot me. Christ with me. Christ before me, Christ behind me. Christ in me, Christ beneath me, Christ above me, Christ on my right. Christ on my left. Christ when I lie down. Christ when I sit down. Christ when I arise, Christ in the heart of everyone who thinks of me. Christ in the mouth of everyone who speaks of me, Christ in the eye that sees me Christ in the ear that hears me. Amen

The Five Finger Prayer by Pope Francis

The thumb is our closest finger; it can remind us to pray for people who are closest to us - praying for our dear ones is a "sweet obligation". Lord, I lift _____ up in prayer ...

The next finger is the index finger; it can remind us to. Pray for those who teach; instruct; and heal us. They need our prayer support as they provide direction to others. Lord, I lift _____ up in prayer ...

The next finger is the tallest; it can remind us to pray for our leaders, governors and other people in authority. These people need God's guidance. Lord, I lift _____ up in prayer ... .

The ring finger is actually our weakest finger; it helps to remind us to pray for the people who are the weakest; the sick; and with problems. They. need our prayers. Lord, I lift _____ up in prayer ...

The little finger is known as the pinky finger. It reminds us to pray for ourselves after we have finished praying for other people. This allows us to identify our own needs better and enables us to pray for ourselves in a better way. Lord, I lift _____ up in prayer ...

The Vocations Prayer

Oh God, we earnestly ask You to bless this Archdiocese with many priests, brothers and sisters who will love You with their while strength and gladly spend their entire lives to serve Your church and to make You known and loved. Bless our families; bless our children; choose from our homes those who are needed for Your work.

Mary, Queen of the clergy, pray for us, pray for our priests, religious and deacons. Obtain fro us many more. Amen.

Prayer Before a Crucifix

Good and gentle Jesus, /   I kneel before You./   I see and I ponder Your five wounds./   My eyes behold what David prophesied about You: /   "They have pierced my hands and feet, /   They have counted all my bones." /   Engrave on me this image of Yourself. /   Fulfill the yearnings of my heart:/   Give me faith, hope and love,/   Repentance for my sins, And true conversion of life. Amen./

* This is a formally indulgenced prayer of the Church; for a simple explanation of indulgences and how they can enrich your spiritual life, please see The Indulgence: A Family Treasure by Joan Welter Czaia, available at www.FortifyingFamiliesofFaith. com.

Prayer for all Vocations

Oh God, I turn to You for providing necessary direction for my life. Help me to discern, discover, and embrace my vocation and Your Divine Will for my life. Am I to serve Your kingdom as wife/mother (husband/father) or in religious service? Whatever Your will, here I am Lord. Help me to wait patiently for Your direction; never let me wander away from Your presence. Amen.

Prayer of Abandonment

Father, I abandon myself into your hands; Do with me what you will.
Whatever you may do, I thank you; I am ready for all, I accept all.
Let only your will be done in me and in all your creatures.
I wish no more than this, O Lord. Into your hands I commend my soul;
I offer it to you with all the love of my heart, for I love you Lord, and so need to give myself, to surrender myself into your hands, without reserve, and with boundless confidence, For you are my Father.   Charles de Foucauld [1858- 1916]

Litany of Humility

O Jesus! meek and humble of heart. Hear me. From the desire of being esteemed. Deliver me Jesus.
From the desire of being loved. Deliver me Jesus.
From the desire of being extolled. Deliver me Jesus.
From the desire of being honored. Deliver me Jesus.
From the desire of being praised. Deliver me Jesus.
From the desire of being preferred to others. Deliver me Jesus.
From the desire of being consulted. Deliver me Jesus.
From the desire of being approved. Deliver me Jesus.
From the fear of being humiliated. Deliver me Jesus.
From the fear of being despised. Deliver me Jesus.
From the fear of suffering rebukes. Deliver me Jesus.

From the fear of being calumniated. Deliver me Jesus.
From the fear of being forgotten. Deliver me Jesus.
From the fear of being ridiculed. Deliver me Jesus.
From the fear of being wronged. Deliver me Jesus.
From the fear of being suspected. Deliver me Jesus.
That others may be loved more than I. Jesus, grant me the grace to desire it.
That others may be esteemed more than I. Jesus, grant me the grace to desire it.
That in the opinion of the world, others may increase and I may decrease. Jesus, grant me the grace to desire it.
That others may be chosen and I set aside. Jesus, grant me the grace to desire it.
We pray this in Jesus' Holy Name. Amen

Fatima Prayer

Oh my Jesus, forgive us our sins, save us from the fires of hell. Lead all souls to Heaven, especially those in most need of Thy mercy.

Praying the Rosary

1. Crucifix: Say the Sign of the Cross and the Apostles Creed
2. Each Large bead: The Lord's Prayer
3. Each Small bead: The Hail Mary
4. Say the Glory Be Prayer & Fatima Prayer after this first set of beads..
5. For each of the next five decades, Announce the Mystery; say the Our Father on the larger bead; say ten Hail Mary's for each small bead; conclude with the Glory Be and the Fatima prayer

Joyful Mysteries: [Monday & Saturday]: The Annunciation of the Angel Gabriel to Mary; The Visitation of Mary with Elizabeth; The Nativity of Our Lord Jesus; the Presentation of Jesus in the Temple; the Finding of Jesus in the Temple.

Luminous Mysteries [Thursday]: The Baptism of our Lord in the River Jordan; The Wedding Feast of Cana; The Proclamation of the Kingdom of God; The Transfiguration of our Lord; The Institution of the Holy Eucharist at the Last Supper.

The Sorrowful Mysteries: [Tuesday and Friday] The Agony in the Garden; the Scourging at the Pillar; the Crowning with Thorns; the Carrying of the Cross; the crucifixion of our Lord.

The Glorious Mysteries; [Sunday and Wednesday] The Transfiguration of our Lord; The Ascension of Jesus into Heaven; the Descent of the Holy Spirit on the Apostles; the Assumption of Mary into Heaven; the Coronation of Mary; as Queen of Heaven and Earth.

Form for the Sacrament of Penance

Forgive me Father, for I have sinned.
It's been about .... weeks/months/years
since my last Confession. These are my sins....

Act of Contrition

Oh my God, I am heartily sorry for having offended Thee. I detest all my sins because I dread the loss of Heaven and the pains of hell, but most of all because they offend Thee, my God, Who art all good and deserving of all my love. I firmly resolve, with the help of Thy grace, to confess my sins, to do penance and to amend my life. Amen.

Date of Confession: **Notes for my Confessions:**

....,..............................
   ....,..............................
....,..............................
   ....,..............................
....,..............................
   ....,..............................
....,..............................
   ....,..............................
....,..............................
   ....,..............................
....,..............................
   ....,..............................
....,..............................
   ....,..............................
....,..............................
   ....,..............................
....,..............................
   ....,..............................
....,..............................

Date of Confession:

Notes for my Confessions:

Putting on the Armor of God

Advances the Virtuous Life

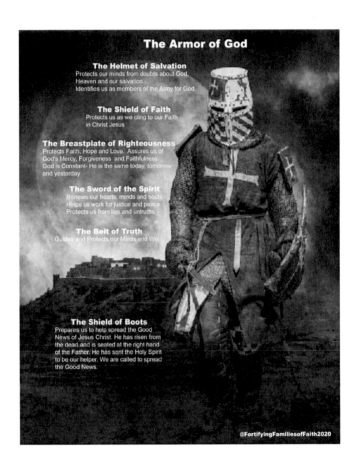

The Cardinal Virtues   **Opposing Vice**

Prudence - good judgment   Poor Judgment
Fortitude - endurance, strength   Lazy
Justice - honorable treatment of others   Injustice
Temperance - restraint, self control, moderation Excessiveness

The Three Theological Virtues

Faith   Disbelief, doubt
Hope   Despair
Charity   Hate

Natural Virtues   **Opposing Vice**

Acceptance   Rejection
Assertiveness   Self-doubt
Authenticity   Disingenuous
Chastity   Lust
Cleanliness   Lack of cleanliness
Commitment   Uncommitted
Compassion   Uncaring
Confidence   Uncertainty
Consideration   Disregard
Contentment   Restlessness
Cooperation   Uncooperative
Courage   Cowardice
Creativity   Lack of Creativity
Determination   Complacency
Encouraging   Discouraging
Enthusiastic   Bored
Ethical   Immoral
Excellence   Mediocrity
Fairness   Unfair
Flexibility   Rigid
Forgiving   Unforgiving
Friendliness   Unfriendly
Generous   Stingy

Natural Virtues	Opposing Vice
Gentleness	Harsh
Gracious	Rude
Grateful	Resentful
Honesty	Dishonest
Humility	Pride
Integrity	Corrupt
Joyful	Morose
Kindness	Cruel
Love	Hate
Loyalty	Betrayal
Moderation	Obsessive
Modesty	Immodesty
Optimistic	Pessimistic
Patience	Impatience
Perseverance	Laziness
Preparedness	Complacency
Purposeful	Lacking purpose
Reliable	Untrustworthy
Respectful	Disrespectful
Responsible	Irresponsible
Reverent	Irreverent
Self-Discipline	Chaotic
Service	Self Centeredness
Sincere	Disingenuousness
Tactful	Clumsy
Temperate	Intemperate
Thankful	Unappreciative
Tolerance	Narrow minded
Trustful	Untrustworthy
Understanding	Egoistical
Wisdom	Lacking Wisdom

This list of natural virtues is only the tip of the iceberg as it pertains to natural virtues. Many virtues are closely related to each other and may even be considered synonyms of the other. The same applies to different vices. While virtues work together to build up our characters, vices work together to tear our characters down.

The Seven Spiritual Works of Mercy

1. Counsel the doubtful
2. Instruct the ignorant
3. Admonish the sinner
4. Comfort the sorrowful
5. Forgive injuries
6. Bear wrongs patiently
7. Pray for the living and the dead.

The Seven Corporal Works of Mercy

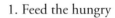

1. Feed the hungry
2. Give drink to the thirsty;
3. Clothe the naked
4. Shelter the homeless
5. Visit the sick
6. Visit the imprisoned
7. Bury the dead.

The Seven Gifts of the Holy Spirit

1. Wisdom   2. Understanding   3. Counsel

4. Knowledge

5. Fortitude   6. Piety   7. Fear of the Lord

The Twelve Fruits of the Holy Spirit

1. Charity   2. Joy   3. Peace   4. Patience   5. Kindness
6. Continence   7. Goodness   8. Faithfulness   9. Fidelity
10. Modesty   11. Chastity   12. Humility.

Notes, etc.

Date: ....

. . . .
. . . .
. . . .
. . . .
. . . .
. . . .
. . . .
. . . .
. . . .
. . . .
. . . .
. . . .
. . . .

Date: ....

. . . .
. . . .
. . . .
. . . .
. . . .
. . . .
. . . .
. . . .
. . . .
. . . .
. . . .
. . . .
. . . .

Notes, etc.

Date: ....

. . . .
. . . .
. . . .
. . . .
. . . .
. . . .
. . . .
. . . .
. . . .
. . . .
. . . .
. . . .
. . . .

Date: ....

. . . .
. . . .
. . . .
. . . .
. . . .
. . . .
. . . .
. . . .
. . . .
. . . .
. . . .
. . . .
. . . .

Notes, etc.

Date: ....

. . . .
. . . .
. . . .
. . . .
. . . .
. . . .
. . . .
. . . .
. . . .
. . . .
. . . .
. . . .
. . . .

Date: ....

. . . .
. . . .
. . . .
. . . .
. . . .
. . . .
. . . .
. . . .
. . . .
. . . .
. . . .
. . . .

Notes, etc.

Date: ....

. . . .
. . . .
. . . .
. . . .
. . . .
. . . .
. . . .
. . . .
. . . .
. . . .
. . . .
. . . .
. . . .

Date: ....

. . . .
. . . .
. . . .
. . . .
. . . .
. . . .
. . . .
. . . .
. . . .
. . . .
. . . .
. . . .
. . . .

Notes, etc.

Date: ....

. . . .
. . . .
. . . .
. . . .
. . . .
. . . .
. . . .
. . . .
. . . .
. . . .
. . . .
. . . .
. . . .

Date: ....

. . . .
. . . .
. . . .
. . . .
. . . .
. . . .
. . . .
. . . .
. . . .
. . . .
. . . .
. . . .
. . . .

Notes, etc.

Date: ....

. . . .
. . . .
. . . .
. . . .
. . . .
. . . .
. . . .
. . . .
. . . .
. . . .
. . . .
. . . .
. . . .

Date: ....

. . . .
. . . .
. . . .
. . . .
. . . .
. . . .
. . . .
. . . .
. . . .
. . . .
. . . .
. . . .
. . . .

Notes, etc.

Date: ....

. . . .
. . . .
. . . .
. . . .
. . . .
. . . .
. . . .
. . . .
. . . .
. . . .
. . . .
. . . .
. . . .

Date: ....

. . . .
. . . .
. . . .
. . . .
. . . .
. . . .
. . . .
. . . .
. . . .
. . . .
. . . .
. . . .

Notes, etc.

Date: ....

. . . .
. . . .
. . . .
. . . .
. . . .
. . . .
. . . .
. . . .
. . . .
. . . .
. . . .
. . . .
. . . .

Date: ....

. . . .
. . . .
. . . .
. . . .
. . . .
. . . .
. . . .
. . . .
. . . .
. . . .
. . . .
. . . .
. . . .

Notes, etc.

Date: ....

. . . .
. . . .
. . . .
. . . .
. . . .
. . . .
. . . .
. . . .
. . . .
. . . .
. . . .
. . . .
. . . .

Date: ....

. . . .
. . . .
. . . .
. . . .
. . . .
. . . .
. . . .
. . . .
. . . .
. . . .
. . . .
. . . .
. . . .

Notes, etc.

Date: ....

. . . .
. . . .
. . . .
. . . .
. . . .
. . . .
. . . .
. . . .
. . . .
. . . .
. . . .
. . . .
. . . .

Date: ....

. . . .
. . . .
. . . .
. . . .
. . . .
. . . .
. . . .
. . . .
. . . .
. . . .
. . . .
. . . .
. . . .